The Constitution and the Court

STUDIES IN
POLITICAL
SCIENCE

The Constitution and the Court

The Development of the Basic Law
Through Judicial Interpretation

Robert S. Hirschfield

Hunter College
of the City University of New York

Random House / New York

PREFACE

This book deals with an essential element in the dynamism of American government: the process of constitutional development through judicial interpretation of the basic law. Demonstrating this process by reference to the Supreme Court's activity in four of the most important problem areas of our time—economic regulation, racial equality, civil liberty, and wartime government—it is designed to illuminate the Court's policymaking role in changing the law of the Constitution to meet the changing needs and aspirations of American society. It is a study of the Supreme Court as a vital instrument in the preservation of a "living" Constitution.

I would like to thank Mr. Charles Lieber of Random House for encouraging me to undertake this project; Mrs. Judith Rutenberg, Miss Mary Carras, and Miss Barbara Susman for typing the manuscript; Professor Walter Murphy of Princeton for commenting on the draft; Mrs. Leonore Hauck and Miss Jane Alles of Random House for directing the production process; Hunter College for a George Shuster Faculty Grant to help defray secretarial expenses; and my wife for assistance at all stages of the work. The book is dedicated to the memory of my parents.

R. S. H.

CONTENTS

The Constitution and the Court

We must never forget that it is a CONSTITUTION *we are expounding . . . a constitution intended to endure for ages to come, and consequently to be adapted to the various crises of human affairs.*

CHIEF JUSTICE JOHN MARSHALL

THE CONSTITUTION, THE COURT, AND THE AMERICAN SYSTEM OF GOVERNMENT

The Idea of Constitutionalism

Every organized political community has a constitution — a system of fundamental principles and procedures by which the society is to be governed. Some of these constitutions are embodied in written documents; others are molded by custom. Some represent only aspirations, others are merely façades, and still others function as the nation's basic law. Of the world's operative written constitutions, the Constitution of the United States is the oldest.

The idea of constitutionalism, as it developed in the Western world from Greco-Roman roots through the medieval period and into modern times, is in essence the idea of government under law, or limited government; with the constitution itself representing an attempt first to define governmental power and then to establish as limits on that power the rights of the governed. In the Anglo-American tradition — particularly as expounded by John Locke and Thomas Jefferson — such rights as freedom of expression, protection against arbitrary detention, ownership of property, and security of one's own person are conceived to be self-evidently necessary to the preservation of an individual's dignity and to the development of his personality. Inherent in all persons, these rights are inviolable and inalienable,

3

and it is the ultimate purpose of the constitution to guarantee them against governmental encroachment.

This theory of rights makes it clear that constitutionalism and totalitarianism are antithetical conceptions. For constitutionalism holds that the power of government, being limited by the rights of the individual, is excluded from significant areas of life; whereas totalitarianism, since it is based on the idea that government and society are coterminous and that governmental power may be applied to every area of human activity, precludes the very concept of individual rights. Thus a totalitarian system cannot in any meaningful sense be constitutional, despite the fact that it may have a "constitution"; and to the extent that individual rights are denied or unrealized, any constitutional system is imperfect.

Theoretically, or at least logically, the idea of constitutionalism is also antithetical to that of democracy. Government "of, by, and for the people" rests on the principle of majoritarianism. But popular majorities or their representatives may decide on policies which violate the rights of individuals or minorities, and an absolute dictatorship which tramples on constitutional guarantees may, after all, have majority support.

Nonetheless, in the United States and the free world generally, constitutionalism and democracy are regarded as inextricably bound together, the constitution being viewed as a framework of rules within which democratic government may proceed in orderly fashion and as a check against the possibility that such government will result in majority tyranny. The fundamental concept in a system of constitutional democracy — reflecting the combination of ideas and attempting to incorporate the best of both — is "majority rule but minority rights." It is a highly sophisticated conception, and it is often very difficult to apply, but it embodies the political ideal of the free society: that government shall represent the will of the many without denying the liberty of any.

The American Constitution

Although democracy did not become a basic ingredient of the American governmental system until after the Jacksonian Revolution of the 1830s, that system was from its inception in 1789 preeminently constitutional. Established in order to "form a more perfect union" and to "secure the blessings of liberty," the Constitution of the United States is, in essence, a contract outlining both the powers and the limits of American government.*

The major purpose of the Constitution's framers was to create a more effective national government than that which had existed under America's first constitution, the Articles of Confederation. Their major problem was to devise a system in which the authority of that government over the states and the individual citizen would not be excessive. The purpose was achieved by empowering the new government to make and execute laws on those subjects which affected the nation as a whole; the problem was resolved by establishing a complex system in which governmental authority was widely distributed and rights were specifically guaranteed.

Thus, with regard to power, the central government's jurisdiction was extended to matters of foreign affairs and defense (international relations, treaties, armed forces, war); to matters of potential conflict among the states (judgment of disputes, regulation of interstate commerce, establishment of uniform rules such as those on duties and excises); to matters of maintaining order throughout the country (calling forth of the militia, suspension of the habeas corpus privilege); and to matters of national finance and services (taxation, appropriation, borrowing, payment of debts, coinage, standardization of weights and measures, postal functions). In addition the national government was given the authority to make all laws which might be "necessary and proper" for effectuating its enumerated powers.

With regard to limitation, the Constitution established three basic principles: federalism, the separation of powers, and the guarantee of individual rights.

The first constitutional principle, federalism, involves the division of all governmental authority in the United States between the national and the state governments, each

*See Appendix A for the text of the Constitution.

being independent with regard to its own sphere of activity, and the citizen being subject to the authority of both. Of the powers delegated to the national government, some (like the war power) are granted to it exclusively, while others (like the taxing power) are held concurrently with the states. As a result of the "necessary and proper" clause, the national government also has that authority which flows by implication from its enumerated powers.

Although certain powers are prohibited to the states by the Constitution, there is no enumeration of those which remain within their sphere of authority. Actually only half of the theory of federalism, that pertaining to the delegation of power to the national government, was included in the original document. But the Tenth Amendment to the Constitution supplied the missing half by adding that all powers "not prohibited by it to the states, are reserved to the states respectively, or to the people." Substantial authority remained in the states, therefore, as a result of both the reserved powers doctrine and the existence of concurrent powers, although the latter were subject to limitation under the provision that statutes and treaties made by the national government shall be "the supreme law of the land."

In sum, the federal principle created a dual system of government in the United States, balancing national and state authority, and limiting both by dividing the totality of governmental power between them.

The separation-of-powers principle is most evident in the Constitution and involves a functional distribution of authority among the three branches of the national government. Each department—the legislative, the executive, and the judicial—is an independent and coordinate organ of the central government, entrusted with its own powers by the basic law itself. The separation of the branches is not absolute, however, for the Constitution includes the corollary principle of "checks and balances," by which each department participates in the activity of the other two.

Congress, for example, may check the President through its power to reject a treaty which he has negotiated; the

President may check Congress by vetoing a bill which it has passed; the Supreme Court may check both by reviewing the constitutionality of their actions; and each of the political branches may check the Court through the President's law-enforcement power or Congress's power to limit that tribunal's appellate jurisdiction. Although the essence of its own function resides exclusively in each of the three branches, they overlap in the exercise of their authority.

Pitting power against power, the system of checks and balances, like the separation-of-powers principle as a whole, represents a conscious attempt by the Framers to prevent the concentration of power in any single agency of government — a phenomenon which Madison, borrowing from Montesquieu, characterized as "the very definition of tyranny" — and to assure the limitation of national governmental authority.

Both federalism and the separation of powers are dual-purpose structural principles. They provide a system within which American government, at both the state and national levels, operates to achieve its goals; and they also provide a framework of protection for the constitutional guarantee of individual liberty, the third principle of the basic law.

This principle, although assumed to be inherent in the Constitution, was not expressly included in the original document but was added in 1791 in the form of the Bill of Rights. Two kinds of rights are guaranteed by these amendments: the substantive freedoms of religion, speech, press, assembly, and petition listed in the First Amendment; and the procedural rights which support those freedoms, listed in Amendments IV through VIII and including the safeguards against deprivation of life, liberty, or property without due process of law, denial of trial by jury, unreasonable searches and seizures, double jeopardy, self-incrimination, excessive bail, and the infliction of cruel and unusual punishments, as well as the other protections traditionally available under the English common law.

The substantive freedoms, and their indispensable procedural supports, are of vital importance to the maintenance of a constitutional system, a fact evidenced by the Framers' admonition that government must not legislate with regard to them. For they embody the fundamental idea and ideal of constitutionalism itself: the protection of individual liberty through the limitation of governmental authority. Thus the Bill of Rights reflects the ultimate values of the American political system and is the crowning glory of the Constitution.

Constitutional Development and the Principle of Judicial Review

Although its fundamental principles are clear enough, the Constitution is a deceptively simple document. It establishes institutions of government, but it virtually ignores the political processes which must breathe life into them; it lists the powers of the national government's three organs, but it does not define those powers; it creates a complex system of inter- and intra-governmental tension and conflict, but it does not attempt to resolve the power struggles which are thereby encouraged. The result of numerous compromises, the Constitution is purposely and necessarily only a broad outline, definite with regard to its general theory of government, but vague and often ambiguous insofar as its application to specific governmental problems is concerned.

By its very nature, therefore, the Constitution creates the difficult task of fitting each particular exercise of power into a general pattern of limitation; of determining what the basic law permits and what it prohibits. But the Constitution is also by nature a flexible document. And this is its most important characteristic — that the absence of specificity and detail leaves it open to change and development. For government, if it is to enjoy the confidence and support of those it governs, must continually respond to the changing conditions and needs of society. And a constitution, if it is to remain the basic law by which the society is governed, must allow for such adaptation. It cannot be a static catalogue of rules binding the nation to the past and constricting its growth. To merit the continued devotion of succeeding generations and to sustain their attachment to its fundamental principles, it must be dynamic, a vehicle of the nation's life, a "living" law. And this, because of its flexibility, the American Constitution has been.

Although governmental and political change always affects the constitutional system, the development of that system is sometimes accomplished without direct reference to the Constitution. The establishment of political parties and processes has to a large extent taken place outside the framework of the basic law; the Cabinet and the rest of the huge executive establishment were created more by presidential and congressional action than by the few relevant words of that law. Indeed many of the most significant aspects of American government and politics have developed out of custom rather than the Constitution.

Equally important developments, however, have involved changes in the Constitution itself. Some of these have been achieved through formal amendments, of which there are now twenty-three. (The latest, enfranchising citizens who live in the District of Columbia, was ratified by the required three-fourths of the states in 1961.) All of the amendments represent significant alterations of the charter, but the first ten, comprising the Bill of Rights, must be considered part of the original document; two others, the Prohibition amendment and its repealer, cancel each other out; and of the remaining eleven, several deal with essentially technical matters, such as electoral college procedure and commencement of the executive's term of office. In all there are only a half-dozen amendments of a really substantive nature — those which deal with the protection of rights and the extension of democracy — and important as they are, it is obvious that they do not begin to account for the vast changes which have occurred in American government during the past 170 years. Accordingly, there is yet another method for achieving constitutional change: interpretation of the Constitution's existing language.

Constitutional interpretation is a technique for preserving both the dynamism and the stability of society, allowing for change within the established framework of the basic law.

But it raises the question of *which* governmental agency shall exercise the transcendent power of determining what the Constitution's words really mean. The intention of the Framers with regard to this problem is not clearly expressed in the document, for it does not specifically entrust to any agency the power to decide whether particular exercises of governmental authority are consistent with the principles of the Constitution.

In *The Federalist* No. 78, however, Hamilton declared that "The interpretation of the laws is the proper and peculiar province of the courts."

> A constitution is, in fact, and must be regarded by the judges, as a fundamental law. It therefore belongs to them to ascertain its meaning, as well as the meaning of any particular act proceeding from the legislative body. If there should happen to be an irreconcilable variance between the two, that which has the superior obligation and validity ought, of course, to be preferred; or, in other words, the Constitution ought to be preferred to the statute, the intention of the people to the intention of their agents.[1]

This was the first authoritative statement of the principle of *judicial review* — the power of the courts, and of the Supreme Court in particular, to test the constitutionality of governmental actions and to declare null and void those actions which fail to meet the test.

The acceptance of this principle as a basic ingredient of the constitutional system was not achieved without a struggle, and it has remained a focus of controversy throughout the nation's history. For the concept of judicial review places the Supreme Court, the organ of government least representative of the people and ostensibly least responsive to their will, at the center of that system, elevating it above the other agencies of government as guardian of the basic law and entrusting it with the special function of defining the general rules under which the society is governed. It institutionalizes the theory of constitutionalism and makes the Supreme Court the major instrument for applying that theory.

[1]Hamilton, Alexander, James Madison, and John Jay, *The Federalist*, Earle edition (New York: Random House, 1937), p. 506.

Interestingly enough, the principle of judicial review was incorporated in the Constitution by the Supreme Court itself. This initial and most important development in the constitutional system arose out of a political struggle between the Federalist and Democratic-Republican (Jeffersonian) parties. Jefferson's victory in the election of 1800 sounded the death knell of the Federalist Party. But in the period preceding his inauguration, the Federalists, still in control of Congress and the Presidency, remodeled the Judiciary Act of 1789 to create a number of judicial positions which President Adams could fill before leaving office. This the outgoing Chief Executive proceeded to do, signing commissions for Federalist judges up until the last moment of his term.

The commissions of some of these "midnight judges" — including one which appointed William Marbury to a justice-ship of the peace in the District of Columbia — remained undelivered, however, when Adams gave way to Jefferson. The new President, through his Secretary of State, James Madison, refused to transfer these documents and Marbury petitioned the Supreme Court to compel delivery, basing his plea on a section of the Judiciary Act of 1789 which conferred on that Court the power to issue writs of mandamus (judicial orders directing governmental officers to perform specific acts) under its original jurisdiction (the constitutional provision by which certain cases come directly to the Supreme Court).

The Court which heard this petition was composed entirely of Federalists, and the Chief Justice, John Marshall, was a prominent member of that party, a former Secretary of State in the Adams administration, and himself newly appointed to the Bench by Adams. It was Marshall who wrote the Court's unanimous and historic opinion.*

*As preparation for reading this opinion and the others that follow, see Appendices B and C: *Judicial Structure, Jurisdiction, and Procedure* and *How to Read a Constitutional Law Case.*

Most of the opinions included in this book have been excerpted, and the citations of prior decisions contained in them have been deleted, for the sake of clarity and brevity.

Marbury v. Madison
1 Cranch 137 (1803)

Mr. Chief Justice Marshall delivered the opinion of the Court:

... In the order in which the court has viewed this subject, the following questions have been considered and decided.

1st. Has the applicant a right to the commission he demands?

2d. If he has a right, and that right has been violated, do the laws of his country afford him a remedy?

3d. If they do afford him a remedy, is it a mandamus issuing from this court?

[*The Court proceeds to discuss the first two points.*]

It is, then, the opinion of the Court,

1st. That by signing the commission of Mr. Marbury, the President of the United States appointed him a justice of peace for the county of Washington, in the District of Columbia; and that the seal of the United States, affixed thereto by the Secretary of State, is conclusive testimony of the verity of the signature, and of the completion of the appointment; and that the appointment conferred on him a legal right to the office for the space of five years.

2d. That, having this legal title to the office, he has a consequent right to the commission; a refusal to deliver which is a plain violation of that right, for which the laws of his country afford him a remedy.

It remains to be inquired whether,

3d. He is entitled to the remedy for which he applies.

[*The Court finds that he is so entitled.*]

This, then, is a plain case for a mandamus, either to deliver the commission, or a copy of it from the record; and it only remains to be inquired,

Whether it can issue from this court.

The act to establish the judicial courts of the United States authorizes the Supreme Court "to issue writs of mandamus in cases warranted by the principles and usages of law, to any courts appointed, or persons holding office, under the authority of the United States."

The Secretary of State, being a person holding an office under the authority of the United States, is precisely within the letter of the description, and if this court is not authorized to issue a writ of mandamus to such an officer, it must be because the law is unconstitutional, and therefore absolutely incapable of conferring the authority, and assigning the duties which its words purport to confer and assign.

The constitution vests the whole judicial power of the United States in one Supreme Court, and such inferior courts as congress shall, from time to time, ordain and establish. This power is expressly extended to all cases arising under the laws of the United States; and, consequently, in some form, may be exercised over the present case; because the right claimed is given by a law of the United States.

In the distribution of this power it is declared that "the Supreme Court shall have original jurisdiction in all cases affecting ambassadors, other public ministers and consuls, and those in which a state shall be a party. In all other cases, the Supreme Court shall have appellate jurisdiction.". . .

If it had been intended to leave it in the discretion of the legislature to apportion the judicial power between the supreme and inferior courts according to the will of that body, it would certainly have been useless to have proceeded further than to have defined the judicial power, and the tribunals in which it should be vested. . . . If congress remains at liberty to give this court appellate jurisdiction, where the constitution has declared their jurisdiction shall be original; and original jurisdiction where the constitution has declared it shall be appellate; the distribution of jurisdiction, made in the constitution, is form without substance. . . .

The authority, therefore, given to the Supreme Court, by the act establishing the judicial courts of the United States, to issue writs of mandamus to public officers, appears not to be warranted by the constitution; and it becomes necessary to inquire whether a jurisdiction so conferred can be exercised.

The question, whether an act, repugnant to the constitution, can become the law of the land, is a question deeply interesting to the United States; but, happily, not of an intricacy proportioned to its interest. It seems only necessary to recognize certain principles, supposed to have been long and well established, to decide it.

That the people have an original right to establish, for their future government, such principles, as, in their opinion, shall most conduce to their own happiness is the basis on which the whole American fabric has been erected. The exercise of this original right is a very great exertion; nor can it, nor ought it, to be frequently repeated. The principles, therefore, so established, are deemed fundamental. And as the authority from which they proceed is supreme and can seldom act, they are designed to be permanent.

This original and supreme will organizes the government, and assigns to different departments their respective powers. It may either stop here, or establish certain limits not to be transcended by those departments.

The government of the United States is of the latter description. The powers of the legislature are defined and limited; and that those limits may not be mistaken, or forgotten, the constitution is written. To what purpose are powers limited, and to what purpose is that limitation committed to writing, if these limits may, at any time, be passed by those intended to be restrained? The distinction between a government with limited and unlimited powers is abolished, if those limits do not confine the persons on whom they are imposed, and if acts prohibited and acts allowed, are of equal obligation. It is a proposition too plain to be contested, that the constitution controls any legislative act repugnant to it; or, that the legislature may alter the constitution by an ordinary act.

Between these alternatives there is no middle ground. The constitution is either a superior paramount law, unchangeable by ordinary means, or it is on a level with ordinary legislative acts, and, like other acts, is alterable when the legislature shall please to alter it.

If the former part of the alternative be true, then a legislative act contrary to the constitution is not law: if the latter part be true, then written constitutions are absurd attempts, on the part of the people, to limit a power in its own nature illimitable.

Certainly all those who have framed written constitutions contemplate them as forming the fundamental and paramount law of the nation, and, consequently, the theory of every such government must be, that an act of the legislature, repugnant to the constitution, is void.

This theory is essentially attached to a written constitution, and, is consequently, to be considered, by this court, as one of the fundamental principles of our society. It is not therefore to be lost sight of in the further consideration of this subject.

If an act of the legislature, repugnant to the constitution, is void, does it, notwithstanding its invalidity, bind the courts, and oblige them to give it effect? Or, in other words, though it be not law, does it constitute a rule as operative as if it was a law? This would be to overthrow in fact what was established in theory; and would seem, at first view, an absurdity too gross to be insisted on. It shall, however, receive a more attentive consideration.

It is emphatically the province and duty of the judicial department to say what the law is. Those who apply the rule to particular cases, must of necessity expound and interpret that rule. If two laws conflict with each other, the courts must decide on the operation of each.

So if a law be in opposition to the constitution; if both the law and the constitution apply to a particular case, so that the court must either decide that case conformably to the law, disregarding the constitution; or conformably to the constitution, disregarding the law; the court must determine which of these conflicting rules governs the case. This is of the very essence of judicial duty.

If, then, the courts are to regard the constitution, and the constitution is superior to any ordinary act of the legislature, the constitution, and not such ordinary act, must govern the case to which they both apply.

Those, then, who controvert the principle that the constitution is to be considered, in court, as a paramount law, are reduced to the necessity of maintaining that courts must close their eyes on the constitution, and see only the law.

This doctrine would subvert the very foundation of all written constitutions. It would declare that an act which, according to the principles and theory of our government, is entirely void, is yet, in practice, completely obligatory. It would declare that if the legislature shall do what is expressly forbidden, such act, notwithstanding the express prohibition, is in reality effectual. It would be giving to the legislature a practical and real omnipotence, with the same breath which professes to restrict their powers within narrow limits. It is prescribing limits, and declaring that those limits may be passed at pleasure.

That it thus reduces to nothing what we have deemed the greatest improvement on political institutions, a written constitution, would of itself be sufficient, in America, where written constitutions have been viewed with so much reverence, for rejecting the construction. But the peculiar expressions of the constitution of the United States furnish additional arguments in favour of its rejection.

The judicial power of the United States is extended to all cases arising under the constitution.

Could it be the intention of those who gave this power, to say that in using it the constitution should not be looked into? That a case arising under the constitution should be decided without examining the instrument under which it arises?

This is too extravagant to be maintained.

In some cases, then, the constitution must be looked into by the judges. And if they can open it at all, what part of it are they forbidden to read or to obey?

There are many other parts of the constitution which serve to illustrate this subject.

It is declared that "no tax or duty shall be laid on articles exported from any state." Suppose a duty on the export of cotton, of tobacco, or of flour; and a suit instituted to recover it. Ought judgment to be rendered in such a case? ought the judges to close their eyes on the constitution, and only see the law?

The constitution declares "that no bill of attainder or ex post facto law shall be passed."

If, however, such a bill should be passed, and a person should be prosecuted under it; must the court condemn to death those victims whom the constitution endeavours to preserve?

"No person," says the constitution, "shall be convicted of treason unless on the testimony of two witnesses to the same overt act, or on confession in open court."

Here the language of the constitution is addressed especially to the courts. It prescribes, directly for them, a rule of evidence not to be departed from. If the legislature should change that rule, and declare one witness, or a confession out of court, sufficient for conviction, must the constitutional principle yield to the legislative act?

From these, and many other selections which might be made, it is apparent, that the framers of the constitution contemplated that instrument as a rule for the government of courts, as well as of the legislature.

Why otherwise does it direct the judges to take an oath to support it? This oath certainly applies in an especial manner, to their conduct in their official character. How immoral to impose it on them, if they were to be used as the instruments, and the knowing instruments, for violating what they swear to support!

The oath of office, too, imposed by the legislature, is completely demonstrative of the legislative opinion on the subject. It is in these words: "I do solemnly swear that I will administer justice without respect to persons, and do equal right to the poor and to the rich; and that I will faithfully and impartially discharge all the duties incumbent on me as   , according to the best of my abilities and understanding, agreeably to the constitution and laws of the United States."

Why does a judge swear to discharge his duties agreeably to the constitution of the United States, if that constitution forms no rule for his government? if it is closed upon him, and cannot be inspected by him?

If such be the real state of things, this is worse than solemn mockery. To prescribe, or to take this oath, becomes equally a crime.

It is also not entirely unworthy of observation, that in declaring what shall be the supreme law of the land, the constitution itself is first mentioned; and not the laws of the United States generally, but those only which shall be made in pursuance of the constitution, have that rank.

Thus, the particular phraseology of the constitution of the United States confirms and strengthens the principle, supposed to be essential to all written constitutions, that a law repugnant to the constitution is void; and that courts, as well as other departments, are bound by that instrument.

The rule must be discharged.

The Doctrine of Judicial Review Attacked

Marshall's specific holding in *Marbury v. Madison* (that the petitioner, although entitled to his commission, could not get a writ of mandamus from the Supreme Court) avoided a direct conflict with the Jefferson Administration. But the crucial point in the case (that the Court, as the final interpreter of the Constitution, could invalidate an Act of Congress) the Jeffersonians, with their negative attitude toward a strong central government and their democratic proclivities, refused to accept.

Because of Marshall's subtle approach in deciding the case, however, there was little they could do to disestablish the doctrine of judicial supremacy in constitutional interpretation; and Marshall himself, aware of the dangers inherent in pushing the Court's power too far, did not invoke the doctrine against a congressional act during the remainder of his thirty-four years on the Bench.

Due in part to the limited nature of national governmental activity during the subsequent period, later Courts adhered to this policy. Though the principle of judicial review was consistently applied to laws of the states — a state act was first declared unconstitutional in 1810 in *Fletcher v. Peck* — not until the *Dred Scott* decision in 1857 did the Court strike down another Act of Congress, and the first case in which it found that a President (Lincoln) had acted beyond his constitutional authority did not come until 1866. On the whole the exercise of judicial power to invalidate actions of the national government has been a significant feature of the constitutional system only since the turn of this century.

But while resort to that power has in fact been more restrained than is often supposed (fewer than 100 congressional acts have been invalidated in 160 years), and despite the general acceptance of judicial review as a fundamental principle of the Constitution, the doctrine has been challenged on many occasions in American history. The most serious attacks, after the initial struggle, have come in the pre-Civil War era, during the early New Deal period, and again in our own time.

Thus the events generating anti-Court attitudes have varied. But the basic argument against judicial review has remained essentially the same. One of the first and best formulations of that argument was presented by Justice John Gibson of the Pennsylvania Supreme Court in 1825. Gibson attempted to rebut the doctrine in a case involving the state court's power to invalidate a statute. A majority of that court, using Marshall's language, held that such power did exist and Gibson dissented.

Eakin v. Raub
12 Sergeant and Rawle 330
(Supreme Court of Pennsylvania, 1825)

Mr. Justice Gibson, dissenting:

... I am aware, that a right to declare all unconstitutional Acts void ... is generally held as a professional [judicial] dogma; but, I apprehend, rather as a matter of faith than of reason. I admit that I once embraced the same doctrine, but without examination, and I shall therefore state the arguments that impelled me to abandon it, with great respect for those by whom it is still maintained. ...

The Constitution and the right of the legislature to pass the Act, may be in collision. But is that a legitimate subject for judicial determination? If it be, the judiciary must be a peculiar organ, to revise the proceedings of the legislature, and to correct its mistakes; And in what part of the Constitution are we to look for this proud preeminence? Viewing the matter in the opposite direction, what would be thought of an Act of Assembly in which it should be declared that the Supreme Court had, in a particular case, put a wrong construction on the Constitution of the United States, and that the judgment should therefore be reversed? It would doubtless be thought a usurpation of judicial power. But it is by no means clear, that to declare a law void which has been enacted according to the forms prescribed in the Constitution, is not a usurpation of legislative power. It is an act of sovereignty; and sovereignty and legislative power are said by Sir William Blackstone to be convertible terms. It is the business of the judiciary to interpret the laws, not scan the authority of the lawgiver; and without the latter, it cannot take cognizance of a collision between a law and the Constitution. So that to affirm that the judiciary has a right to judge of the existence of such collision, is to take for granted the very thing to be proved. . . .

But it has been said to be emphatically the business of the judiciary, to ascertain and pronounce what the law is; and that this necessarily involves a consideration of the Constitution. It does so: but how far? If the judiciary will inquire into anything beside the form of enactment, where shall it stop? There must be some point of limitation to such an inquiry; for no one will pretend, that a judge would be justifiable in calling for the election returns, or scrutinizing the qualifications of those who composed the legislature. . . .

In theory, all the organs of the government are of equal capacity; or, if not equal, each must be supposed to have superior capacity only for those things which peculiarly belong to it; and, as legislation peculiarly involves the consideration of those limitations which are put on the law-making power, and the interpretation of the laws when made, involves only the construction of the laws themselves, it follows that the construction of the constitution in this particular belongs to the legislature, which ought therefore to be taken to have superior capacity to judge of the constitutionality of its own acts. But suppose all to be of equal capacity in every respect, why should one exercise a controlling power over the rest? That the judiciary is of superior rank, has never been pretended, although it has been said to be co-ordinate. It is not easy, however, to comprehend how the power which gives law to all the rest, can be of no more than equal rank with one which receives it, and is answerable to the former for the observance of its statutes. . . .

Every one knows how seldom men think exactly alike on ordinary subjects; and a government constructed on the principle of assent by all its parts, would be inadequate to the most simple operations. The notion of a complication of counter checks has been carried to an extent in theory, of which the framers of the Constitution never dreamt. When the entire sovereignty was separated into its elemen-

tary parts, and distributed to the appropriate branches, all things
incident to the exercise of its powers were committed to each branch
exclusively. The negative which each part of the legislature may
exercise, in regard to the acts of the other, was thought sufficient to
prevent material infractions of the restraints which were put on the
power of the whole; for, had it been intended to interpose the judiciary as an additional barrier, the matter would surely not have been
left in doubt. The judges would not have been left to stand on the
insecure and ever shifting ground of public opinion as to construc-
tive powers: they would have been placed on the impregnable
ground of an express grant. . . .

    But the judges are sworn to support the Constitution, and are
they not bound by it as the law of the land? In some respects they
are. In the very few cases in which the judiciary, and not the legislature, is the immediate organ to execute its provisions they are
bound by it in preference to any Act of Assembly to the contrary.
In such cases, the Constitution is a rule to the courts. But what I
have in view in this inquiry, is the supposed right of the judiciary to
interfere, in cases where the Constitution is to be carried into effect
through the instrumentality of the legislature, and where that organ
must necessarily first decide on the constitutionality of its own act.
The oath to support the Constitution is not peculiar to the judges,
but is taken indiscriminately by every officer of the government,
and is designed rather as a test of the political principles of the man,
than to bind the officer in the discharge of his duty. . . . But granting
it to relate to the official conduct of the judge, as well as every other
officer and not to his political principles, still it must be understood
in reference to supporting the Constitution, only as far as that may
be involved in his official duty; and, consequently, if his official duty
does not comprehend an inquiry into the authority of the legislature,
neither does his oath. . . .

    But do not the judges do a positive act in violation of the Consti-
tution, when they give effect to an unconstitutional law? Not if the
law has been passed according to the forms established in the Constitution. The fallacy of the question is, in supposing that the
judiciary adopts the Acts of the Legislature as its own; whereas the
enactment of a law and the interpretation of it are not concurrent
acts, and as the judiciary is not required to concur in the enactment,
neither is it in the breach of the Constitution which may be the
consequence of the enactment. The fault is imputable to the legislature, and on it the responsibility exclusively rests. In this respect,
the judges are in the predicament of jurors who are bound to serve
in capital cases, although unable, under any circumstances, to rec-

oncile it to their duty to deprive a human being of life. To one of these, who applied to be discharged from the panel, I once heard it remarked by an eminent and humane judge, "You do not deprive a prisoner of life by finding him guilty of a capital crime: you but pronounce his case to be within the law, and it is therefore those who declare the law, and not you, who deprive him of life."

For these reasons, I am of opinion that it rests, ultimately, with the people, in whom full and absolute sovereign power resides, to correct abuses in legislation, by instructing their representatives to repeal the obnoxious act. What is wanting to plenary power in the government, is reserved by the people for their own immediate use; and to redress an infringement of their rights in this repect, would seem to be an accessory of the power thus reserved. It might, perhaps, have been better to vest the power in the judiciary; as it might be expected that its habits of deliberation, and the aid derived from the arguments of counsel, would more frequently lead to accurate conclusions. On the other hand, the judiciary is not infallible; and an error by it would admit of no remedy but a more distinct expression of the public will, through the extraordinary medium of a convention; whereas, an error by the legislature admits of a remedy by an exertion of the same will, in the ordinary exercise of the right of suffrage,— a mode better calculated to attain the end, without popular excitement.

The Scope and the Limits of Judicial Power

While there is much force in the democratic argument against judicial interpretation of the basic law, and though the actual power of the Supreme Court has varied from period to period, the doctrine of judicial review has long been firmly established in the American constitutional system. And it has had a profound effect on the nation's economic, social, and political development. For the ultimate result of the doctrine is to make the Supreme Court a *policymaking* organ of government.

When the Court interprets or reinterprets the Constitution to permit expansion of national governmental power over the economy, for example, or to prohibit state activities which deny the equal protection of the laws to some of its citizens, or to safeguard the right of free speech against either state or national authority, it is in effect "making law." It does not legislate in the same sense that Congress enacts statutes, nor in the same way that the President or an administrative agency may set down rules having the force of law. But judicial decisions approving or disapproving the policy determinations of other governmental organs are inevitably policy determinations themselves. And indeed, since they are based on the fundamental law, they are fundamental policy determinations, governing the future operations of the legislative and executive departments, as well as of the states.

The existence of such great power in the Supreme Court raises the question of whether there are any effective restraints on the judiciary. The Court acts as a check on the other agencies of government, but are there any checks on the Court? The answer is "yes" and the checks are of three sorts: constitutional, political, and self-imposed.

Both Congress and the President have constitutional powers which may be used to restrain the Court. The structure of the national judicial system and the jurisdiction of the Court itself are both subject to congressional control, since it is the legislature which establishes the lower federal courts and regulates the types of cases (comprising by far the largest number) which the Supreme Court may hear under its appellate jurisdiction. Together, Congress, through its office-creating power, and the President (with the consent of the Senate), through his appointing power, control the size of the Court, making it possible for the two political departments to bring about a shift in the judicial branch's interpretation of the Constitution by enlarging its personnel. In addition, Congress has the power to initiate constitutional amendments which may be designed to overcome the effects of judicial decisions, and it may impeach any or all of the Justices.

The amending process, of course, brings the states into the system of judicial restraint, since three-fourths of them must ratify an amendment; in fact all of the congressional checks reflect state power to a certain extent, since Congress (and especially the Senate) is, after all, composed of state representatives. Finally, there are important limits on the Court at both the beginning and the end of the judicial process. The Court does not survey the problems of American society and decide which ones require judicial attention; it only considers problems which are brought before it in the form of legal "cases or controversies." And since no judicial decision is self-enforcing, after the Court has acted it is ultimately the President who must assure compliance with such decisions through his power to execute the law.

None of these constitutional restraints on the judiciary has been applied with any regularity. But the post-Civil War Congress did curtail judicial review of the Reconstruction Acts; the Court's size has been changed on five occasions, and on a number of others (the latest in 1937 during the New Deal period) it has been threatened with "packing"; Federalist Justice Chase was impeached, though not convicted, by the Jeffersonians; and the Eleventh Amendment repudiated a judicial decision, as did the Fourteenth and Sixteenth. With regard to presidential actions restraining the Court, there have been few direct encounters. However, Jackson once refused to carry out a judicial decision, and Lincoln ignored a circuit court ruling of Chief Justice Taney in 1861. Conversely, the Court's desegregation decision was enforced in Little Rock only as a result of presidential action. In all, the constitutional powers available to restrain the Court are formidable, but they are infrequently used.

More consistently applied, and more effective, are political restraints in the form of pressures generated by other governmental organs and by public opinion. For if the Court acts as a check on democracy, it is also affected by and responsive to the popular will. It may not "follow the election returns," but it cannot ignore the force of electoral support for the political branches. If the nation as a whole has clearly expressed its approval of major governmental policies, and particularly if that approval continues over an extended period of time, the Court cannot maintain a position which goes counter to the political decision and also sustain that widespread respect for the law on which its own position and power ultimately depend. As with the other organs of government, popular support is the basic source of and popular hostility is the most effective restraint on judicial power.

Thus, while President Roosevelt was unsuccessful in his 1937 attempt to "pack" the Court, his effort focused attention on judicial obstruction of the New Deal reform program and created pressures impelling a change in the judiciary's attitude. Similarly, pressure generated by the contemporary conservative attacks on the Court have had an effect on several recent decisions dealing with civil liberties. There can be no doubt that the Justices, despite the aura of detachment and dispassion which surrounds them, are sensitive to public opinion and conscious of political realities.

Recognition of the constitutional and political power potentially available to check judicial authority has also led the Supreme Court to impose restraints on itself. It has, for example, developed a whole catalogue of "cautionary considerations" or "rules of self-restraint" to which it adheres in general (though by no means always). According to these rules, the Court, in reviewing an Act of Congress, will not pass on the motives of the legislature or on the wisdom of the legislation enacted; and it will presume that a statute is constitutional until that presumption is overcome by the challenging party. In addition, it will not give advisory opinions; it will not "anticipate a question of constitutional law in advance of the necessity of deciding it"; it will not "formulate a rule of constitutional law broader than is required by the precise facts" of the case to which the rule is applied; it will not address itself to a constitutional question if there is some other ground on which to dispose of a case, and if a statute is involved, it will "first ascertain whether a construction of the statute is fairly possible by which the question may be avoided."[1]

A related form of limitation on the Court is the doctrine of *stare decisis,* under which cases are to be determined according to the rule laid down in prior decisions dealing with similar situations. If it were strictly followed this doctrine would, of course, prevent any change in the law. But it is not binding, and while the Court will often go to great

---

[1] These "cautionary considerations" were outlined by Justice Brandeis in *Ashwander v. T.V.A.,* 297 U.S. 288, 346 (1936).

lengths in attempting to demonstrate its adherence to precedent, and thereby avoid reversing itself, the variety of rules established over the course of its history now gives the Justices a vast reservoir from which to choose an appropriate precedent supporting virtually any decision.

A more significant principle of self-restraint is the doctrine of "political questions," excluding from the Court's purview those issues which are not susceptible of judicial determination. Just what issues fall under this doctrine, however, the Court itself decides. Thus "gerrymandering" of election districts for purely partisan purposes is a political question, according to the Court, but as a device for limiting Negro voting rights it is not. The doctrine of political questions has been applied most consistently in the field of international relations, leaving the problems in this area to be determined by the President and Congress, but it is an ill-defined rule and may be expanded or contracted in the Court's discretion.

Finally, and of particular significance today, the Court has developed a strict rule of self-restraint with regard to governmental operations in time of war. The reasons are obvious: when the nation's survival is at stake, constitutional principles may have to give way to military necessity; and the judges of that necessity must be the political leaders of the government, not the members of the Supreme Court. Consequently, the most serious problems of wartime government have on the whole been regarded as political questions *par excellence,* and with regard to them the Court has consistently restrained itself rather than the political agencies entrusted with the nation's defense.

The Supreme Court and Constitutional Development

To view the Supreme Court realistically, it is essential to recognize all of these limitations on its power. But none of this vitiates the fact that the Court has the final authority to interpret the meaning of the basic law, and that it alone can place the imprimatur of constitutionality on the public policies which are tested before its Bench. This function is the key to the Court's important role in American government. For by giving or withholding such approval it can itself make policy, basing its determinations of constitutionality on the wide range of alternative interpretations in its store of precedents and incorporating in those determinations the policy views of a majority of its own members.

Thus the Supreme Court has real power, and it is an active participant in the governmental process. Notwithstanding the contrary view of American mythology, it is a *political* organ of government, and the social, economic, and political philosophies of its members are no less relevant in making the rules under which the society is governed than the President's or the Congressman's. But this does not mean that American government is "undemocratic," or that the judicial power is as great as the power of the political organs. On the contrary, in practical terms the Court is the weakest of the governmental agencies which share authority in the American system, and while it has on occasion attempted to block popularly supported policy decisions, taken as a whole its record of response to democratic aspirations compares favorably with the records of its elected counterparts. Indeed the Court has continued to exist and to command the respect of the nation because it has consistently interpreted the Constitution so that it would meet the nation's needs and conform with the popular will.

It is this process of adapting the basic law to the changing needs and aspirations of the society that is meant by the term *constitutional development*. The Supreme Court is not the only agency of government involved in this process, for in addition to interpretative judicial decisions the contemporary Constitution has also been shaped by presidential practices instituted primarily as the result of crises and making the Presidency the focal position in American government, by congressional acts elaborating the constitutional outline and establishing many of the government's operational features, and by a whole catalogue of political customs forming the basis of American democracy. But even these nonjudicial aspects of constitutional development are ultimately concretized by judicial acceptance, and despite the often unrecognized significance of political factors in molding the basic law, the Court's relationship to the Constitution remains special and unique.

The materials which follow are designed to illuminate that relationship and to demonstrate the dynamic process of constitutional development through judicial interpretation. Dealing with four of the most important issues of our time — economic regulation, racial equality, civil liberty, and wartime government — they reveal the Supreme Court's vital role in making the Constitution a "living" law for American society.

CHAPTER I

GOVERNMENT
AND THE ECONOMY

The Problem of National Control
Over Economic Affairs

Conflicting Views of National Power

One of the most important reasons for establishment of
the Constitution was the recognized need for greater central
authority in regulating the nation's economic affairs. But the
constitutional statement empowering Congress to "regulate
commerce . . . among the several States" is not very clear.
What kinds of economic activity does the word "commerce"
comprehend? Is the congressional power to be exclusive
or may the states also regulate commerce? What if an economic activity affects the national economy but takes place
entirely within one state? These and many other questions
were left unanswered by the Framers, and they have been
the focus of a continuing conflict between opposing views
of government's role in economic affairs.

The problem of interpreting the commerce clause and
those other parts of the Constitution relevant to the economy
has historically occupied more of the Supreme Court's time
and energy than any other. And few problems have involved
the Court in deeper controversy, for its decisions in this
field have effected policies determining the basic social and
economic (as well as political) structure of the American
community. The essential issue in this still unresolved con-

flict is the extent to which economic affairs should be subject to governmental supervision and control; and in its attempts to deal with this issue the Court has reflected the change of attitude toward socio-economic problems which the nation itself has undergone.

In this field there has been no consistent line of constitutional development, but rather a fluctuation of judicial opinion falling roughly into four periods:

The first period—extending from the establishment of the Constitution to the end of John Marshall's reign on the Court—was dominated by the great Chief Justice's Federalist views. As expressed in a number of cases, the first and most important being *Gibbons v. Ogden* (1824), the Marshallian position was that Congress's power comprehended all aspects of commercial life; that it was a plenary, absolute, and complete power, allowing the legislature to prescribe the rules by which commerce would be governed; that its exercise superseded any state attempts to regulate commerce; and that it included the regulation of economic activity even if conducted wholly within one state. Significantly, Marshall failed to say that Congress's power was exclusive, and on later occasions his opinions included language which was more acceptable to states' righters. But the underlying conception remained, that in economic affairs, as in all other essential areas of national life, Americans were one people.

The second period covered Roger Taney's tenure as Chief Justice—from 1835 through the Civil War—and was characterized by a modification of the Court's prior position in favor of greater state power over commerce. The most important case during this period was *Cooley v. Board of Wardens* (1852) where an attempt was made to clarify the rules which had been developed over the preceding quarter century. Congress alone, said the Court, could act on subjects national in scope and requiring uniform regulation; but with regard to subjects local in character and not requiring uniform regulation, the states might legislate in the absence of congressional action. Subsequent national legislation would supersede any state laws, and in cases of conflict between the two, national law would prevail. Thus the

Taney Court more definitely injected the federal principle into the area of economic affairs, although it did not radically alter the Marshallian view.

In the third period—from the end of the Civil War through the early 1930s—issues related to the economic system were predominant on the American scene, for this was an era of tremendous economic expansion and of concomitantly serious social problems. All of the strains and tensions resulting from this "industrial revolution" were reflected in decisions of the Supreme Court, as that tribunal undertook to resolve the conflicts between competing socioeconomic theories. In general the Court aligned itself with those forces opposed to economic regulation, but despite that bias it is difficult to find a clear pattern in its opinions. For the Justices were rather generous in their attitude toward regulation by the states (acting under their "police power" to protect the health, safety, morals, and general welfare of their citizens), and though they generally looked with disfavor on national governmental attempts at regulation, in a number of instances those efforts were also upheld.

Thus, with regard to national legislation, the Court held in *United States v. E. C. Knight Co.* (1895) that a sugar-refining monopoly was not subject to regulation under the Sherman Act, because its production activities were "local" in character and affected interstate commerce only "indirectly." If such activities could be regulated by Congress, said the Chief Justice, "comparatively little of business operations and affairs would be left for State control." Nonetheless, in *Swift & Co. v. United States* (1905), the Court recognized the new trends in business activity and held that a meat-packing monopoly was unlawful under the Act because its operations, though geographically local, had more than accidental or remote effects on the flow of commerce among the states. Later still, however, this broad view of the commerce power was rejected in *Hammer v. Dagenhart* (1918), as the Court returned to the Sugar Trust decision, distinguished between production and distribution, and invalidated Congress's attempt to prohibit the transportation in interstate commerce of goods produced by child labor.

This confused and confusing approach to interpretation of the commerce power continued throughout the third period of conflict over economic issues. But if there was no clear line of development in the judicial attitude toward those issues, by the time of the Great Depression a dominant view had been adopted by the Court and embodied in the Constitution. That view, combining the federal principle and laissez-faire economic theory, emphasized the limits rather than the powers of the federal government and resulted in the negation of efforts to deal on a national scale with the increasingly serious social and economic problems of a complexly interdependent industrial economy.

The New Deal and the Court

The fourth period of conflict in this area of constitutional development began with the Great Depression of the 1930s, was climaxed by a battle-royal between the Court and the President, and ended in a shift of judicial attitude which opened the way for a new conception of government's role in regulating socio-economic affairs.

When Franklin D. Roosevelt assumed the Presidency in March 1933, the economic depression which had begun with the stock market "crash" of 1929 was at a critical point. The national income had declined by over 50 per cent, farm foreclosures and business failures were at an all-time high, industrial production had virtually ceased, between ten and fifteen million workers were unemployed. The nation faced its gravest domestic emergency since the Civil War.

In his Inaugural Address, the new President recognized this fact and made clear his determination to treat the economic crisis as though it were a war. Acting quickly and decisively, FDR bridged the separation-of-powers and instituted a period of presidentially-directed legislative activity unparalleled in American history. Out of this "Hundred Days" of effort came a stream of legislation constituting the initial program of the New Deal. Many of these measures were designed to provide relief for those who were hit hardest by the Depression; others were designed to reinvigorate the economy and stimulate recovery. All were based on the philosophy that the federal government under the existing

conditions had both the power and the responsibility to regulate economic affairs for the general welfare of the nation.

The New Deal program represented the most comprehensive attempt at economic regulation in American history,
unprecedented in its sweeping encroachment on powers
traditionally reserved to the states, in its limitation of contractual and property rights, and in its delegations of authority
to the President to effectuate legislative policy. But the
situation which had given rise to this departure from the
previous conception of government's role in economic affairs
was also unprecedented. The big question was whether, in
view of this fact, the Supreme Court would sublimate its bias
against national regulation and place the stamp of constitutionality on the New Deal.

There was no immediate answer, for the members of the
Court were themselves deeply divided on the basic issues.
Of the nine Justices, four — Van Devanter, McReynolds,
Sutherland, and Butler — were strict-constructionists and
staunchly conservative in their attitude toward social and
economic regulation; three — Brandeis, Stone, and Cardozo
— were disposed to flexible interpretation of the fundamental
law and a broadening of national power over the economic
system; Roberts and Chief Justice Hughes occupied the center of this cleft Bench and were the "swing men" on whom
most of the Court's decisions would turn.

As a result of this internal division, the Court's initial
decisions regarding Depression policies established no clear
judicial position. In fact, during 1934, the Justices gave
Congress and the President some reason to hope for a favorable attitude toward the New Deal by upholding (5-4) two
state emergency acts limiting contractual rights and fixing
prices under the police power. *(Home Building and Loan
Association v. Blaisdell; Nebbia v. New York.)*

But then, in January 1935, came the first indication that
national regulatory efforts would meet a different fate, as
one section of the National Industrial Recovery Act (NIRA)
was declared invalid on the ground that Congress had improperly delegated legislative power to the President.
(Panama Refining Co. v. Ryan.) Never before had the Court
struck down a federal statute for this reason, and its invo-

cation of the separation-of-powers principle was particularly ominous because so many New Deal measures included broad delegation of rule-making authority to the executive.

The impact of this decision was somewhat softened when the Court narrowly upheld the government's power to determine the monetary standard and allowed the abrogation of contract provisions requiring payment in gold. *(The Gold Clause Cases.)* But Justice Roberts then shifted back to the conservative bloc to invalidate the Railroad Retirement Act on the ground that establishment of a pension system for employees was "really and essentially related solely to the social welfare of the worker, and therefore remote from any regulation of commerce as such." *(Railroad Retirement Board v. Alton R.R. Co.)*

This holding with regard to legislative power under the commerce clause went to the heart of congressional efforts to meet the Depression on a national basis, and it was a prelude to the full-scale judicial attack against the New Deal which began on May 27, 1935, when the Court declared the entire NIRA unconstitutional.

The Recovery Act was the most innovative and controversial of the early New Deal measures. The reasons for its passage, the constitutional authority on which it was based, and the purposes it sought to achieve were noted in its first section:

> A national emergency productive of widespread unemployment and disorganization of industry, which burdens interstate commerce, affects the public welfare, and undermines the standards of living of the American people, is hereby declared to exist. It is hereby declared to be the policy of Congress to remove obstructions to the free flow of interstate and foreign commerce which tend to diminish the amount thereof; and to provide for the general welfare by promoting the organization of industry for the purpose of cooperative action among trade groups, to induce and maintain united action of labor and management under adequate governmental sanctions and supervision, to eliminate unfair competitive practices, to promote the fullest possible utilization of the present productive capacity of industries, to avoid undue restriction of production (except as may be temporarily required), to increase the consumption of industrial

and agricultural products by increasing purchasing power, to
reduce and relieve unemployment, to improve standards of labor,
and otherwise to rehabilitate industry and to conserve natural
resources.[1]

To effectuate this policy the President was empowered to
promote industry-wide agreements in the various sectors
of the economy. These agreements were to be embodied in
"codes of fair competition" governing such matters as wages,
hours, and trade practices in the industry. The codes were
to be proposed by industry associations and approved by
the President, or in the absence of agreement by the associations the President was to prescribe a code. The determination of rules and standards to be applied in establishing
the codes was left largely to the President.

In the case which tested the constitutionality of this Act,
a Brooklyn slaughterhouse operator who purchased live
poultry at a New York City market to which it had been
shipped from outside the state and then resold it to consumers in the city was indicted for violating and for conspiring to violate the wages-and-hours provisions of the
"Live Poultry Code," as well as a requirement involving
the selection of poultry at markets. He was convicted, and
the Court of Appeals sustained the conviction, though only
as to the selection provision. On petitions for review from
both the dealer and the government the Supreme Court
granted certiorari.

Schechter Poultry Corporation v. United States
295 U.S. 495 (1935)

Mr. Chief Justice Hughes delivered the opinion of the Court:[2]

... *First.* Two preliminary points are stressed by the government
with respect to the appropriate approach to the important questions
presented. We are told that the provision of the statute authorizing
the adoption of codes must be viewed in the light of the grave national crisis with which Congress was confronted. Undoubtedly, the

[1] The National Industrial Recovery Act is 48 *United States Statutes-at-
Large* 195 (1933).

[2] Although the opinion dealt with two subjects — the delegation of legislative
power to the President and the regulation of commerce by Congress — the
excerpts include here are related primarily to the commerce problem.

conditions to which power is addressed are always to be considered when the exercise of power is challenged. Extraordinary conditions may call for extraordinary remedies. But the argument necessarily stops short of an attempt to justify action which lies outside the sphere of constitutional authority, Extraordinary conditions do not create or enlarge constitutional power. The Constitution established a national government with powers deemed to be adequate, as they have proved to be both in war and peace, but these powers of the national government are limited by the constitutional grants. Those who act under these grants are not at liberty to transcend the imposed limits because they believe that more or different power is necessary. Such assertions of extra-constitutional authority were anticipated and precluded by the explicit terms of the Tenth Amendment, "The powers not delegated to the United States by the Constitution, nor prohibited by it to the States, are reserved to the States respectively, or to the people."

The further point is urged that the national crisis demanded a broad and intensive co-operative effort by those engaged in trade and industry, and that this necessary co-operation was sought to be fostered by permitting them to initiate the adoption of codes. But the statutory plan is not simply one for voluntary effort. It does not seek merely to endow voluntary trade or industrial associations or groups with privileges or immunities. It involves the coercive exercise of the law-making power. The codes of fair competition which the statute attempts to authorize are codes of laws. If valid, they place all persons within their reach under the obligation of positive law, binding equally those who assent and those who do not assent. Violations of the provisions of the codes are punishable as crimes.

Second. The question of the delegation of legislative power.

[*The Court proceeds to discuss this question, noting particularly the President's broad discretionary power under § 3 to "effectuate the policy" of the Act.*]

To summarize and conclude upon this point: § 3 of the Recovery Act is without precedent. It supplies no standards for any trade, industry or activity. It does not undertake to prescribe rules of conduct to be applied to particular states of fact determined by appropriate administrative procedure. Instead of prescribing rules of conduct, it authorizes the making of codes to prescribe them. For that legislative undertaking, § 3 sets up no standards, aside from the statement of the general aims of rehabilitation, correction and expansion described in § 1. In view of the scope of that broad declaration, and of the nature of the few restrictions that are imposed, the discretion of the President in approving or prescribing codes, and thus enacting laws for the government of trade and industry throughout the country, is virtually unfettered. We think that the code-making authority thus conferred is an unconstitutional delegation of legislative power.

Third. The question of the application of the provisions of the Live Poultry Code to intrastate transactions. Although the validity of the codes (apart from the question of delegation) rests upon the commerce clause of the Constitution, § 3 (a) is not in terms limited to interstate and foreign commerce. From the generality of terms, and from the argument of the Government at the bar it would appear that § 3 (a) was designed to authorize codes without that limitation. But under § 3 (f) penalties are confined to violations of a code provision "in any transaction in or affecting interstate or foreign commerce." This aspect of the case presents the question whether the particular provisions of the Live Poultry Code, which the defendants were convicted for violating and for having conspired to violate, were within the regulating power of Congress.

These provisions relate to the hours and wages of those employed by defendants in their slaughterhouses in Brooklyn and to the sales there made to retail dealers and butchers.

(1) Were these transactions *"in"* interstate commerce? Much is made of the fact that almost all the poultry coming to New York is sent there from other States. But the code provisions, as here applied, do not concern the transportation of the poultry from other States to New York, or the transactions of the commission men or others to whom it is consigned, or the sales made by such consignees to defendants. When defendants had made their purchases, whether at the West Washington Market in New York City or at the railroad terminals serving the city, or elsewhere, the poultry was trucked to their slaughterhouses in Brooklyn for local disposition. The interstate transactions in relation to that poultry then ended. Defendants held the poultry at their slaughterhouse markets for slaughter and local sale to retail dealers and butchers, who in turn sold directly to consumers. Neither the slaughtering nor the sales by defendants were transactions in interstate commerce. . . .

The undisputed facts thus afford no warrant for the argument that the poultry handled by defendants at their slaughterhouse markets was in a *"current"* or *"flow"* of interstate commerce and was thus subject to congressional regulation. The mere fact that there may be a constant flow of commodities into a State does not mean that the flow continues after the property has arrived and has become commingled with the mass of property within the State and is there held solely for local disposition and use. So far as the poultry herein questioned is concerned, the flow in interstate commerce had ceased. The poultry had come to a permanent rest within the State. It was not held, used or sold by defendants in relation to any further transactions in interstate commerce and was not destined for transportation to other States. . . .

(2) Did the defendants' transactions directly "affect" interstate commerce so as to be subject to Federal regulation? The power of Congress extends not only to the regulation of transactions which are part of interstate commerce, but to the protection of that commerce from injury. It matters not that the injury may be due to the conduct of those engaged in intrastate operations. Thus, Congress may protect the safety of those employed in interstate transportation "no matter what may be the source of the dangers which threaten it." Defendants [however] have been convicted, not upon direct charges of injury to interstate commerce or of interference with persons engaged in that commerce, but of violations of certain provisions of the Live Poultry Code and of conspiracy to commit these violations. Interstate commerce is brought in only upon the charge that violations of these provisions—as to hours and wages of employes and local sales—"*affected*" interstate commerce.

In determining how far the Federal Government may go in controlling intrastate transactions upon the ground that they "affect" interstate commerce, there is a necessary and well-established distinction between direct and indirect effects. The precise line can be drawn only as individual cases arise, but the distinction is clear in principle. Direct effects are illustrated by the railroad cases we have cited. as, e. g., the effect of failure to use prescribed safety appliances on railroads which are the highways of both interstate and intrastate commerce, injury to an employe engaged in interstate transportation by the negligence of an employe engaged in an intrastate movement, the fixing of rates for intrastate transportation which unjustly discriminate against interstate commerce. But where the effect of intrastate transactions upon interstate commerce is merely indirect, such transactions remain within the domain of State power. If the commerce clause were construed to reach all enterprises and transactions which could be said to have an indirect effect upon interstate commerce, the Federal authority would embrace practically all the activities of the people and the authority of the State over its domestic concerns would exist only by sufferance of the Federal Government. Indeed, on such a theory, even the development of the State's commercial facilities would be subject to Federal control.

... [The] distinction between direct and indirect effects of intrastate transactions upon interstate commerce must be recognized as a fundamental one, essential to the maintenance of our constitutional system. Otherwise, as we have said, there would be virtually no limit to the Federal power, and for all practical purposes we should have a completely centralized government. We must consider the provisions here in question in the light of this distinction.

The question of chief importance relates to the provisions of the Code as to the hours and wages of those employed in defendants' slaughterhouse markets. It is plain that these requirements are imposed in order to govern the details of defendants' management of their local business. The persons employed in slaughtering and selling in local trade are not employed in interstate commerce. Their hours and wages have no direct relation to interstate commerce. The question of how many hours these employes should work and what they should be paid differs in no essential respect from similar questions in other local businesses which handle commodities brought into a State and there dealt in as a part of its internal commerce. This appears from an examination of the considerations urged by the Government with respect to conditions in the poultry trade. Thus, the Government argues that hours and wages affect prices; that slaughterhouse men sell at a small margin above operating costs; that labor represents 50 to 60 per cent of these costs; that a slaughterhouse operator paying lower wages or reducing his cost by exacting long hours of work translates his saving into lower prices; that this results in demands for a cheaper grade of goods, and that the cutting of prices brings about a demoralization of the price structure. Similar conditions may be adduced in relation to other businesses. The argument of the Government proves too much. If the Federal Government may determine the wages and hours of employes in the internal commerce of a State, because of their relation to cost and prices and their indirect effect upon interstate commerce, it would seem that a similar control might be exerted over other elements of cost, also affecting prices, such as the number of employes, rents, advertising, methods of doing business, etc. All the processes of production and distribution that enter into cost could likewise be controlled. If the cost of doing an intrastate business is in itself the permitted object of Federal control, the extent of the regulation of cost would be a question of discretion and not of power.

The Government also makes the point that efforts to enact State legislation establishing high labor standards have been impeded by the belief that unless similar action is taken generally, commerce will be diverted from the States adopting such standards, and that this fear of diversion has led to demands for Federal legislation on the subject of wages and hours. The apparent implication is that the Federal authority under the commerce clause should be deemed to extend to the establishment of rules to govern wages and hours in intrastate trade and industry generally throughout the country, thus overriding the authority of the States to deal with domestic problems arising from labor conditions in their internal commerce.

It is not the province of the Court to consider the economic advantages or disadvantages of such a centralized system. It is sufficient to say that the Federal Constitution does not provide for it. Our growth and development have called for wide use of the commerce power of the Federal Government in its control over the expanded activities of interstate commerce and in protecting that commerce from burdens, interferences and conspiracies to restrain and monopolize it. But the authority of the Federal Government may not be pushed to such an extreme as to destroy the distinction, which the commerce clause itself establishes, between commerce "among the several States" and the internal concerns of a State. The same answer must be made to the contention that is based upon the serious economic situation which led to the passage of the Recovery Act—the fall in prices, the decline in wages and employment, and the curtailment of the market for commodities. Stress is laid upon the great importance of maintaining wage distributions which would provide the necessary stimulus in starting "the cumulative forces making for expanding commercial activity." Without in any way disparaging this motive, it is enough to say that the recuperative efforts of the Federal Government must be made in a manner consistent with the authority granted by the Constitution.

We are of the opinion that the attempt through the provisions of the Code to fix the hours and wages of employes of defendants in their intrastate business was not a valid exercise of Federal Power. . . .

In view of these conclusions, we find it unnecessary to discuss other questions which have been raised as to the validity of certain provisions of the code under the due process clause of the Fifth Amendment.

On both the grounds we have discussed, the attempted delegation of legislative power and the attempted regulation of intrastate transactions which affect interstate commerce only indirectly, we hold the code provisions here in question to be invalid and that the judgment of conviction must be reversed.

The Court Fight

The *Schechter* decision was less important because it doomed the NIRA (which had not been very effective) than because it reaffirmed the Court's restrictive attitude toward governmental power in regulating the national economy. And the political branches were particularly concerned not only because the other "Hundred Day" measures were coming up for review, but because even more significant socio-economic legislation was at the moment in the process of being enacted. For the 1935 session of Congress was engaged in passing a number of laws designed to bring about basic reforms in the economic system, and that body of legislation — constituting the second and permanent New Deal program — would also have to be reviewed by the Court. If the Justices persisted in their demolition work, the reform program would suffer the same fate as the recovery program, and with the *Schechter* decision it seemed clear that no other result could be expected unless there was a change in either the attitude or the personnel of the Court. This soon became even clearer.

Undeterred by the growing wave of criticism which had greeted its previous decisions, in January 1936 the Court declared the Agricultural Adjustment Act unconstitutional in *United States v. Butler*. That Act was another pillar of the original New Deal program and involved an attempt by Congress to regulate the agricultural economy through resort to the taxing power. Justice Roberts found it a little difficult to demonstrate that the legislature had transcended its authority, since the power to tax for the general welfare and for regulatory purposes had never been denied. But, he said, taxing devices could not be used as part of a plan to control farm production, because agricultural regulation was "a matter beyond the powers delegated to the federal government." The general welfare clause of the Constitution could not be interpreted to permit the destruction of all state powers and the establishment of broad national authority over the economy. Moreover, in providing for processing taxes on farm commodities and for benefit payments to farmers signing acreage control contracts, the Act wrongfully expropriated money "from one group for the benefit of another." Finally, argued Roberts, the AAA plan was not really voluntary, since refusal to participate meant the loss of advantages, and "the power to confer or withhold unlimited benefits is the power to coerce or destroy."

In his opinion Roberts also gave evidence that the Court was aware of the criticism directed against it:

> It is sometimes said that the Court assumes a power to overrule or control the action of the people's representatives. This is a misconception. . . . When an act of Congress is appropriately challenged in the courts . . . the judicial branch of the Government has only one duty—to lay the Article of the Constitution which is invoked beside the statute which is challenged and to decide whether the latter squares with the former. . . . The only power it has, if such it may be called, is the power of judgment. This court neither approves nor condemns any legislative policy.

But Justice Stone, joined by Justices Brandeis and Cardozo, angrily disagreed with both the decision and the majority's attempt to avoid responsibility for its policy determinations. The majority opinion, he declared, was "a tortured construction of the Constitution . . . addressed to the mind accustomed to believe that it is the business of courts to sit in judgment on the wisdom of legislative action." In the absence of a check on judicial review, it was incumbent on the Justices to exercise self-restraint. "Courts," said Stone, "are not the only agency of government that must be assumed to have the capacity to govern," and he quoted from Justice Holmes, "It must be remembered that legislators are the ultimate guardians of the liberties and welfare of the people in quite as great a degree as the courts."

This reminder that the Court was supposed to be a "nonpolitical" organ of government fell on deaf ears, however. Although in its next decision the right of the government-owned Tennessee Valley Authority to sell electricity in competition with private companies was upheld *(Ashwander v. T.V.A.)*, on May 18 the Court struck down the Bituminous Coal Conservation Act.

The opinion in this case, *Carter v. Carter Coal Co.,* was

virtually a review of all the Court's objections to New Deal legislation. Designed to regulate working conditions in the mining industry and to fix prices for the sale of coal, the statute looked to the general welfare, interstate commerce, and taxation clauses of the Constitution for authority. In turn, each of these provisions was narrowly interpreted by Justice Sutherland so as to preclude national legislative action. Speaking for a Court which split 5-4 and 6-3 (Hughes joined the liberal minority on some points) he found that the excise tax which had been imposed to support the regulatory scheme was not a true tax, but a penalty imposed on non-compliant producers; that the effect of mining conditions on interstate commerce was only indirect; and that the federal government had no plenary power to legislate for the general welfare. In relation to this last point his opinion was particularly restrictive, holding that there was no inherent federal power which extended to matters affecting the nation as a whole, even though these were matters "with which the states severally cannot deal or cannot adequately deal."

> Much stress is put upon the evils which come from the struggle between employers and employees over the matter of wages, working conditions, the right of collective bargaining, etc., and the resulting strikes, curtailment and irregularity of production and effect on prices; and it is insisted that interstate commerce is *greatly* affected thereby. But ... the conclusive answer is that the evils are all local evils over which the federal government has no legislative control.... Such effect as they may have upon commerce, however extensive it may be, is secondary and indirect. An increase in the greatness of the effect adds to its importance. It does not alter its character.

The opinion also held that in establishing a system under which majorities of owners and miners were authorized to determine conditions of labor for their areas Congress had improperly delegated its legislative power, and that the Act's wages-and-hours provisions violated due process of law requirements.

Recognizing that this decision threw doubt on the constitutionality of the soon-to-be-tested National Labor Relations (Wagner) Act and other reform measures, Brandeis, Cardozo, and Stone again reproved their brethren for using the judicial power to negate governmental policies with which they disagreed. But as the Court's term came to a close, the conservative majority handed down yet another decision unfavorable to the Administration. While the coal case had limited congressional attempts to bring about labor-management reform, it had seemed to leave open the possibility that the states could act in this area. Now even this possibility was eliminated, as five Justices voted down a New York law establishing machinery to determine minimum wage rates for women and children. *(Morehead v. New York ex rel. Tipaldo.)*

Fixing wages, declared Justice Butler, deprived employees of their freedom to make contracts and violated the due process clause of the Fourteenth Amendment. The Chief Justice dissented, pointing out that contract rights had often been restricted in the public interest; and Brandeis and Cardozo joined in Justice Stone's incensed blast at the conservatives, which pointed out the "grim irony in speaking of the freedom of contract of those who, because of their economic necessities, give their services for less than is needful to keep body and soul together."

> It is difficult to imagine any grounds other than our own personal economic predilections, for saying that the contract of employment is any the less an appropriate subject of legislation than are scores of others, in dealing with which this Court has held that legislatures may curtail individual freedom in the public interest.

The Depression emergency, said Stone, had made necessary a new and broader approach to economic problems. "A generation ago they were for the individual to solve; today they are the burden of the nation."

The "Court-Packing" Plan

Throughout the period of judicial attack on the New Deal, President Roosevelt had remained relatively silent. He had encouraged Congress to modify and reenact some of those measures which the Court had invalidated, and despite one occasion on which he suggested that "doubts as to constitutionality" should not be permitted to block suggested legislation, he had been quite cautious in his references to judicial activity. During the 1935 Court term, this attitude may well have reflected the President's recognition of the fact that, for all its damage to his program, the invalidation of the initial New Deal program had been largely *ex post facto,* since the worst part of the economic crisis had already passed before the judiciary declared that the emergency measures which had been in effect for over two years were unconstitutional. Moreover, the NIRA had been on its last legs when the Court put it out of its misery, and many other early statutes obviously required reappraisal. But the decisions of 1936 posed a threat to those measures which were designed to endure beyond the crisis that had induced their enactment, and it was this threat to the permanent efforts of his Administration which precipitated Mr. Roosevelt's fight with the Court.

The President was not yet ready, however, to engage in his bitter struggle with the judicial branch. In a press conference on the day after the minimum wage decision he denounced the Court for having created a "no-man's-land" where neither the state nor the federal government could function, but he refused to comment on how he intended to meet the situation. With a presidential election only a few months off, FDR preferred to postpone action until after the nation had indicated its approval of his first Administration. In any event, he was obviously wary of a frontal attack against the "sacred institution." Although he had considered drastic legislative measures and an appeal to the people if the Court had invalidated the Gold Clause Act in 1935, the Democratic election platform did not contain any proposal for judicial reform and Roosevelt avoided the subject during the campaign.

The President's great victory in November 1936 did not, therefore, include a specific mandate to reform the Court. But it nonetheless represented an unqualified vote of confidence in his leadership and in his policies. Since that leadership and those policies were threatened by narrow judicial interpretation of the basic law, and since the conservative Justices had made it clear that they were disinclined to "follow the election returns," it followed logically that an attempt to force compliance from the Court would not lack popular support. And the need for such an attempt seemed imperative as FDR reassumed office, for the Fifth Circuit Court of Appeals had already declared the Wagner Act unconstitutional.

At least three alternatives were open to the President in formulating a plan to neutralize the Supreme Court: its reviewing power might be limited by a constitutional amendment, it might be deprived of jurisdiction in certain areas by an act of Congress, or the legislature might expand its membership. Each of these possibilities, however, had objectionable features. The amending process would be long, difficult, and uncertain; besides which, any really effective amendment would have revolutionized the established governmental system. A congressional act limiting the Court's jurisdiction over matters which raised constitutional issues might itself be subject to judicial veto. The third alternative —enlargement of the Court's membership—though it could be presented as merely a plan to increase judicial efficiency, was rather obvious in its purpose. On the other hand, this approach would be quick, clearly constitutional, and comparatively moderate.

The President liked the enlargement method, and on February 5, 1937, he sent to Congress his message recommending reorganization of the judiciary. The major provision of this plan allowed for the retirement of all Justices over 70; if a Justice failed to retire, he could remain in office, but the President would then be empowered to appoint an additional member to the Court. Since six Justices were then past the proposed retirement age (the oldest was Brandeis at 81), the plan would have made possible a fifteen-man Court with a majority of at least eight or nine sympathetic to the New Deal point of view.

The Roosevelt proposal—promptly dubbed "the Court-packing plan"—unleashed a storm of protest, as FDR was accused of attempting to invade judicial independence and of having dictatorial ambitions. The Court itself remained judiciously silent and apparently calm throughout the ensuing struggle, but to its defense rushed the press, the bar, private organizations, and a congressional coalition of Republicans, Southern Democrats, and anti-Roosevelt liberals. Chief Justice Hughes, along with Justice Roberts, played an important role behind the scenes, but the sole instance of direct judicial participation in the fight occurred when Hughes demolished Roosevelt's specious argument regarding judicial inefficiency, by stating, in a letter to Senator Wheeler, that the Court was abreast of its work and that "the present number of justices is thought to be large enough so far as the prompt, adequate, and efficient conduct of the work of the Court is concerned."[1]

The Justices could not avoid being the center of the controversy, however, nor could they escape feeling the pressures which were generated by that controversy. Having involved themselves in a serious political dispute, they were now necessarily exposed to the hot climate of political life. They maintained their dignity, but they could not help being concerned about the Court's reputation and its position as the "nonpolitical" arbiter of the constitutional system.

Throughout the short but tense period of presidential-judicial warfare, Hughes and Roberts were subjected to the greatest pressure, for they were the conservative members least committed to nullification of the New Deal program, the "swing men" on whom the Court's decisions turned. The Chief Justice represented the exact center of the Court, neither adamantly opposed to the Administration's program nor incapable of responding to the necessities of the situation. He was also the most politically experienced man on the Bench, aware of the extent to which congressional action on the reorganization bill would ultimately depend on the Court's attitude toward those reform measures then before it, and conscious of the fact that the present widespread defense of judicial independence might forthwith be transformed into an equally widespread demand for judicial limi-

---

[1]Chief Justice Hughes' letter is included as part of the record of the *Hearings on the Judiciary Reorganization Bill (S.1392)*, United States Senate, Committee on the Judiciary, 75th Congress, 1st session (Washington: Government Printing Office, 1937).

tation if the Court persisted in blocking social and economic reforms.

With a stalemate in Congress (reflecting the popular dilemma, Congress wanted both an independent judiciary and the New Deal reforms) and with the integrity of the Court at stake, Hughes allied himself with the liberals. Impelled by the same considerations, Roberts decided to re-examine his position, and in March, when the Court handed down its opinion on the constitutionality of Washington State's minimum wage law, he was counted in favor of reversing the year-old New York decision and upholding the regulation of wage rates for women. The Chief Justice, who had dissented in the previous case, now spoke for a five-man liberal majority and held that freedom of contract and due process had not been violated. "The community," he said, "may direct its lawmaking power to correct the abuse which springs from employers' selfish disregard of the public interest." *(West Coast Hotel Co. v. Parrish.)* On the same day an amended Farm Mortgage Act was upheld unanimously *(Wright v. Mountain Trust Bank),* and shortly thereafter a new railway labor act was also pronounced valid *(Virginian Railway Co. v. System Federation No. 40).* Coerced by the threat of reorganization, the Court was shifting into line beside the political branches.

The climax of the Court fight came on April 12, 1937 — less than two years after the *Schechter* case and only two months after the Court-packing plan had been sent to Congress — when Roberts joined Brandeis, Cardozo, Hughes, and Stone in declaring the Wagner Act constitutional. That Depression-induced measure was labor's "Magna Carta," guaranteeing to workers the right to organize and bargain collectively with their employers. But in prohibiting "any unfair labor practices affecting interstate commerce" it raised the question of Congress's power to regulate activities whose relation to such commerce was only "indirect." In the *Schechter* and *Carter* cases, the Court had denied Congress that power; now these former decisions were ignored and the commerce clause was interpreted broadly to allow a general expansion of legislative authority over the nation's economic life.

In the case before the Court, the National Labor Relations Board had ordered one of the nation's largest steel producers to "cease and desist" from engaging in certain unfair labor practices forbidden by Congress. Upon the company's failure to comply, the NLRB had petitioned the Court of Appeals to enforce its order. That court denied the petition, and the Supreme Court granted certiorari to review the constitutionality of the Labor Relations Act.

National Labor Relations Board v.
Jones & Laughlin Steel Company
301 U.S. 1 (1937)

Mr. Chief Justice Hughes delivered the opinion of the Court:

...*First. The scope of the Act.*—The Act is challenged in its entirety as an attempt to regulate all industry, thus invading the reserved powers of the States over their local concerns. It is asserted that the references in the Act to interstate and foreign commerce are colorable at best; that the Act is not a true regulation of such commerce or of matters which directly affect it but on the contrary has the fundamental object of placing under the compulsory supervision of the Federal government all industrial labor relations within the nation....

If this conception of terms, intent and consequent inseparability were sound, the Act would necessarily fall by reason of the limitation upon the Federal power which inheres in the constitutional grant, as well as because of the explicit reservation of the Tenth Amendment. The authority of the Federal government may not be pushed to such an extreme as to destroy the distinction, which the commerce clause itself establishes, between commerce "among the several States" and the internal concerns of a State. That distinction between what is national and what is local in the activities of commerce is vital to the maintenance of our Federal system.

But we are not at liberty to deny effect to specific provisions, which Congress has constitutional power to enact, by superimposing upon them inferences from general legislative declarations of an ambiguous character, even if found in the same statute. The cardinal principle of statutory construction is to save and not to destroy. We have repeatedly held that as between two possible interpretations of a statute, by one of which it would be unconstitutional and by the other valid, our plain duty is to adopt that which will save the act. Even to avoid a serious doubt the rule is the same....

We think it clear that the National Labor Relations Act may be construed so as to operate within the sphere of constitutional authority. The jurisdiction conferred upon the Board, and invoked in this instance, is found in § 10 (a), which provides:

"Sec. 10 (a). The Board is empowered, as hereinafter provided, to prevent any person from engaging in any unfair labor practice (listed in § 8) affecting commerce." . . .

"The term 'affecting commerce' means in commerce, or burdening or obstructing commerce or the free flow of commerce, or having led or tending to lead to a labor dispute burdening or obstructing commerce or the free flow of commerce."

This definition is one of exclusion as well as inclusion. The grant of authority to the Board does not purport to extend to the relationship between all industrial employees and employers. Its terms do not impose collective bargaining upon all industry regardless of effects upon interstate or foreign commerce. It purports to reach only what may be deemed to burden or obstruct that commerce and, thus qualified, it must be construed as contemplating the exercise of control within constitutional bounds. . . . Whether or not particular action does affect commerce in such a close and intimate fashion as to be subject to Federal control, and hence to lie within the authority conferred upon the Board, is left by the statute to be determined as individual cases arise. We are thus to inquire whether in the instant case the constitutional boundary has been passed.

Second. The unfair labor practices in question. — The unfair labor practices found by the Board are those defined in § 8, subdivisions (1) and (3). These provide:

"Sec. 8. It shall be an unfair labor practice for an employer —

"(1) To interfere with, restrain, or coerce employees in the exercise of the rights guaranteed in § 7."

"(3) By discrimination in regard to hire or tenure of employment or any term or condition of employment to encourage or discourage membership in any labor organization. . . . "

Section 8, subdivision (1), refers to § 7, which is as follows:

"Sec. 7. Employees shall have the right to self-organization, to form, join, or assist labor organizations, to bargain collectively through representatives of their own choosing, and to engage in concerted activities, for the purpose of collective bargaining or other mutual aid or protection."

Thus, in its present application, the statute goes no further than to safeguard the right of employees to self-organization and to select representatives of their own choosing for collective bargaining or other mutual protection without restraint or coercion by their employer.

That is a fundamental right. Employees have as clear a right to organize and select their representatives for lawful purposes as the respondent has to organize its business and select its own officers and agents. Discrimination and coercion to prevent the free exercise of the right of employees to self-organization and representation is a proper subject for condemnation by competent legislative authority. Long ago we stated the reason for labor organizations. We said that they were organized out of the necessities of the situation; that a single employee was helpless in dealing with an employer; that he was dependent ordinarily on his daily wage for the maintenance of himself and family; that if the employer refused to pay him the wages that he thought fair, he was nevertheless unable to leave the employ and resist arbitrary and unfair treatment; that union was essential to give laborers opportunity to deal on an equality with their employer.... Fully recognizing the legality of collective action on the part of employees in order to safeguard their proper interests, we said that Congress was not required to ignore this right but could safeguard it. Congress could seek to make appropriate collective action of employees an instrument of peace rather than of strife. We said that such collective action would be a mockery if representation were made futile by interference with freedom of choice. Hence the prohibition by Congress of interference with the selection of representatives for the purpose of negotiation and conference between employers and employees, "instead of being an invasion of the constitutional right of either, was based on the recognition of the rights of both."

Third. The application of the Act to employees engaged in production. — The principle involved. — Respondent says that whatever may be said of employees engaged in interstate commerce, the industrial relations and activities in the manufacturing department of respondent's enterprise are not subject to Federal regulation. The argument rests upon the proposition that manufacturing in itself is not commerce.... [But] the fact that the employees here concerned were engaged in production is not determinative. The question remains as to the effect upon interstate commerce of the labor practice involved. In the A. L. A. Schechter Poultry Corp. Case, supra, we found that the effect there was so remote as to be beyond the Federal power. To find "immediacy or directness" there was to find it "almost everywhere," a result inconsistent with the maintenance of our Federal system. In the Carter Case, supra, the Court was of the opinion that the provisions of the statute relating to production were invalid upon several grounds, — that there was improper delegation of legislative power, and that the requirements not only went beyond any sustainable measure of protection of interstate commerce but were also inconsistent with due process. These cases are not controlling here.

Fourth. Effects of the unfair labor practice in respondent's enterprise. — Giving full weight to respondent's contention with respect to a break in the complete continuity of the "stream of commerce" by reason of respondent's manufacturing operations, the fact remains that the stoppage of those operations by industrial strife would have a most serious effect upon interstate commerce. In view of respondent's farflung activities, it is idle to say that the effect would be indirect or remote. It is obvious that it would be immediate and might be catastrophic. We are asked to shut our eyes to the plainest facts of our national life and to deal with the question of direct and indirect effects in an intellectual vacuum. Because there may be but indirect and remote effects upon interstate commerce in connection with a host of local enterprises throughout the country, it does not follow that other industrial activities do not have such a close and intimate relation to interstate commerce as to make the presence of industrial strife a matter of the most urgent national concern. When industries organize themselves on a national scale, making their relation to interstate commerce the dominant factor in their activities, how can it be maintained that their industrial labor relations constitute a forbidden field into which Congress may not enter when it is necessary to protect interstate commerce from the paralyzing consequences of industrial war? We have often said that interstate commerce itself is a practical conception. It is equally true that interferences with that commerce must be appraised by a judgment that does not ignore actual experience.

Experience has abundantly demonstrated that the recognition of the right of employees to self-organization and to have representatives of their own choosing for the purpose of collective bargaining is often an essential condition of industrial peace. Refusal to confer and negotiate has been one of the most prolific causes of strife. This is such an outstanding fact in the history of labor disturbances that it is a proper subject of judicial notice and requires no citation of instances. . . .

These questions have frequently engaged the attention of Congress and have been the subject of many inquiries. The steel industry is one of the great basic industries of the United States, with ramifying activities affecting interstate commerce at every point. The Government aptly refers to the steel strike of 1919-1920 with its far-reaching consequences. The fact that there appears to have been no major disturbance in that industry in the more recent period did not dispose of the possibilities of future and like dangers to interstate commerce which Congress was entitled to foresee and to exercise its protective power to forestall. It is not necessary again to detail the facts as to respondent's enterprise. Instead of being beyond the pale, we think that it presents in a most striking way the close and intimate relation which a manufacturing industry may have to interstate commerce and we have no doubt that Congress had constitutional authority to safeguard the right of respondent's employees to self-organization and freedom in the choice of representatives for collective bargaining.

Fifth. The means which the Act employs. — *Questions under the due process clause and other constitutional restrictions.* — Respondent asserts its right to conduct its business in an orderly manner without being subjected to arbitrary restraints. What we have said points to the fallacy in the argument. Employees have their correlative right to organize for the purpose of securing the redress of grievances and to promote agreements with employers relating to rates of pay and conditions of work. Restraint for the purpose of preventing an unjust interference with that right cannot be considered arbitrary or capricious. . . .

The Act has been criticised as one-sided in its application; that it subjects the employer to supervision and restraint and leaves untouched the abuses for which employees may be responsible; that it fails to provide a more comprehensive plan, — with better assurances of fairness to both sides and with increased chances of success in bringing about, if not compelling, equitable solutions of industrial disputes affecting interstate commerce. But we are dealing with the power of Congress, not with a particular policy, or with the extent to which policy should go. We have frequently said that the legislative authority, exerted within its proper field, need not embrace all the evils within its reach. The Constitution does not forbid "cautious advance, step by step," in dealing with the evils which are exhibited in activities within the range of legislative power. The question in such cases is whether the legislature, in what it does prescribe, has gone beyond constitutional limits.

The procedural provisions of the Act are assailed. But these provisions, as we construe them, do not offend against the constitutional requirements governing the creation and action of administrative bodies. . . .

Our conclusion is that the order of the Board was within its competency and that the Act is valid as here applied. The judgment of the Circuit Court of Appeals is reversed and the cause is remanded for further proceedings in conformity with this opinion.

Mr. Justice McReynolds dissenting:

Mr. Justice Van Devanter, Mr. Justice Sutherland, Mr. Justice Butler and I are unable to agree with the decisions just announced. . . .

The Court as we think departs from well-established principles followed in A. L. A. Schechter Poultry Corp. v. United States, and Carter v. Carter Coal Co. Upon the authority of those decisions . . . the power of Congress under the commerce clause does not extend to relations between employers and their employees engaged in manufacture, and therefore the Act conferred upon the National Labor Relations Board no authority in respect of matters covered by the questioned orders. . . . No decision or judicial opinion to the contrary has been cited, and we find none. Every consideration brought forward to uphold the Act before us was applicable to support the Acts held unconstitutional in causes decided within two years. . . .

The Constitution still recognizes the existence of states with indestructible powers; the Tenth Amendment was supposed to put them beyond controversy. . . .

That Congress has power by appropriate means, not prohibited by the Constitution, to prevent direct and material interference with the conduct of interstate commerce is settled doctrine. But the interference struck at must be direct and material, not some mere possibility contingent on wholly uncertain events; and there must be no impairment of [guaranteed] rights. . . .

A New Court and a New Policy

The *Jones & Laughlin* decision, as one wag put it, was "the switch in time that saved nine." And that appraisal may not have been far from the mark. For if a shocked nation had sprung to the defense of the Court, and if a Congress grown restive after five years of executive domination had resisted encroachment on judicial independence, still both the people and a majority of their representatives supported those social and economic policies which the Court had blocked. There can be little doubt that continued judicial obstructionism whould have resulted in some form of limitation on the Court's power.

However, with the shift in judicial attitude, Congress rejected the reorganization plan. The Court had thus won

the battle—but it had lost the war. For a broad national
power over economic affairs was now recognized and embodied in the Constitution.

This was confirmed at the end of May when the Social
Security Act was upheld. Although the majority opinion in
the *Butler* case a year earlier had stated that neither the
general welfare nor the taxing power could be used to support a scheme whose purpose was economic regulation, the
Court now found both to be proper bases for such governmental action. Unemployment relief, said Justice Cardozo
in *Steward Machine Company v. Davis,* was a legitimate object of federal expenditure under the general welfare provision, and credit allowances for taxes paid into state
unemployment compensation funds did not represent a
"weapon of coercion impairing the autonomy of the States."
The Act was a valid attempt to solve pressing problems
through the "cooperation of State and Federal Governments."

Having set its new course, in 1939 the Court upheld a
refurbished Agricultural Adjustment Act which provided
for the establishment of marketing quotas on certain farm
commodities. The opinion was written by none other than
Justice Roberts (author of the first AAA opinion three years
before) who said that "any rule, such as that embodied in
the Act, which is intended to foster, protect and conserve . . .
commerce, or to prevent the flow of commerce from working
harm to the people of the nation, is within the competence
of Congress." *(Mulford v. Smith.)*

Two years later the Fair Labor Standards Act, the last
major New Deal measure, was also upheld in *United States
v. Darby Lumber Company.* The FLSA was a wages-and-
hours law which prohibited the shipment in interstate commerce of goods produced in violation of the standards set
by Congress. Its terms were much like those used in the
child labor law which the Court had declared unconstitutional in 1918 in *Hammer v. Dagenhart,* but the Act was
nonetheless held to be a valid exercise of legislative authority, as Mr. Justice Stone disposed of the prior decision
with little ceremony:

In that case it was held by a bare majority of the Court over the powerful and now classic dissent of Mr. Justice Holmes . . . that Congress was without power to exclude the products of child labor from interstate commerce. The reasoning and conclusion of the Court's opinion there cannot be reconciled with the conclusion which we have reached, that the power of Congress under the Commerce Clause is plenary to exclude any article from interstate commerce subject only to the specific prohibitions of the Constitution. . . . The conclusion is inescapable that *Hammer v. Dagenhart* was a departure from the principles which have prevailed in the interpretation of the Commerce Clause both before and since the decision and that such vitality, as a precedent, as it then had has long since been exhausted. It should be and now is overruled.

By the end of 1941 seven of the Court's members were Roosevelt appointees (all but Stone and Roberts of the 1933-37 Bench had either died or retired) and Stone had been elevated to the Chief Justiceship. There was no longer any question regarding the validity of national economic regulation, and in the last significant case in this area of constitutional development the new Court held that the scope of the regulatory power was virtually as broad as Congress might choose to make it.

The case involved the Agricultural Adjustment Act of 1938, under which "marketing quotas" were assigned to individual farmers as part of a national plan to stabilize agricultural production. The plan was to be suspended if more than one-third of the farmers affected disapproved it in a referendum. Once adopted, however, the plan would bind the farmers to produce no more than their assigned quotas. Penalties were provided for excess production. A farmer, Roscoe Filburn, sowed 11.9 acres and harvested 239 bushels of wheat in excess of his allotment. None of the wheat was intended for interstate commerce, and all of it was, in fact, consumed on his own farm. Penalized for exceeding his quota, Filburn sought an injunction against Secretary of Agriculture Wickard. The district court granted the injunction on grounds which did not involve the commerce power, but in reversing that decision the Supreme Court directed attention to the major point of national legislative authority.

Wickard v. Filburn
317 U.S. 111 (1942)

Mr. Justice Jackson delivered the opinion of the Court:

... Appellee says that [the regulation involved] is a regulation of production and consumption of wheat. Such activities are, he urges, beyond the reach of congressional power under the Commerce Clause, since they are local in character, and their effects upon interstate commerce are at most "indirect." In answer the Government argues that the statute regulates neither production nor consumption, but only marketing; and, in the alternative, that if the Act does go beyond the regulation of marketing it is sustainable as a "necessary and proper" implementation of the power of Congress over interstate commerce.

The Government's concern lest the Act be held to be a regulation of production or consumption rather than of marketing is attributable to a few dicta and decisions of this Court which might be understood to lay it down that activities such as "production," "manufacturing," and "mining" are strictly "local" and, except in special circumstances which are not present here, cannot be regulated under the commerce power because their effects upon interstate commerce are, as matter of law, only "indirect." Even today, when this power has been held to have great latitude, there is no decision of this Court that such activities may be regulated where no part of the product is intended for interstate commerce or intermingled with the subjects thereof. We believe that a review of the course of decision under the Commerce Clause will make plain, however, that questions of the power of Congress are not to be decided by reference to any formula which would give controlling force to nomenclature such as "production" and "indirect" and foreclose consideration of the actual effects of the activity in question upon interstate commerce.

[*The Court proceeds to review its prior commerce decisions.*]

... The present Chief Justice has said in summary of the present state of the law: "The commerce power is not confined in its exercise to the regulation of commerce among the states. It extends to those activities intrastate which so affect interstate commerce, or the exertion of the power of Congress over it, as to make regulation of them appropriate means to the attainment of a legitimate end, the effective execution of the granted power to regulate interstate commerce.... The power of Congress over interstate commerce is plenary and complete in itself, may be exercised to its utmost extent, and acknowledges no limitations other than are prescribed in the Constitution.... It follows that no form of state activity can constitutionally thwart the regulatory power granted by the commerce clause to Congress. Hence the reach of that power extends to those intrastate activities which in a substantial way interfere with or obstruct the exercise of the granted power." United States v. Wrightwood Dairy Co.

Whether the subject of the regulation in question was "production," "consumption," or "marketing" is, therefore, not material for purposes of deciding the question of federal power before us. That an activity is of local character may help in a doubtful case to determine whether Congress intended to reach it. The same consideration might help in determining whether in the absence of congressional action it would be permissible for the state to exert its power on the subject matter, even though in so doing it to some degree affected interstate commerce. But even if appellee's activity be local and though it may not be regarded as commerce, it may still, whatever its nature, be reached by Congress if it exerts a substantial economic effect on interstate commerce, and this irrespective of whether such effect is what might at some earlier time have been defined as "direct" or "indirect."

The parties have stipulated a summary of the economics of the wheat industry. Commerce among the states in wheat is large and important. Although wheat is raised in every state but one, production in most states is not equal to consumption. Sixteen states on average have had a surplus of wheat above their own requirements for feed, seed, and food. Thirty-two states and the District of Columbia, where production has been below consumption, have looked to these surplus-producing states for their supply as well as for wheat for export and carry-over.

The wheat industry has been a problem industry for some years. Largely as a result of increased foreign production and import restrictions, annual exports of wheat and flour from the United States during the ten-year period ending in 1940 averaged less than 10 per cent of total production, while during the 1920's they averaged more than 25 per cent. The decline in the export trade has left a large surplus in production which in connection with an abnormally large supply of wheat and other grains in recent years caused congestion in a number of markets; tied up railroad cars; and caused elevators in some instances to turn away grains, and railroads to institute embargoes to prevent further congestion....

The effect of consumption of home-grown wheat on interstate commerce is due to the fact that it constitutes the most variable factor in the disappearance of the wheat crop. Consumption on the farm where grown appears to vary in an amount greater than 20 per cent of average production. The total amount of wheat consumed as food varies but relatively little, and use as seed is relatively constant.

The maintenance by government regulation of a price for wheat undoubtedly can be accomplished as effectively by sustaining or increasing the demand as by limiting the supply. The effect of the statute before us is to restrict the amount which may be produced for market and the extent as well to which one may forestall resort to the market by producing to meet his own needs. That appellee's own contribution to the demand for wheat may be trivial by itself is not enough to remove him from the scope of federal regulation where, as here, his contribution, taken together with that of many others similarly situated, is far from trivial.

It is well established by decisions of this Court that the power to regulate commerce includes the power to regulate the prices at which commodities in that commerce are dealt in and practices affecting such prices. One of the primary purposes of the Act in question was to increase the market price of wheat and to that end to limit the volume thereof that could affect the market. It can hardly be denied that a factor of such volume and variability as home-consumed wheat would have a substantial influence on price and market conditions. This may arise because being in marketable condition such wheat overhangs the market and if induced by rising prices tends to flow into the market and check price increases. But if we assume that it is never marketed, it supplies a need of the man who grew it which would otherwise be reflected by purchases in the open market. Home-grown wheat in this sense competes with wheat in commerce. The stimulation of commerce is a use of the regulatory function quite as definitely as prohibitions or restrictions thereon. This record leaves us in no doubt that Congress may properly have considered that wheat consumed on the farm where grown if wholly outside the scheme of regulation would have a substantial effect in defeating and obstructing its purpose to stimulate trade therein at increased prices.

It is said, however, that this Act, forcing some farmers into the market to buy what they could provide for themselves, is an unfair promotion of the markets and prices of specializing wheat growers. It is of the essence of regulation that it lays a restraining hand on the self-interest of the regulated and that advantages from the regulation commonly fall to others. The conflicts of economic interest between the regulated and those who advantage by it are wisely left under our system to resolution by the Congress under its more flexible and responsible legislative process. Such conflicts rarely lend themselves to judicial determination. And with the wisdom, workability, or fairness, of the plan of regulation we have nothing to do. . . .

Appellee's [further] claim that the Act works a deprivation of due process . . . is not persuasive. Control of total supply, upon which the whole statutory plan is based, depends upon control of individual supply. Appellee's claim is not that his quota represented less than a fair share of the national quota, but that the Fifth Amendment requires that he be free from penalty of planting wheat and disposing of his crop as he sees fit.

We do not agree. In its effort to control total supply, the Government gave the farmer a choice which was, of course, designed to encourage co-operation and discourage nonco-operation. The farmer who planted within his allotment was in effect guaranteed a minimum return much above what his wheat would have brought if sold on a world market basis. Exemption from the applicability of quotas was made in favor of small producers. The farmer who produced in excess of his quota might escape penalty by delivering his wheat to the Secretary or by storing it with the privilege of sale without penalty in a later year to fill out his quota, or irrespective of quotas if they are no longer in effect, and he could obtain a loan of 60 per cent of the rate for co-operators, or about 59 cents a bushel, on so much of his wheat as would be subject to penalty if marketed. Finally, he might make other disposition of his wheat, subject to the penalty. It is agreed that as the result of the wheat programs he is able to market his wheat at a price "far above any world price based on the natural reaction of supply and demand." We can hardly find a denial of due process in these circumstances, particularly since it is even doubtful that appellee's burdens under the program outweigh his benefits. It is hardly lack of due process for the Government to regulate that which it subsidizes. . . .

That appellee is the worse off for the aggregate of this legislation does not appear; it only appears that if he could get all that the Government gives and do nothing that the Government asks, he would be better off than this law allows. To deny him this is not to deny him due process of law.

Reversed.

Conclusion: A New Conception Based on an Old Tradition

With *Wickard v. Filburn* the judicial reinterpretation of the national government's economic regulatory power was completed. In scope and effect that power was now virtually unlimited. But this post-1937 view of the commerce clause and the other constitutional provisions related to economic affairs was neither "new" nor "revolutionary." For the Marshall Court had also spoken of congressional authority as being plenary, complete, and applicable to all economic activity which affected the nation generally. The result of the dramatic events of 1937-42 was a "constitutional revolution" only in comparison with the restrictive concept of national power during the preceding half century. In longer perspective, the philosophy expressed by the liberalized Court of the late 1930s and early 1940s was in the older Marshallian tradition, viewing the American people as a single nation and the national government as the constitutionally established instrument for meeting their common problems.

But whether acceptance of the New Deal represented a revolution or a reaffirmation in the judicial attitude toward government's role in economic affairs, one clear consequence of decisions like *Wickard* was that the Supreme Court largely removed itself from the field of socio-economic policymaking. Problems requiring judicial decision have continued to arise in this area of national life, of course, but since the New Deal period the Court has consistently approved the policies formulated by the government's political organs.

Thus, for the Court—as for the entire nation—the Depression marked the end of one era and the beginning of another. New problems soon moved forward on the national scene, and increasingly the Court's attention was directed to new fields of constitutional development. The most significant of these involved the meaning of individual freedom and equality in American society, and it is in the important problem areas of civil rights and civil liberties that judicial activity has been greatest during the contemporary period.

CHAPTER II

RACIAL DISCRIMINATION AND CIVIL RIGHTS

The Problem of Equality in Education

Civil War and Civil Rights

Because of the historical context in which it arose, the problem of racial discrimination is inextricably bound up with the constitutional principle of federalism. Although the Civil War was triggered by the controversy over slavery, the underlying issue in that conflict involved the relationship between the nation and the states. And while the Union victory confirmed the emancipation of the Negro slaves, it also secured the doctrine of national supremacy against the claim of the Southern states to "sovereign rights." The full import of this connection between national authority and racial equality was not to be realized for almost a century, however. For despite its ultimate effect on federalism, the Civil War did not destroy that principle, and upon returning to the Union the Southern states proceeded to use their "reserved powers" as a means of imposing restrictions on the newly freed Negro.

The immediate result of this attempt to undo the verdict of the battlefield was a resort to the national legislative power to protect the Negro citizen against his own state by assuring his rights under the laws of the United States. In 1866 Congress passed a Civil Rights Act designed to outlaw the postwar Southern "Black Codes" and safeguard the

Negroes' legal status by guaranteeing to citizens "of every race and color . . . in every State and Territory . . . full and equal benefit of all laws and proceedings for the security of person and property, as is enjoyed by white citizens. . . . "

This legislative action to translate one of the war's objectives into law, was followed two years later by adoption of the Fourteenth Amendment, the central constitutional provision related to racial equality. That Amendment, which was eventually to become a watershed of the constitutional system, provided in its first section that:

> All persons born or naturalized in the United States, and subject to the jurisdiction thereof, are citizens of the United States and of the state wherein they reside. No state shall make or enforce any law which shall abridge the privileges or immunities of citizens of the United States; nor shall any state deprive any person of life, liberty, or property without due process of law; nor deny to any person within its jurisdiction the equal protection of the law.

Three additional Acts designed to enforce the Fourteenth and Fifteenth Amendment guarantees of equal civil rights for Negroes were passed by Congress in 1870, 1871, and 1875. The first primarily protected voting rights, the second was aimed against those persons and organizations (like the Ku Klux Klan) who interfered with the exercise of civil rights, and the third assured all citizens the right to "free and equal enjoyment" of public conveyances, inns, theatres, and other places of amusement.

These efforts of the Reconstruction Congress in the decade after the Civil War were not supplemented by additional legislation until 1957. But more important, the initial congressional attempts to guarantee racial equality were themselves quickly nullified by the Supreme Court. Ignoring the legislature's intention, and substituting its own interpretation of the Fourteenth Amendment, the postwar Court proceeded to deprive that provision of its essential meaning and significance. Although the Court noted in 1873 (in the *Slaughterhouse Cases*) that the Fourteenth Amendment's "pervading purpose" was the protection of Negro rights, it rejected the argument that the Amendment had basically altered the previous conception of federalism and indicated that it would take a very conservative view of the new constitutional provision.

And that is precisely what happened when, in the *Civil Rights Cases* of 1883, the Court said that Congress, in enacting enforcement legislation, had misunderstood the Amendment and as a result had exceeded its legislative authority. Only "state action," literally and narrowly conceived, was constitutionally prohibited, according to Justice Bradley, and regardless of the public nature or effect of private discriminatory activities, no restrictions could be imposed by the federal government. "Individual invasion of individual rights is not the subject matter of the Amendment," said the Court. "Until some State law has been passed, or some State action through its officers or agents has been taken, adverse to the rights of citizens sought to be protected by the Fourteenth Amendment, no legislation of the United States under said Amendment, nor any proceeding under such legislation, can be called into activity."

This limited view of the equal protection available under the Fourteenth Amendment, as Justice Harlan protested in his dissent, sacrificed both the "substance and spirit" of the provision. But in setting a course which modified the Fourteenth Amendment and allowed for a return in the South to conditions approaching ante-bellum "normalcy" the Court probably reflected the prevailing national sentiment. For in the post-Reconstruction period of industrial development and increased business activity, there was a widespread desire to forget the antagonisms of the past and concentrate on the opportunities of the present. Some white people in the North were outraged by passage in the Southern states of legislation which required segregation of the races in schools, parks, conveyances, and other public and semi-public facilities, but as the nation moved into an era of great economic expansion, the plight of the Negro was largely ignored and the issue of racial equality was relegated to the background of the constitutional arena.

The "Separate But Equal" Doctrine

The hallmark of this national sublimation of concern for Negro rights — and the touchstone of judicial interpretation in the racial equality field for over a half century — was the "separate but equal" doctrine, enunciated by the Supreme Court in 1896. The case in which this doctrine arose involved an 1890 Louisiana statute providing that "all railway companies carrying passengers in their coaches in this state shall provide equal but separate accommodations for the white and colored races. . . . " Anyone sitting in a section of a train set aside for persons of the opposite race was subject to a fine of $25 or to a term of twenty days in jail. A man of one-eighth Negro blood, Homer Plessy, refused to vacate a seat in a railway car reserved for whites, and was arrested for violating the statute. He brought suit for a writ of prohibition against the judge, John Ferguson, before whom he was to be tried. The Supreme Court of Louisiana denied the writ, and Plessy appealed to the United States Supreme Court. There the state court's decision was affirmed 7-1, the single but significant dissent being written by Mr. Justice Harlan.

Plessy v. Ferguson
163 U.S. 537 (1896)

Mr. Justice Brown delivered the opinion of the Court:

The constitutionality of this act is attacked upon the ground that it conflicts both with the 13th Amendment of the Constitution, abolishing slavery, and the 14th Amendment, which prohibits certain restrictive legislation on the part of the states.

1. That it does not conflict with the 13th Amendment, which abolished slavery and involuntary servitude, except as a punishment for crime, is too clear for argument.

A statute which implies merely a legal distinction between the white and colored races — a distinction which is founded in the color of the two races, and which must always exist so long as white men are distinguished from the other race by color — has no tendency to destroy the legal equality of the two races, or re-establish a state of involuntary servitude. . . .

2. By the 14th Amendment, all persons born or naturalized in the United States, and subject to the jurisdiction thereof, are made

citizens of the United States and of the state wherein they reside; and the states are forbidden from making or enforcing any law which shall abridge the privileges or immunities of citizens of the United States, or shall deprive any person of life, liberty, or property without due process of law, or deny to any person within their jurisdiction the equal protection of the laws....

The object of the amendment was undoubtedly to enforce the absolute equality of the two races before the law, but in the nature of things it could not have been intended to abolish distinctions based upon color, or to enforce social, as distinguished from political, equality, or a commingling of the two races upon terms unsatisfactory to either. Laws permitting, and even requiring their separation in places where they are liable to be brought into contact do not necessarily imply the inferiority of either race to the other, and have been generally, if not universally, recognized as within the competency of the state legislatures in the exercise of their police power. The most common instance of this is connected with the establishment of separate schools for white and colored children, which have been held to be a valid exercise of the legislative power even by courts of states where the political rights of the colored race have been longest and most earnestly enforced....

It is claimed by the plaintiff in error that, in any mixed community, the reputation of belonging to the dominant race, in this instance the white race, is *property*, in the same sense that a right of action, or of inheritance, is property. Conceding this to be so, for the purposes of this case, we are unable to see how this statute deprives him of, or in any way affects his right to, such property. If he be a white man and assigned to a colored coach, he may have his action for damages against the company for being deprived of his so-called property. Upon the other hand, if he be a colored man and be so assigned, he has been deprived of no property, since he is not lawfully entitled to the reputation of being a white man.

In this connection it is also suggested by the learned counsel for the plaintiff in error that the same argument that will justify the state legislature in requiring railways to provide separate accommodations for the two races will also authorize them to require separate cars to be provided for people whose hair is of a certain color, or who are aliens, or who belong to certain nationalities, or to enact laws requiring colored people to walk upon one side of the street, and white people upon the other, or requiring white men's houses to be painted white, and colored men's black, or their vehicles or business signs to be of different colors, upon the theory that one side of the street is as good as the other, or that a house or vehicle of one color is as good as one of another color. The reply to all this is that every exercise of the police power must be reasonable, and extend only to such laws as are enacted in good faith for the promotion of the public good, and not for the annoyance or oppression of a particular class. . . .

So far, then, as a conflict with the 14th Amendment is concerned, the case reduces itself to the question whether the statute of Louisiana is a reasonable regulation, and with respect to this there must necessarily be a large discretion on the part of the legislature. In determining the question of reasonableness it is at liberty to act with reference to the established usages, customs, and traditions of the people, and with a view to the promotion of their comfort, and the preservation of the public peace and good order. Gauged by this standard, we cannot say that a law which authorizes or even requires the separation of the two races in public conveyances is unreasonable or more obnoxious to the 14th Amendment than the acts of Congress requiring separate schools for colored children in the District of Columbia, the constitutionality of which does not seem to have been questioned, or the corresponding acts of state legislatures.

We consider the underlying fallacy of the plaintiff's argument to consist in the assumption that the enforced separation of the two races stamps the colored race with a badge of inferiority. If this be so, it is not by reason of anything found in the act, but solely because the colored race chooses to put that construction upon it. The argument necessarily assumes that if, as has been more than once the case, and is not unlikely to be so again, the colored race should become the dominant power in the state legislature, and should enact a law in precisely similar terms, it would thereby relegate the white race to an inferior position. We imagine that the white race, at least, would not acquiesce in this assumption. The argument also assumes that social prejudices may be overcome by legislation, and that equal rights cannot be secured to the negro except by an enforced commingling of the two races. We cannot accept this proposition. If the two races are to meet on terms of social equality, it must be the result of natural affinities, a mutual appreciation of each other's merits and a voluntary consent of individuals. As was said by the court of appeals of New York in *People* v. *Gallagher,* "this end can neither be accomplished nor promoted by laws which conflict with the general sentiment of the community upon whom they are designed to operate. When the government, therefore, has secured to each of its citizens equal rights before the law and equal opportunities for improvement and progress, it has accomplished the end for which it is organized and performed all of the functions respecting social advantages with which it is endowed." Legislation is powerless to eradicate racial instincts or to abolish distinctions based upon physical differences, and the attempt to do so can only result in accentuating the difficulties of the present situation. If the civil and political rights of both races be equal, one cannot be inferior to the other civilly or politically. If one race be inferior to the other socially, the Constitution of the United States cannot put them upon the same plane.

It is true that the question of the proportion of colored blood necessary to constitute a colored person, as distinguished from a white person is one upon which there is a difference of opinion in the different states, some holding that any visible admixture of black blood stamps the person as belonging to the colored race; others that it depends upon the preponderance of blood; and still others that the predominance of white blood must only be in the proportion of three fourths. But these are questions to be determined under the laws of each state and are not properly put in issue in this case. Under the allegation of his petition it may undoubtedly become a question of importance whether, under the laws of Louisiana, the petitioner belongs to the white or colored race.

The judgment of the court below is therefore affirmed.

Mr. Justice Harlan dissenting:

... In respect of civil rights, common to all citizens, the Constitution of the United States does not, I think, permit any public authority to know the race of those entitled to be protected in the enjoyment of such rights....

It was said in argument that the statute of Louisiana does not discriminate against either race, but prescribes a rule applicable alike to white and colored citizens. But this argument does not meet the difficulty. Everyone knows that the statute in question had its origin in the purpose, not so much to exclude white persons from railroad cars occupied by blacks, as to exclude colored people from coaches occupied by or assigned to white persons....

It is one thing for railroad carriers to furnish, or to be required by law to furnish, equal accommodations for all whom they are under a legal duty to carry. It is quite another thing for government to forbid citizens of the white and black races from traveling in the same public conveyance, and to punish officers of railroad companies for permitting persons of the two races to occupy the same passenger coach. If a state can prescribe as a rule of civil conduct, that whites and blacks shall not travel as passengers in the same railroad coach, why may it not so regulate the use of the streets of its cities and towns as to compel white citizens to keep on one side of the street and black citizens to keep on the other? Why may it not upon like grounds, punish whites and blacks who ride together in street cars or in open vehicles on a public road or street? Why may it not require sheriffs to assign whites to one side of a court-room and blacks to the other? And why may it not also prohibit the commingling of the two races in the galleries of legislative halls or in public assemblages convened for the political questions of the day? Further, if this statute of Louisiana is consistent with the personal liberty of citizens, why may not the state require the separation in railroad coaches of native and naturalized citizens of the United States, or of Protestants and Roman Catholics?

The answer given at the argument to these questions was that regulations of the kind they suggest would be unreasonable, and could not, therefore, stand before the law. . . . But I do not understand that the courts have anything to do with the policy or expediency of legislation. . . . Statutes must always have a reasonable construction. Sometimes they are to be construed strictly; sometimes literally, in order to carry out the legislative will. But however construed, the intent of the legislature is to be respected, if the particular statute in question is valid, although the courts, looking at the public interests, may conceive the statute to be both unreasonable and impolitic. If the power exists to enact a statute, that ends the matter so far as the courts are concerned. . . .

The white race deems itself to be the dominant race in this country. And so it is, in prestige, in achievements, in education, in wealth, and in power. So, I doubt not that it will continue to be for all time, if it remains true to its great heritage and holds fast to the principles of constitutional liberty. But in view of the Constitution, in the eye of the law, there is in this country no superior, dominant, ruling class of citizens. There is no caste here. Our Constitution is color-blind, and neither knows nor tolerates classes among citizens. In respect of civil rights, all citizens are equal before the law. The humblest is the peer of the most powerful. The law regards man as man, and takes no account of his surroundings or of his color when his civil rights as guaranteed by the supreme law of the land are involved. It is therefore to be regretted that this high tribunal, the final expositor of the fundamental law of the land, has reached the conclusion that it is competent for a state to regulate the enjoyment by citizens of their civil rights solely upon the basis of race.

In my opinion, the judgment this day rendered will, in time, prove to be quite as pernicious as the decision made by this tribunal in the *Dred Scott Case.* . . . The present decision, it may well be apprehended, will not stimulate aggressions, more or less brutal and irritating, upon the admitted rights of colored citizens, but will encourage the belief that it is possible, by means of state enactments, to defeat the beneficent purposes which the people of the United States had in view when they adopted the recent amendments of the Constitution.

... The destinies of the two races in this country are indissolubly linked together, and the interests of both require that the common government of all shall not permit the seeds of race hate to be planted under the sanction of law.... State enactments, regulating the enjoyment of civil rights, upon the basis of race, and cunningly devised to defeat legitimate results of the war, under the pretense of recognizing equality of rights, can have no other result than to render permanent peace impossible and to keep alive a conflict of races, the continuance of which must do harm to all concerned. This question is not met by the suggestion that social equality cannot exist between the white and black races in this country. That argument, if it can be properly regarded as one, is scarcely worthy of consideration, for social equality no more exists between two races when traveling in a passenger coach or a public highway than when members of the same races sit by each other in a street car or in the jury box, or stand or sit with each other in a political assembly, or when they use in common the streets of a city or town, or when they are in the same room for the purpose of having their names placed on the registry of voters, or when they approach the ballot-box in order to exercise the high privilege of voting....

The arbitrary separation of citizens, on the basis of race, while they are on a public highway, is a badge of servitude wholly inconsistent with the civil freedom and the equality before the law established by the Constitution. It cannot be justified upon any legal grounds.

If evils will result from the commingling of the two races upon public highways established for the benefit of all, they will be infinitely less than those that will surely come from state legislation regulating the enjoyment of civil rights upon the basis of race. We boast of the freedom enjoyed by our people above all other peoples. But it is difficult to reconcile that boast with a state of the law which, practically, puts the brand of servitude and degradation upon a large class of our fellow citizens, our equals before the law. The thin disguise of "equal" accommodations for passengers in railroad coaches will not mislead anyone, or atone for the wrong this day done....

I am of opinion that the statute of Louisiana is inconsistent with the personal liberty of citizens, white and black, in that state, and hostile to both the spirit and letter of the Constitution of the United States. . . .

Separate But Really Equal

Applied by the Supreme Court to all areas of "social" relations, the separate-but-equal doctrine in effect "constitutionalized" discrimination by permitting the legal segregation of Negro citizens. It was, nonetheless, to remain the law of the land for almost sixty years, and its history was to be the principal measure of the nation's—and the Court's—changing attitude toward the meaning of racial equality.

Significant steps in the direction of abrogating the segregation doctrine would eventually be taken; but during the generation following its establishment, the Court either upheld that doctrine without significant modification or, whenever possible, avoided discussing the basic issue altogether. This judicial acquiescence in the use of state power to separate the races and discriminate against Negroes extended to a variety of activities, from transportation to amusements to housing. The field in which the most important developments were ultimately to take place, however, was public education, and it is in that field that the process of constitutional change through judicial interpretation is most clearly seen.

In the first case involving educational facilities, *Cumming v. Richmond County Board of Education* (1899), the Court held unanimously that equal protection of the laws had not been denied by the board's decision to convert a Negro high school into a Negro elementary school without providing another high school for Negroes to match the one available for whites. And in 1908 a Kentucky law requiring the segregation of white and colored students in private as well as public institutions was upheld on the ground that the law merely amended the college charter, which the state had issued under its power to create corporations, and that the constitutional rights of individuals were not involved. *(Berea College v. Kentucky.)*

The Court had yet to rule directly on the question of educational segregation, but nonetheless by 1927 it was firmly committed to the separate-but-equal doctrine in this area, holding in *Gong Lum v. Rice* — where, under a Mississippi segregation statute, a Chinese child was required to attend a Negro school — that the type of dispute involved had been "many times decided to be within the constitutional power of the state legislature to settle without intervention of the federal courts under the Federal Constitution."

Despite this definite, and almost exasperated, affirmation of the states' power to maintain segregated education, however, the Court would within a decade begin the process of reevaluating the separate-but-equal doctrine.

A number of external factors were important in bringing about this new attitude on the Court. First of all, the Negro's economic, social, and political position changed significantly between 1900 and 1930. Drawn to the urban centers of the North by the promise of greater economic opportunity and social mobility, many Negroes had obtained an education and achieved status in their communities. Leadership developed, and as their numbers grew, Negroes formed a powerful political minority in many areas. Increasingly conscious of their second-class citizenship, and increasingly able to press for equality, they began to demand an end to discrimination against themselves and their Negro fellow-citizens in the South.

In addition, as America moved from its attachment to the 19th century conception of rugged individualism to its more socially conscious attitudes of the mid-20th century, the illogic and illiberalism of racial discrimination became more apparent to white as well as colored citizens. And, finally, in the later 1930s, the government of the United States itself, and the Supreme Court in particular, underwent significant change as a result of the Great Depression and the New Deal response to it.

The major problems of the Depression were, of course, economic rather than racial; but the approach adopted to meet them had two results of great importance for future developments in the field of racial relations: (1) it established a pattern for the national assumption of traditional state power, and (2) it brought forth a liberalized Court, more concerned with the protection of individual and minority rights than with property and states' rights, and more attuned to the implementation of national policies than to strict maintenance of the federal system.

The effect of all these changes in American government and society began to be felt almost immediately after the "new" (i.e. New Deal) Court was constituted. This body heard its first case involving the separate-but-equal doctrine in 1938, and at once it became apparent that while the Court might continue to accept the principle of separation, it would also insist that the states satisfy the requirement of equality.

The case was brought to the Court (with the aid of the National Association for the Advancement of Colored People) by a Negro citizen of Missouri who had been refused admission to the law school of the segregated state university. Missouri had no Negro law school, but pending the establishment of such an institution, the state had authorized officials of the university to arrange and pay for the attendance of any Negro resident at an unsegregated university in an adjacent state. The petitioner, Lloyd Gaines, contended that the university's refusal to admit him to the law school of his own state constituted a denial of the equal protection of the laws guaranteed under the Fourteenth Amendment. He sought a writ of mandamus to compel the university's registrar, S. W. Canada, to admit him. The Supreme Court of Missouri affirmed a denial of the writ, and the United States Supreme Court granted certiorari.

Missouri ex rel. Gaines v. Canada
305 U.S. 337 (1938)

Mr. Chief Justice Hughes delivered the opinion of the Court:

... The clear and definite conclusions of the state court in construing the pertinent state legislation narrow the issue. The action of the curators, who are representatives of the State in the management of the state university, must be regarded as state action. The state constitution provides that separate free public schools shall

be established for the education of children of African descent (Art.
11, § 3), and by statute separate high school facilities are supplied
for colored students equal to those provided for white students.
While there is no express constitutional provision requiring that the
white and negro races be separated for the purpose of higher education, the state court on a comprehensive review of the state statutes held that it was intended to separate the white and negro races
for that purpose also. Referring in particular to Lincoln University,
the court deemed it to be clear "that the Legislature intended to
bring the Lincoln University up to the standard of the University of
Missouri, and give to the whites and negroes an equal opportunity
for higher education—the whites at the University of Missouri, and
the negroes at Lincoln University." Further, the court concluded
that the provisions of § 9622 [of the state law] to the effect that negro
residents "may attend the university of any adjacent State with
their tuition paid, pending the full development of Lincoln University," made it evident "that the Legislature did not intend that
negroes and whites should attend the same university in this state."
In that view it necessarily followed that the curators of the University of Missouri acted in accordance with the policy of the State
in denying petitioner admission to its School of Law upon the sole
ground of his race.

In answering petitioner's contention that this discrimination
constituted a denial of his constitutional right, the state court has
fully recognized the obligation of the State to provide negroes with
advantages for higher education substantially equal to the advantages afforded to white students. The State has sought to fulfill that
obligation by furnishing equal facilities in separate schools, a method the validity of which has been sustained by our decisions. *(Plessy
v. Ferguson.)* Respondent's counsel have appropriately emphasized
the special solicitude of the State for the higher education of negroes
as shown in the establishment of Lincoln University, a state institution well conducted on a plane with the University of Missouri so
far as the offered courses are concerned. It is said that Missouri is a
pioneer in that field and is the only State in the Union which has established a separate university for negroes on the same basis as the
state university for white students. But, commendable as is that action, the fact remains that instruction in law for negroes is not now
afforded by the State, either at Lincoln University or elsewhere
within the State, and that the State excludes negroes from the advantages of the law school it has established at the University of
Missouri....

The state court stresses the advantages that are afforded by the
law schools of the adjacent States, Kansas, Nebraska, Iowa and

Illinois, which admit non-resident negroes. The court considered that these were schools of high standing where one desiring to practice law in Missouri can get "as sound, comprehensive, valuable legal education" as in the University of Missouri; that the system of education in the former is the same as that in the latter and is designed to give the students a basis for the practice of law in any State where the Anglo-American system of law obtains; that the law school of the University of Missouri does not specialize in Missouri law and that the course of study and the case books used in the five schools are substantially identical. Petitioner insists that for one intending to practice in Missouri there are special advantages in attending a law school there, both in relation to the opportunities for the particular study of Missouri law and for the observation of the local courts, and also in view of the prestige of the Missouri law school among the citizens of the State, his prospective clients. Proceeding with its examination of relative advantages, the state court found that the difference in distances to be traveled afforded no substantial ground of complaint and that there was an adequate appropriation to meet the full tuition fees which petitioner would have to pay.

We think that these matters are beside the point. The basic consideration is not as to what sort of opportunities other States provide, or whether they are as good as those in Missouri, but as to what opportunities Missouri itself furnishes to white students and denies to negroes solely upon the ground of color. The admissibility of laws separating the races in the enjoyment of privileges afforded by the State rests wholly upon the quality of the privileges which the laws give to the separated groups within the State. The question here is not of a duty of the State to supply legal training, or of the quality of the training which it does supply, but of its duty when it provides such training to furnish it to the residents of the State upon the basis of an equality of right. By the operation of the laws of Missouri a privilege has been created for white law students which is denied to negroes by reason of their race. The white resident is afforded legal education within the State; the negro resident having the same qualifications is refused it there and must go outside the State to obtain it. That is a denial of the equality of legal right to the enjoyment of the privilege which the State has set up, and the provision for the payment of tuition fees in another State does not remove the discrimination.

The equal protection of the laws is "a pledge of the protection of equal laws." Manifestly, the obligation of the State to give the protection of equal laws can be performed only where its laws operate, that is, within its own jurisdiction. It is there that the equality of legal right must be maintained. That obligation is imposed by the Constitution upon the States severally as governmental entities,— each responsible for its own laws establishing the rights and duties of persons within its borders. It is an obligation the burden of which cannot be cast by one State upon another, and no State can be excused from performance by what another State may do or fail to do. That separate responsibility of each state within its own sphere is of the essence of statehood maintained under our dual system. It seems to be implicit in respondents' argument that if other States did not provide courses for legal education, it would nevertheless be the constitutional duty of Missouri when it supplied such courses for white students to make equivalent provision for negroes. But that plain duty would exist because it rested upon the State independently of the action of other States. We find it impossible to conclude that what otherwise would be an unconstitutional discrimination, with respect to the legal right to the enjoyment of opportunities within the State, can be justified by requiring resort to opportunities elsewhere. That resort may mitigate the inconvenience of the discrimination but cannot serve to validate it.

Nor can we regard the fact that there is but a limited demand in Missouri for the legal education of negroes as excusing the discrimination in favor of whites. . . . Whether or not particular facilities shall be provided may doubtless be conditioned upon there being a reasonable demand therefor, but, if facilities are provided, substantial equality of treatment . . . cannot be refused. It is the individual who is entitled to the equal protection of the laws, and if [for example] he is denied by a common carrier, acting in the matter under the authority of a state law, a facility or convenience in the course of his journey which under substantially the same circumstances is furnished to another traveler, he may properly complain that his constitutional privilege has been invaded.

Here, petitioner's right was a personal one. It was as an individual that he was entitled to the equal protection of the laws, and the State was bound to furnish him within its borders facilities for legal education substantially equal to those which the State there afforded for persons of the white race, whether or not other negroes sought the same opportunity.

It is urged, however, that the provision for tuition outside the State is a temporary one,—that it is intended to operate merely pending the establishment of a law department for negroes at Lincoln University. While in that sense the discrimination may be termed temporary, it may nevertheless continue for an indefinite period by reason of the discretion given to the curators of Lincoln University and the alternative of arranging for tuition in other States, as permitted by the state law as construed by the state court, so long as the curators find it unnecessary and impracticable to provide facilities for the legal instruction of negroes within the State. In that view, we cannot regard the discrimination as excused by what is called its temporary character.... We are of the opinion that the ruling was error, and that petitioner was entitled to be admitted to the law school of the State University in the absence of other and proper provision for his legal training within the State.

The judgment of the Supreme Court of Missouri is reversed and the cause is remanded for further proceedings not inconsistent with this opinion.

Separate opinion of Mr. Justice McReynolds:

Considering the disclosures of the record, the Supreme Court of Missouri arrived at a tenable conclusion and its judgment should be affirmed. That court well understood the grave difficulties of the situation and rightly refused to upset the settled legislative policy of the State by directing a mandamus....

For a long time Missouri has acted upon the view that the best interest of her people demands separation of whites and negroes in schools. Under the opinion just announced, I presume she may abandon her law school and thereby disadvantage her white citizens without improving petitioner's opportunities for legal instruction; or she may break down the settled practice concerning separate schools and thereby, as indicated by experience, damnify both races. Whether by some other course it may be possible for her to avoid condemnation is matter for conjecture.

The State has offered to provide the negro petitioner opportunity for study of the law — if perchance that is the thing really desired — by paying his tuition at some near-by school of good standing. This is far from unmistakable disregard of his rights and in the circumstances is enough to satisfy any reasonable demand for specialized training. It appears that never before has a negro applied for admission to the Law School and none has ever asked that Lincoln University provide legal instruction.

The problem presented obviously is a difficult and highly practical one. A fair effort to solve it has been made by offering adequate opportunity for study when sought in good faith. The State should not be unduly hampered through theorization inadequately restrained by experience....

Mr. Justice Butler concurs in the above views.

Separate Cannot Be Equal

With the *Gaines* decision the groundwork was laid for an increasingly insistent attack on the separate-but-equal doctrine. That attack did not begin in earnest until after World War II had come to a close, but during the war pressure for the achievement of racial equality grew, as large numbers of Negroes entered the nation's military service, and as still others, seeking defense work, moved into the urban areas of the North.

These wartime pressures resulted in action by that part of the national government which was politically and practically willing and able to act. Thus President Truman, by executive order, instituted policies of desegregation in the armed forces and nondiscrimination in industries operating under defense contracts. And immediately after the war, in 1946, he created the President's Committee on Civil Rights, which, in addition to its reports on racial discrimination in housing, transportation, employment and other fields, found that in the South

> With respect to education...the "separate but equal" rule has not been obeyed in practice. There is a marked difference in quality between the educational opportunities offered white children and Negro children in the separate schools. Whatever test is used—expenditure per pupil, teachers' salaries, the number of pupils per teacher, transportation of students, adequacy of school buildings and educational equipment, length of school term, extent of curriculum—Negro students are invariably at a disadvantage. Opportunities for Negroes in public institutions of higher education in the South—particularly at the professional graduate school level—are severely limited.[1]

These presidentially initiated policies and studies added to the growing attack against discriminatory practices in American society, but paralleling this increased activity to secure equality for the Negro was a stiffening of Southern resistance to civil rights programs. The fortress for this

[1]From the Report of The President's Committee on Civil Rights, *To Secure These Rights* (Washington: Government Printing Office, 1947), pp. 62-63.

defense of States' Rights was Congress, and particularly the Senate, where a continuing coalition of Southern Democrats and conservative Republicans, using various techniques, was able to block all attempts at civil rights legislation.

If the legislative route to racial equality was closed, however, the Supreme Court had indicated that it would be a congenial forum in which to press the issue. Therefore, those who sought action on civil rights (and especially the NAACP, which financed many of the test cases) began a campaign of mounting intensity in the courts. Although efforts in other areas of discrimination—transportation, restrictive covenants, and voting—were also made, the most important area of attack, and the one in which the most significant decisions were handed down, continued to be education.

The emphasis in the postwar cases was still on the point that public educational facilities for Negroes were not *in fact* equal to those provided for whites, and the particular facilities attacked were still at the upper levels of education —professional and graduate schools. There were good reasons for this. Insofar as the limited approach to the issue was concerned, while the Court had shown a determination to insist on real equality in educational facilities, it had not yet revealed any disposition to invalidate the concept of segregation itself. With regard to the strategy adopted, concentration on the highest levels of education had at least three advantages: (1) the fact of inequality was most evident at the graduate level, not only because the existing Negro facilities were clearly inferior, but because in most of the Southern states there were no upper-level facilities at all; (2) the states would have no practical alternatives to accepting integration in their graduate schools, since financially and otherwise it would simply be impossible for them to create duplicate university systems for Negroes; and (3) the degree of Southern resistance would be less if only higher levels of education were affected, since desegregation of graduate schools (or even colleges) would involve only a small number of Negroes and, therefore, would not be viewed as a "social revolution."

The next education decision in effect constituted a post-script to the *Gaines* case, as the Court held, in *Sipuel v. Oklahoma State Regents* (1948), that a Negro student was not only "entitled to secure legal education afforded by a state institution," but that she could not be kept waiting for her education while the state sought to meet the equality requirement by building a separate institution. The Court did not specify what action the state should take, but the hint was clear, and in an attempt to avoid the unpleasant alternative now facing them, many Southern states quickly established separate graduate schools for Negroes.

In 1950, however, the Court blocked this last maneuver to maintain segregation in public higher education by carrying the logic of the "separate-but-really-equal" position to its ultimate conclusion. In *Sweatt v. Painter,* the first of two education cases decided unanimously on the same day, the petitioner, having been denied admission to the University of Texas Law School, had refused to attend a separate Negro law school provided by the state on the ground that it was an inferior institution. The Court, after comparing the two schools' facilities, concluded that:

> . . . the University of Texas Law School possesses to a far greater degree those qualities which are incapable of objective measurement but which make for greatness in a law school. Such qualities, to name but a few, include reputation of the faculty, experience of the administration, position and influence of the alumni, standing in the community, traditions and prestige. It is difficult to believe that one who had a free choice between these law schools would consider the question close.
>
> Moreover, although the law is a highly learned profession, we are well aware that it is an intensely practical one. The law school, the proving ground for legal learning and practice, cannot be effective in isolation from the individuals and institutions with which the law interacts. Few students and no one who has practiced law would choose to study in an academic vacuum, removed from the interplay of ideas and the exchange of views with which the law is concerned. The law school to which Texas is willing to admit petitioner excludes from its student body members of the racial groups which number 85% of the population of the State and include most of the lawyers, witnesses,

jurors, judges and other officials with whom petitioner will inevitably be dealing when he becomes a member of the Texas Bar. With such a substantial and significant segment of society excluded, we cannot conclude that the education offered petitioner is substantially equal to that which he would receive if admitted to the University of Texas Law School.

The *Sweatt* opinion was not, therefore, concerned with the mere physical differences between two educational institutions. Rather, the Court held that the very fact of segregation deprived the Negro student of association with most of those persons upon whom his professional career would depend, and that because of these practical and intangible factors, a law school limited to the members of a minority group could not satisfy the requirements of the separate-but-equal rule.

In the companion case, *McLaurin v. Oklahoma State Regents,* the Court went even further in adding new dimensions to the meaning of equality. Here, Oklahoma, following the *Gaines* and *Sipuel* decisons, had amended its law to permit the attendance of Negro students at the state university if the course of instruction in a Negro school was inadequate, but the instruction of such students was to be on a "segregated basis." Under this new provision, a Negro student, having been admitted to the university's graduate school of education, was assigned to a desk on the mezzanine floor of the library, to a designated table and special eating time in the cafeteria, and to a classroom seat in a row reserved for colored students.

These restrictions imposed by the university in complying with the state law, said the Court, constituted a denial of the equal protection of the laws.

> [The] result is that appellant is handicapped in his pursuit of effective graduate instruction. Such restrictions impair and inhibit his ability to study, to engage in discussions and exchange views with other students, and, in general, to learn his profession. . . .
>
> There is a vast difference — a Constitutional difference — between restrictions imposed by the state which prohibit the intellectual commingling of students, and the refusal of individ-

uals to commingle where the state presents no such bar....
Appellant, having been admitted to a state-supported graduate
school, must receive the same treatment at the hands of the
state as students of other races.

The two 1950 decisions made it clear that no segregated
institution of higher education could meet the new test of
equality. They also made it clear that the Court had gone as
far as it could go in interpreting away the separate-but-equal
doctrine. But the Justices had yet to say that the principle
of segregation was itself unconstitutional.

As the pressure for such a pronouncement increased,
the focus of attack shifted from the upper levels of education to the primary and secondary school levels. Here
Southern resistance would be all-out, but if the concept of
racial equality was to be meaningful it could not be limited
to the least significant area of Negro education. At the end
of 1952, the Court heard arguments in five public school
cases involving the educational segregation laws of Kansas,
South Carolina, Virginia, Delaware, and the District of
Columbia. All had been appealed from lower court decisions
upholding segregation while insisting on equality of facilities.
In June 1953, the Court announced that the cases would be
reargued the following October, and requested that counsel
answer a series of questions concerning the intention of the
Fourteenth Amendment's framers in regard to the education issue, the power of the judiciary to abolish segregation,
and the proper procedure to be followed if the Court were
to declare its abolition.

On May 17, 1954—with the attention of both the nation
and the world fixed on it—the Court handed down its historic unanimous decision in the desegregation cases.

Brown v. Board of Education
347 U.S. 483 (1954)

Mr. Chief Justice Warren delivered the opinion of the Court:

... In each of [these] cases, minors of the Negro race, through their
legal representatives, seek the aid of the courts in obtaining admission to the public schools of their community on a nonsegregated

basis. In each instance, they had been denied admission to schools attended by white children under laws requiring or permitting segregation according to race. This segregation was alleged to deprive the plaintiffs of the equal protection of the laws under the Fourteenth Amendment . . . .

The plaintiffs contend that segregated public schools are not "equal" and cannot be made "equal," and that hence they are deprived of the equal protection of the laws. Because of the obvious importance of the question presented, the Court took jurisdiction. Argument was heard in the 1952 Term, and reargument was heard this Term on certain questions propounded by the Court.

Reargument was largely devoted to the circumstances surrounding the adoption of the Fourteenth Amendment in 1868. It covered exhaustively consideration of the Amendment in Congress, ratification by the states, then existing practices in racial segregation, and the views of proponents and opponents of the Amendment. This discussion and our own investigation convince us that, although these sources cast some light, it is not enough to resolve the problem with which we are faced. At best, they are inconclusive. The most avid proponents of the post-War Amendments undoubtedly intended them to remove all legal distinctions among "all persons born or naturalized in the United States." Their opponents, just as certainly, were antagonistic to both the letter and the spirit of the Amendments and wished them to have the most limited effect. What others in Congress and the state legislatures had in mind cannot be determined with any degree of certainty.

An additional reason for the inconclusive nature of the Amendment's history, with respect to segregated schools, is the status of public education at that time. In the South, the movement toward free common schools, supported by general taxation, had not yet taken hold. Education of white children was largely in the hands of private groups. Education of Negroes was almost nonexistent, and practically all of the race were illiterate. In fact, any education of Negroes was forbidden by law in some states. Today, in contrast, many Negroes have achieved outstanding success in the arts and sciences as well as in the business and professional world. It is true that public school education at the time of the Amendment had advanced further in the North, but the effect of the Amendment on Northern States was generally ignored in the congressional debates. Even in the North, the conditions of public education did not approximate those existing today. The curriculum was usually rudimentary; ungraded schools were common in rural areas; the school term was but three months a year in many states; and compulsory school attendance was virtually unknown. As a consequence, it is not surprising that there should be so little in the history of the Fourteenth Amendment relating to its intended effect on public education.

In the first cases in this Court construing the Fourteenth Amendment, decided shortly after its adoption, the Court interpreted it as proscribing all state-imposed discriminations against the Negro race. The doctrine of "separate but equal" did not make its appearance in this Court until 1896 in the case of Plessy v. Ferguson, supra, involving not education but transportation. American courts have since labored with the doctrine for over half a century. In this Court, there have been six cases involving the "separate but equal" doctrine in the field of public education. In Cumming v. County Board of Education and Gong Lum v. Rice, the validity of the doctrine itself was not challenged. In more recent cases, all on the graduate school level, inequality was found in that specific benefits enjoyed by white students were denied to Negro students of the same educational qualifications. Missouri ex rel. Gaines v. Canada; Sipuel v. University of Oklahoma; Sweatt v. Painter; McLaurin v. Oklahoma State Regents. In none of these cases was it necessary to re-examine the doctrine to grant relief to the Negro plaintiff. And in Sweatt v. Painter, supra, the Court expressly reserved decision on the question whether Plessy v. Ferguson should be held inapplicable to public education.

In the instant cases, that question is directly presented. Here, unlike Sweatt v. Painter, there are findings below that the Negro and white schools involved have been equalized, or are being equalized, with respect to buildings, curricula, qualifications and salaries of teachers, and other "tangible" factors. Our decision, therefore, cannot turn on merely a comparison of these tangible factors in the Negro and white schools involved in each of the cases. We must look instead to the effect of segregation itself on public education.

In approaching this problem, we cannot turn the clock back to 1868 when the Amendment was adopted, or even to 1896 when Plessy v. Ferguson was written. We must consider public education in the light of its full development and its present place in American life throughout the Nation. Only in this way can it be determined if segregation in public schools deprives these plaintiffs of the equal protection of the laws.

Today, education is perhaps the most important function of state and local governments. Compulsory school attendance laws and the great expenditures for education both demonstrate our recognition of the importance of education to our democratic society.

It is required in the performance of our most basic public responsibilities, even service in the armed forces. It is the very foundation of good citizenship. Today it is a principal instrument in awakening the child to cultural values, in preparing him for later professional training, and in helping him to adjust normally to his environment. In these days, it is doubtful that any child may reasonably be expected to succeed in life if he is denied the opportunity of an education. Such an opportunity, where the state has undertaken to provide it, is a right which must be made available to all on equal terms.

We come then to the question presented: Does segregation of children in public schools solely on the basis of race, even though the physical facilities and other "tangible" factors may be equal, deprive the children of the minority group of equal educational opportunities? We believe that it does.

In Sweatt v. Painter, supra, in finding that a segregated law school for Negroes could not provide them equal educational opportunities, this Court relied in large part on "those qualities which are incapable of objective measurement but which make for greatness in a law school." In McLaurin v. Oklahoma State Regents, supra, the Court, in requiring that a Negro admitted to a white graduate school be treated like all other students, again resorted to intangible considerations: ". . . his ability to study, to engage in discussions and exchange views with other students, and, in general, to learn his profession." Such considerations apply with added force to children in grade and high schools. To separate them from others of similar age and qualifications solely because of their race generates a feeling of inferiority as to their status in the community that may affect their hearts and minds in a way unlikely ever to be undone. The effect of this separation on their educational opportunities was well stated by a finding in the Kansas case by a court which nevertheless felt compelled to rule against the Negro plaintiffs:

"Segregation of white and colored children in public schools has a detrimental effect upon the colored children. The impact is greater when it has the sanction of the law; for the policy of separating the races is usually interpreted as denoting the inferiority of the negro group. A sense of inferiority affects the motivation of a child to learn. Segregation with the sanction of law, therefore, has a tendency to [retard] the educational and mental development of Negro children and to deprive them of some of the benefits they would receive in a racial[ly] integrated school system."

Whatever may have been the extent of psychological knowledge at the time of Plessy v. Ferguson, this finding is amply supported by modern authority. Any language in Plessy v. Ferguson contrary to this finding is rejected.

We conclude that in the field of public education the doctrine of "separate but equal" has no place. Separate educational facilities are inherently unequal. Therefore, we hold that the plaintiffs and others similarly situated for whom the actions have been brought are, by reason of the segregation complained of, deprived of the equal protection of the laws guaranteed by the Fourteenth Amendment. This disposition makes unnecessary any discussion whether such segregation also violates the Due Process Clause of the Fourteenth Amendment. . . .

Since Brown v. Board of Education was decided under the Fourteenth Amendment, it did not apply to the District of Columbia. Segregation in the schools of the nation's capital was declared unconstitutional in a companion case, Bolling v. Sharpe:

. . . We have this day held that the Equal Protection Clause of the Fourteenth Amendment prohibits the states from maintaining racially segregated public schools. The legal problem in the District of Columbia is somewhat different, however. The Fifth Amendment, which is applicable in the District of Columbia, does not contain an equal protection clause as does the Fourteenth Amendment which applies only to states. But the concepts of equal protection and due process, both stemming from our American ideal of fairness, are not mutually exclusive. The "equal protection of the laws" is a more explicit safeguard of prohibited unfairness than "due process of law," and, therefore, we do not imply that the two are always interchangeable phrases. But, as this Court has recognized, discrimination may be so unjustifiable as to be violative of due process. . . .

Liberty under law extends to the full range of conduct which the individual is free to pursue, and it cannot be restricted except for a proper governmental objective. Segregation in public education is not reasonably related to any proper governmental objective, and thus it imposes on Negro children of the District of Columbia a burden that constitutes an arbitrary deprivation of their liberty in violation of the Due Process Clause.

In view of our decision that the Constitution prohibits the states from maintaining racially segregated public schools, it would be unthinkable that the same Constitution would impose a lesser duty on the Federal Government. We hold that racial segregation in the public schools of the District of Columbia is a denial of the due process of law guaranteed by the Fifth Amendment to the Constitution.

The Enforcement of Desegregation

Because of the complex problems involved in implementing desegregation, the Court restored *Brown v. Board of Education* and its companion cases to the docket and scheduled further hearings for April 1955. The Attorney General of the United States was invited to appear, as were the attorneys general of all states requiring or permitting segregation in their public schools. In addition a number of other persons and organizations were allowed to participate as *amici curiae*. All of this was quite unusual, as was the amount of time (fourteen hours) which was given to the reargument, and it indicated the Court's concern regarding the significant policy decision it had made. On May 31, 1955 the enforcement decree was handed down.

Brown v. Board of Education
(Enforcement Decision)
349 U.S. 294 (1955)

Mr. Chief Justice Warren delivered the opinion of the Court:

These cases were decided on May 17, 1954. The opinions of that date, declaring the fundamental principle that racial discrimination in public education is unconstitutional, are incorporated herein by reference. All provisions of federal, state, or local law requiring or permitting such discrimination must yield to this principle. There remains for consideration the manner in which relief is to be accorded....

Full implementation of these constitutional principles may require solution of varied local school problems. School authorities have the primary responsibility for elucidating, assessing, and solving these problems; courts will have to consider whether the action of school authorities constitutes good faith implementation of the governing constitutional principles. Because of their proximity to local conditions and the possible need for further hearings, the courts which originally heard these cases can best perform this judicial appraisal. Accordingly, we believe it appropriate to remand the cases to those courts.

In fashioning and effectuating the decrees, the courts will be guided by equitable principles. Traditionally, equity has been characterized by a practical flexibility in shaping its remedies and by a facility for adjusting and reconciling public and private needs. These cases call for the exercise of these traditional attributes of equity power. At stake is the personal interest of the plaintiffs in admission to public schools as soon as practicable on a nondiscriminatory basis. To effectuate this interest may call for elimination of a variety of obstacles in making the transition to school systems operated in accordance with the constitutional principles set forth in our May 17, 1954, decision. Courts of equity may properly take into account the public interest in the elimination of such obstacles in a systematic and effective manner. But it should go without saying that the vitality of these constitutional principles cannot be allowed to yield simply because of disagreement with them.

While giving weight to these public and private considerations, the courts will require that the defendants make a prompt and reasonable start toward full compliance with our May 17, 1954, ruling. Once such a start has been made, the courts may find that additional time is necessary to carry out the ruling in an effective manner. The burden rests upon the defendants to establish that such time is necessary in the public interest and the earliest practicable date. To that end, the courts may consider problems related to administration, arising from the physical condition of the school plant, the school transportation system, personnel, revision of school districts and attendance areas into compact units to achieve a system of determining admission to the public schools on a nonracial basis, and revision of local laws and regulations which may be necessary in solving the foregoing problems. They will also consider the adequacy of any plans the defendants may propose to meet these problems and to effectuate a transition to a racially nondiscriminatory school system. During this period of transition, the courts will retain jurisdiction of these cases.

The judgments below, except that in the Delaware case, are accordingly reversed and remanded to the District Courts to take such proceedings and enter such orders and decrees consistent with this opinion as are necessary and proper to admit to public schools on a racially nondiscriminatory basis with all deliberate speed the parties to these cases. The judgment in the Delaware case — ordering the immediate admission of the plaintiffs to schools previously attended by white children — is affirmed on the basis of the principles stated in our May 17, 1954, opinion, but the case is remanded to the Supreme Court of Delaware for such further pro-

ceedings as that court may deem necessary in light of this opinion.
It is so ordered.

Conclusion: With All Deliberate Speed

The school desegregation decision climaxed an eighty-year effort to realize the Fourteenth Amendment's promise of a "color-blind" Constitution. Its broad statement of a new principle immediately became the basis for declaring segregation unconstitutional in public recreational facilities, public housing, and intrastate bus transportation. And it also gave impetus to congressional activity aimed at securing more effective protection of Negro political rights. The first such legislation since the Civil War was passed in 1957, and Congress enacted still another voting rights statute on the eve of the 1960 presidential elections.

But despite these marks of progress toward the elimination of discrimination in American society, in the states most affected the desegregation decision has encountered formidable resistance, as opposition has been organized by White Citizens Councils and abetted by state governors and legislators. Moreover, many non-Southern constitutional strict-constructionists have joined the segregationists in condemning the *Brown* decision. Their contention is that the decision violated both of the Constitution's structural principles — federalism (by invading the states' reserved power over education) and the separation of powers (by "legislating" a new educational policy for the nation). Defenders of the Court and its decision have countered with the argument that even the reserved powers cannot be exercised to deny constitutional rights, that the definition of such rights is a function of the Supreme Court, and that the Court does not make law in the legislative sense when it interprets or reinterprets the Constitution.

Further criticism has been directed at the Court's adoption of psycho-sociological data as a basis for its decision; while still other attacks (less substantial but no less vehement) have accused the Court, on the one hand, of ignoring the "majority rule" principle by overriding white majority sentiment in the South, and on the other, of ignoring the "minority rights" principle by imposing the national majority will on the white Southern minority. Finally, the Justices have been charged with reading into the basic law their own predilections concerning racial relations in American society, and with propagandizing for Afro-Asian consumption.

Most serious of all, however, has been the concerted effort to avoid compliance with the desegregation ruling which began immediately after announcement of the enforcement plan. A number of Southern state legislatures passed resolutions condemning the Court's action and "interposing" the sovereignty of the states against the alleged encroachment on their reserved powers. In 1956 most of the Southern senators and representatives in Congress signed a declaration advocating resistance to desegregation by "all lawful means." And all of the "Deep South" states began to seek practical ways of obviating the decision, the most significant of which contemplated the establishment of private school systems or the use of pupil placement plans.

A high point of active Southern resistance was reached in 1957 with a riotous situation in Little Rock, Arkansas, traceable to the Governor and state legislature and necessitating the use of federal troops to achieve school integration.[1] The Court responded in a firm decision rising out of this incident. With every Justice listed as author of the opinion (including the three who had come to the Bench since the *Brown* decision), *Cooper v. Aaron* reiterated the desegregation principle, condemned violence as a means of resisting its application, and warned against the use of subterfuges to avoid compliance with it. The constitutional protection against discrimination in public school education, said the Court, "can neither be nullified openly and directly by state legislators or state executive or judicial officers, nor nullified indirectly by them through evasive schemes for segregation whether attempted 'ingeniously or ingenuously.'" State support of segregated schools "through any arrangement, management, funds, or property" would be unconstitutional.

[1] An even more serious crisis occurred in 1962, when rioting over the admission of a Negro student, James Meredith, to the University of Mississippi resulted in two deaths and required the use of 15,000 federal troops to maintain order.

School desegregation cases continue to enter the judicial mill, and the final resolution of this problem is still a long way off, involving as it does not only the acceptance of a new rule of law but the intellectual and emotional reorientation of a whole society. Nonetheless, as of 1963 some form of compliance with the Court's decision — though often only token in nature — had been achieved in each of the 21 states which required or permitted racial segregation in their public educational systems at the time of that decision. Concomitantly the focus of anti-discrimination efforts has been shifting to the areas of political rights (registration, voting), economic pressure (boycotts, fair employment practices legislation), and moral suasion (sit-ins, freedom rides). Having accomplished much in the courts during the past twenty years, Negro and white advocates of racial equality are turning their attention increasingly toward the centers of political, rather than judicial, action.

However, most of these contemporary efforts raise issues which must ultimately be reviewed in the courts, and thus the Supreme Court will not be on the sidelines in future civil rights controversies. Just as it was largely responsible for embodying the concept of racial discrimination in the nation's basic law originally, and just as it later played the major role in rejecting that concept and establishing racial equality as a principle of today's Constitution, so will the Court continue to be an active participant in resolving the problem which — both at home and abroad — is regarded as a major test of America's attachment to its own ideals.

CHAPTER III

NATIONAL SECURITY AND CIVIL LIBERTY

The Problem of Free Political Belief and Expression

The Constitutional Guarantee of Liberty

"Congress," says the Constitution, "shall make no law respecting an establishment of religion, or prohibiting the free exercise thereof; or abridging the freedom of speech or of the press; or the right of the people peaceably to assemble, and to petition the government for a redress of grievances."

Here, in the First Amendment of the Bill of Rights, is expressed the fundamental idea and ideal of the free society: the protection of individual liberty through the limitation of governmental authority. Moreover, that concept is expressed in absolute terms—"Congress shall make *no* law" —indicating the importance attached to the substantive freedoms and ostensibly placing them beyond the purview of governmental power. In interpreting these words, however, the courts have always recognized that while there may be a constitutional presumption in favor of liberty, "reasonable" limitations on its exercise are not precluded by the basic law. The great problem has been to determine just what restrictions on freedom *are* reasonable and to achieve a balance between the liberties of the individual and the interests of society.

Despite the fundamental nature of the First Amendment,

few controversies centered around it for over 125 years
after establishment of the constitutional system. The Alien
and Sedition Acts of 1798, proscribing criticism of the government or its officers in broad terms, raised serious
questions of civil liberty, but they were never tested in the
Supreme Court. And some of Lincoln's extralegal suppres-
sions of speech and press during the Civil War raised similar
questions, though again no direct judicial test of their
validity arose.

It was not until World War I that important issues regarding these basic guarantees began to appear in the constitutional arena. The focus of the controversy that arose then
was freedom of speech—or more specifically, freedom of
political belief and expression—and that controversy has
raged ever since, reaching its highest pitch in the 1920s and
the 1950s. Largely as a result of the continuing struggle with
communism, it remains one of the most important problems
of our time.

That the genesis of this problem was a war is significant,
though not surprising, since it is in periods of grave national
crisis that the desire for security may outweigh the desire
for liberty and that patriotic fervor may degenerate into
hysterical attacks on nonconformity. Moreover, in such
periods the balance between liberty and authority is inevitably weighted in favor of authority, thus creating the dilemma which President Lincoln recognized at the Civil War's
inception when he asked: "Must a government, of necessity,
be too *strong* for the liberties of its own people, or too *weak*
to maintain its own existence?"[1]

The Supreme Court has had to face this dilemma on
many occasions in deciding cases which require that it
balance individual freedom against national security. And
in no area of constitutional law has it experienced greater
difficulty in finding satisfactory solutions. For few issues
are more contentious than whether the Constitution should
protect the expression of revolutionary doctrines, and as

[1] From Lincoln's Message to Congress of July 4, 1861. See James Richardson, ed., *Messages and Papers of the Presidents,* 10 vols. (Washington:
Government Printing Office, 1896-1899), VI, 20, 23.

the threat of international communism has become increasingly clear, few issues have generated more conflicting pressures on the Court.

As a result, the history of judicial decisions in this problem area reveals no consistent line of development—though the Court has repeatedly attempted to formulate "rules" for deciding free speech cases—but has been characterized instead by periodic expansion or contraction of individual liberty in response to changes in the climate of national and international affairs. With regard to freedom of political belief and expression, the Court has been more a barometer of public opinion than a maker of public policy.

The "Clear and Present Danger" Rule

During World War I, genuine concern regarding the nation's unity in meeting its first foreign conflict, coupled with a xenophobic attitude deeply ingrained in American society and a fear that the emergency would bring about radical changes in the prevailing socio-economic pattern, gave rise to legislation restricting activities which Congress considered detrimental to the crisis effort. The first of these measures was the Espionage Act of 1917, which prohibited willful actions intended to hinder successful prosecution of the war, including false statements interfering with military operations; attempts to cause insubordination, disloyalty, mutiny, or refusal of duty in the armed forces; and obstruction of recruiting or enlistment into the military services. The penalty for violation of the Act was a fine of up to $10,000, or imprisonment for up to twenty years, or both.

The second wartime measure was the Sedition Law amendment to the Espionage Act, passed in May 1918. This statute broadened the Act's restrictive language and added a number of new offenses, including the obstruction of war bond sales and the urging of a curtailment of war production. It also prohibited the uttering, printing, writing, or publishing of any disloyal, profane, scurrilous, or abusive language, or of other language intended to cause contempt, scorn, contumely, or disrepute regarding the form of government of the United States, the Constitution, the flag, or the uniform. And in addition, it forbade the advocating, teaching, defending, or suggesting that such acts be done, as well as any speech or activity supporting or favoring the enemy cause.[1]

This sweeping statute went beyond the request for additional legislation which the Attorney General had made of Congress, and in terms of its actual effect on individual civil liberties was the most restrictive measure in American history. Added to these congressional acts, and completing the picture of legislative attempts to limit speech during the World War I period, were a number of state laws passed in response to public pressure and equally or more restrictive in their impact on individual rights.

The Espionage Act was vigorously enforced by the Justice Department, with the result that almost 2000 prosecutions were instituted and 900 convictions obtained, most of them for expressions of opinion regarding the nature and conduct of the war. This governmental activity gave rise to a number of cases, the first of which reached the Supreme Court in 1919. The case involved the general secretary of the Socialist Party, Charles Schenck, who had participated in printing and distributing to men called into the military service leaflets allegedly designed to cause insubordination and obstruction of the draft. Indicted under the Espionage Act, he claimed that the statute abridged the freedom of speech and press guaranteed him by the First Amendment, but was convicted in federal district court. He appealed from the judgment, and the Supreme Court granted certiorari. Since this was the first time it had been called upon to interpret the meaning of the free-speech guarantee, the Court's major problem was to formulate some "rule" or standard for testing the legitimacy of attempts to restrict that substantive right.

Schenck v. United States
249 U.S. 47 (1919)

Mr. Justice Holmes delivered the opinion of the Court:

[1]The Espionage Act is 40 *Statutes-at-Large* 217 (1917); the Sedition Law amendment to that Act, 40 *Statutes-at-Large* 553 (1918).

This is an indictment in three counts. The first charges a conspiracy to violate the Espionage Act of June 15, 1917, by causing and attempting to cause insubordination, etc., in the military and naval forces of the United States, and to obstruct the recruiting and enlistment service of the United States, when the United States was at war with the German Empire; to wit, that the defendant wilfully conspired to have printed and circulated to men who had been called and accepted for military service under the Act of May 18, 1917, a document set forth and alleged to be calculated to cause such insubordination and obstruction. The count alleges overt acts in pursuance of the conspiracy, ending in the distribution of the document set forth. The second count alleges a conspiracy to commit an offense against the United States; to wit, to use the mails for the transmission of matter declared to be nonmailable by title 12, § 2, of the Act of June 15, 1917, to wit, the above-mentioned document, with an averment of the same overt acts. The third count charges an unlawful use of the mails for the transmission of the same matter and otherwise as above. The defendants were found guilty on all the counts. They set up the 1st Amendment to the Constitution forbidding Congress to make any law abridging the freedom of speech or of the press. . . .

The document in question, upon its first printed side, recited the 1st section of the 13th Amendment, said that the idea embodied in it was violated by the Conscription Act, and that a conscript is little better than a convict. In impassioned language it intimated that conscription was despotism in its worst form and a monstrous wrong against humanity, in the interest of Wall street's chosen few. It said: "Do not submit to intimidation"; but in form at least confined itself to peaceful measures, such as a petition for the repeal of the act. The other and later printed side of the sheet was headed, "Assert Your Rights." It stated reasons for alleging that anyone violated the Constitution when he refused to recognize "your right to assert your opposition to the draft," and went on: "If you do not assert and support your rights, you are helping to deny or disparage rights which it is the solemn duty of all citizens and residents of the United States to retain." It described the arguments on the other side as coming from cunning politicians and a mercenary capitalist press, and even silent consent to the Conscription Law as helping to support an infamous conspiracy. It denied the power to send our citizens away to foreign shores to shoot up the people of other lands, and added that words could not express the condemnation such cold-blooded ruthlessness deserves, etc., etc., winding up, "You must do your share to maintain, support, and uphold the rights of the people of this country." Of course the document would not have been sent unless it had been intended to have some effect, and we do not see what effect it could be expected to have upon persons subject to the draft except to influence them to obstruct the carrying of it out. The defendants do not deny that the jury might find against them on this point.

But it is said, suppose that that was the tendency of this circular, it is protected by the 1st Amendment to the Constitution. Two of the strongest expressions are said to be quoted respectively from well-known public men. It well may be that the prohibition of laws abridging the freedom of speech is not confined to previous restraints, although to prevent them may have been the main purpose.... We admit that in many places and in ordinary times the defendants, in saying all that was said in the circular, would have been within their constitutional rights. But the character of every act depends upon the circumstances in which it is done. The most stringent protection of free speech would not protect a man in falsely shouting fire in a theater, and causing a panic. It does not even protect a man from an injunction against uttering words that may have all the effect of force. The question in every case is whether the words used are used in such circumstances and are of such a nature as to create a clear and present danger that they will bring about the substantive evils that Congress has a right to prevent. It is a question of proximity and degree. When a nation is at war many things that might be said in time of peace are such a hindrance to its effort that their utterance will not be endured so long as men fight, and that no court could regard them as protected by any constitutional right. It seems to be admitted that if an actual obstruction of the recruiting service were proved, liability for words that produced that effect might be enforced. The Statute of 1917, in § 4, punishes conspiracies to obstruct as well as actual obstruction. If the act (speaking, or circulating a paper), its tendency and the intent with which it is done, are the same, we perceive no ground for saying that success alone warrants making the act a crime....

Judgments affirmed.

Development of the Restrictive Rules

The "clear and present danger" rule was the first authoritative judicial test applicable to limitations on freedom of speech, and it was immediately applied to a series of postwar Espionage Act cases. A week after *Schenck* the Court, with Justice Holmes again writing the unanimous opinions, upheld two more convictions under the Act. In *Frohwerk v. United States,* the publication in a German-language newspaper of articles questioning the constitutionality of the draft and the purposes of the war was held to meet the test; and in *Debs v. United States,* the conviction of America's foremost Socialist leader for attempting to cause insubordination in the armed forces and to obstruct the draft was affirmed, although his speech was not directed to military personnel and did not advocate resistance to conscription.

The result in the first case involving the Sedition Law amendments of 1918 was similar. In *Abrams v. United States* (1919), the petitioner had been convicted for printing and distributing leaflets attacking the capitalist system as the workers' only enemy, denouncing President Wilson as a "hypocritical coward" for sending troops to Russia during the revolution, and urging a general strike in the munitions industry. A majority of the Court affirmed the conviction, finding that this activity was intended "to excite, at the supreme crisis of the war, disaffection, sedition, riots, and . . . revolution in this country for the purpose of embarrassing and if possible defeating the military plans of the Government in Europe."

By this time, however, Holmes (the author of the new rule governing political expression) had begun to question its application solely for restrictive purposes, and joined by Justice Brandeis, he dissented on the ground that the actions involved did not constitute the "present danger of immediate evil" or indicate an intention to bring it about which would warrant governmental interference with free expression of opinion.

Deriding the notion that the publication of a "silly leaflet by an unknown man, without more, would present any immediate danger that its opinions would hinder the success of the government arms or have an appreciable tendency to do so," Holmes asserted his belief that "the defendants had as much right to publish as the government has the right to publish the Constitution of the United States now vainly invoked by them." The Justice then delivered his most famous defense of free speech and thought:

> [When] men have realized that time has upset many fighting
> faiths, they come to believe even more than they believe the
> foundations of their own conduct that the ultimate good desired
> is better reached by free trade in ideas — that the best test of truth
> is the power of the thought to get itself accepted in the competi-
> tion of the market, and that truth is the only ground upon which
> their wishes can safely be carried out. That at any rate is the
> theory of our Constitution. It is an experiment, as all life is an
> experiment.

Holmes then attempted to fit the clear-and-present-danger
test into the framework of this general theory:

> While that experiment is part of our system I think that we should
> be eternally vigilant against attempts to check the expression
> of opinions that we loathe and believe to be fraught with death,
> unless they so imminently threaten immediate interference with
> the lawful and pressing purposes of the law that an immediate
> check is required to save the country.... Only the emergency
> that makes it immediately dangerous to leave the correction of
> evil counsels to time warrants making any exception to the
> sweeping command, "Congress shall make no law . . . abridging
> the freedom of speech."

The attempt of Holmes and Brandeis to convince the
Court of the clear-and-present-danger test's protective aspect did not succeed, and they dissented repeatedly in subsequent cases. In *Schaefer v. United States* (1920), after the
majority had upheld a conviction for reprinting German-
language articles allegedly subversive of the war effort on
the ground that whatever the real effect of the articles may
have been their "tendency" was bad, Brandeis warned
against projecting a restrictive attitude into the postwar
period and insisted that the clear-and-present-danger test
was best viewed as "a rule of reason." "Correctly applied,"
he said, "it will preserve the right of free speech both from
suppression by tyrannous, well-meaning majorities, and
from abuse by irresponsible fanatical minorities."

The "bad tendency" test so casually adopted in *Schaefer*
was picked up in the next major free-speech case. Holmes
and Brandeis had sought to emphasize that governmental interference with speech or press must be limited to instances

in which the relationship between the expression and the allegedly unlawful act was proximate and direct rather than remote and indirect, or in which the expression created a danger, both evident and immediate, of bringing about an illegal action. However, in *Gitlow v. New York* (1925), the Court accepted the "bad tendency" test of the challenged state law and thereby adopted a theory of indirect causation.

Gitlow had published a document similar to the *Communist Manifesto* and was convicted of violating the New York Criminal Anarchy Act of 1902. That law defined certain kinds of words as incitements to illegal action and prohibited their expression regardless of the speaker's or publisher's intention. The first question raised in this case was whether or not the First Amendment guarantees of free speech and press were applicable against the states under the Fourteenth Amendment. The Court, seemingly oblivious to the importance of its ruling, simply assumed that these freedoms were "among the fundamental personal rights and 'liberties' protected . . . from impairment by the States" and thus brought a significant new principle into the Constitution.

But insofar as the statute under attack was concerned, the Court sustained its constitutionality, holding that it was not an arbitrary or unreasonable exercise of the state's police power. "A simple revolutionary spark," said Mr. Justice Sanford, "may kindle a fire that, smoldering for a time, may burst into a sweeping and destructive conflagration." The state need not wait until the threat of destruction becomes imminent or immediate, he declared, but may "suppress the threatened danger in its incipiency." Again Holmes and Brandeis dissented, pointing out that "every idea is an incitement" and expressing the opinion that Gitlow's "redundant discourse . . . had no chance of starting a present conflagration."

The last in this series of postwar cases restricting free speech was *Whitney v. California* in 1927. Here the petitioner was convicted of violating the California Syndicalism Act of 1919 by assisting in organizing the California Communist Labor Party and by joining and attending meetings of that party, which advocated and taught the violent over-

throw of established government. The Court again refused
to disturb a state legislative determination that a danger requiring restrictive measures existed. If a "reasonable man"
could have reached the same conclusion as the legislature,
then the statute's validity must be sustained. Holmes and
Brandeis concurred in the result of this case, but not in the
reasoning. Commenting once more on the manner of applying the clear-and-present-danger test, Brandeis said:

> Those who won our independence ... did not exalt order at the
> cost of liberty. To courageous, self-reliant men, with confidence
> in the power of free and fearless reasoning applied through the
> processes of popular government, no danger flowing from speech
> can be deemed clear and present, unless the incidence of the evil
> apprehended is so imminent that it may befall before there is
> opportunity for full discussion. If there be time to expose through
> discussion the falsehoods and fallacies, to avert the evil by the
> processes of education, the remedy to be applied is more speech,
> not enforced silence. Only an emergency can justify repression.
> Such must be the rule if authority is to be reconciled with free-
> dom. Such, in my opinion, is the command of the Constitution.
> It is therefore always open to Americans to challenge a law
> abridging free speech and assembly by showing that there was
> no emergency justifying it.

Temporary Modification of the Restrictive Rules

By the 1930s the tensions of World War I had faded, the
"Red Scare" of the previous decade had run its course, and
indeed in 1933 diplomatic relations had been established
with the Soviet Union. Moreover, the United States was
in the process of achieving major socio-economic reforms,
and in 1937 the Supreme Court itself was liberalized.

All of these factors were reflected in a series of judicial
decisions modifying the restrictions which had been imposed
on free speech during the postwar period, as the Court reversed the convictions of a woman who had displayed a red
flag at a summer camp (*Stromberg v. California,* 1931), of
a speaker at a meeting called by the Communist Party to
protest police violence against strikers (*De Jonge v. Oregon,*
1937), and of an organizer seeking Negro support for the
Communist Party (*Herndon v. Lowry,* 1937). The "security

of the Republic, the very foundation of Constitutional government," said Chief Justice Hughes in *De Jonge,* lies in maintaining the opportunity for free political discussion "to the end that government may be responsive to the voice of the people and that changes, if desired, may be obtained by peaceful means."

Thus the first phase of the civil liberties controversy came to an end with the enunciation of a policy more protective of the right to express unpopular political views. But this change in attitude was to be short-lived, as the earlier restrictive policy was soon reinstituted under the pressures generated by another period of national emergency.

Hot War, Cold War, and Internal Security

The free-speech issue flared up again as a result of World War II and its aftermath. There were few incursions on First Amendment rights while the global conflict was in progress, and it seemed that the nation might be spared a repetition of the World War I experience.[1] But when relations between the Allies broke down almost immediately after victory was achieved, and when the tensions between the free and Communist worlds resulted in the phenomenon of protracted "cold war," the problem of restricting Communist activity in the interest of national security became the focus of political and constitutional attention.

Although Congress had passed only three major internal security laws from the establishment of the Constitution to the outbreak of World War II, during the fifteen years after 1940 it enacted a number of statutes dealing with that problem and directed primarily against Communist activity in the United States. The most important measures of this nature included: the Alien Registration (Smith) Act of 1940, the Internal Security (McCarran) Act of 1950, the Immigration and Nationality Act of 1952, and the Communist Control Act of 1954. In addition, the Hatch Act of 1939 and the

[1]Although it was not related to the problem of political freedom, one of the most serious invasions of constitutional rights in American history—the treatment of Japanese-Americans on the West Coast—did occur during World War II. This problem is discussed in the next chapter.

Labor-Management Relations (Taft-Hartley) Act of 1947 also contained anti-Communist provisions. Moreover, by the mid-1950s almost all the states had passed their own internal security laws.

This body of legislation, taken as a whole, represented the most serious and concerted attempt to restrict political thought and expression in the nation's history, and the question of its constitutionality confronted the Supreme Court with some of the most difficult decisions it has ever been called upon to make.

Ostensibly aimed against Fascist as well as Communist activity, the Smith Act was the first peacetime sedition law since 1798. Destined to become the center of the free speech controversy in the postwar period, its purpose was to outlaw activities whose goal was the overthrow of American government by force or violence. The Act's major provisions made it unlawful:

(1) to intentionally impair the loyalty, morale, or discipline of the armed forces;

(2) to knowingly or willfully advocate, abet, advise, or teach the duty, necessity, desirability, or propriety of overthrowing or destroying any government in the United States by force or violence;

(3) to organize or help to organize any society, group, or assembly of persons who teach, advocate, or encourage the overthrow or destruction of any government in the United States by force or violence; or knowing its purposes to be or become a member of or affiliated with such an organization;

(4) to attempt or conspire to commit any of the listed acts.

The penalty for violating the Act was a fine of not more than $10,000 or imprisonment for not more than ten years, or both.[1]

The Smith Act was invoked only twice before the end of World War II. In 1941 eighteen members of the Trotskyite Socialist Workers Party were convicted under its conspiracy provisions, and in 1942 twenty-eight alleged Nazi sympa-

---

[1]The Alien Registration (Smith) Act is 54 *Statutes-at-Large* 670 (1940).

thizers were indicted under the provisions against interference with the armed forces, but after an incomplete trial and a lapse of almost three years, the indictment was dismissed for failure to prosecute.

Then, in 1948, the eleven top leaders of the American Communist Party were indicted under the Act, and one of the most important free-speech trials in American history began. The executive secretary of the Communist Political Association, Eugene Dennis, and his cohorts were charged with wilfully and knowingly conspiring to organize the Communist Party of the United States and to teach and advocate the overthrow of the government by force and violence. Their stormy and sensational trial (five defense attorneys were convicted of contempt as a result of the proceedings) ran for nine months in the federal district court of Judge Harold Medina in New York City. At its end, Medina's charge to the jury included a ruling that "as a matter of law there is sufficient danger of a substantive evil that the Congress has a right to prevent to justify the application of the statute under the First Amendment."

The defendants were convicted, and the convictions were upheld in a Court of Appeals opinion (written by Judge Learned Hand) which broadened the clear-and-present-danger test to allow for restriction of the particular activities involved in the case. The Supreme Court granted certiorari to review the constitutionality of the Smith Act. Its 6-2 decision was handed down on June 4, 1951, at the height of the cold war, for as the case had progressed through the courts, East-West tensions had exploded in 1950 in the Korean conflict.

Dennis v. United States
341 U.S. 494 (1951)

Mr. Chief Justice Vinson announced the judgment of the Court:

... Our limited grant of the writ of certiorari has removed from our consideration any question as to the sufficiency of the evidence to support the jury's determination that petitioners are guilty of the offense charged. Whether on this record petitioners did in fact ad-

vocate the overthrow of the Government by force and violence is
not before us, and we must base any discussion of this point upon
the conclusions stated in the opinion of the Court of Appeals, which
treated the issue in great detail. That court held that the record in
this case amply supports the necessary finding of the jury that petitioners, the leaders of the Communist Party in this country, were
unwilling to work within our framework of democracy, but intended
to initiate a violent revolution whenever the propitious occasion
appeared....

I.

It will be helpful in clarifying the issues to treat next the contention that the trial judge improperly interpreted the statute by charging that the statute required an unlawful intent before the jury could
convict. More specifically, he charged that the jury could not find
the petitioners guilty under the indictment unless they found that
petitioners had the intent "to overthrow the government by force
and violence as speedily as circumstances permit."

... The structure and purpose of the statute demand the inclusion
of intent as an element of the crime. Congress was concerned with
those who advocate and organize for the overthrow of the Government. Certainly those who recruit and combine for the purpose of
advocating overthrow intend to bring about that overthrow. We
hold that the statute requires as an essential element of the crime
proof of the intent of those who are charged with its violation to
overthrow the Government by force and violence....

II.

The obvious purpose of the statute is to protect existing Government, not from change by peaceable, lawful and constitutional
means, but from change by violence, revolution and terrorism. That
it is within the *power* of the Congress to protect the Government
of the United States from armed rebellion is a proposition which
requires little discussion. Whatever theoretical merit there may be
to the argument that there is a "right" to rebellion against dictatorial
governments [it] is without force where the existing structure of the
government provides for peaceful and orderly change. We reject
any principle of governmental helplessness in the face of preparation
for revolution, which principle, carried to its logical conclusion,
must lead to anarchy. No one could conceive that it is not within
the power of Congress to prohibit acts intended to overthrow the

Government by force and violence. The question with which we are concerned here is not whether Congress has such *power*, but whether the *means* which it has employed conflict with the First and Fifth Amendments to the Constitution.

One of the bases for the contention that the means which Congress has employed are invalid takes the form of an attack on the face of the statute on the grounds that by its terms it prohibits academic discussion of the merits of Marxism-Leninism, that it stifles ideas and is contrary to all concepts of a free speech and a free press. . . .

The very language of the Smith Act negates the interpretation which petitioners would have us impose on that Act. It is directed at advocacy, not discussion. Thus, the trial judge properly charged the jury that they could not convict if they found that petitioners did "no more than pursue peaceful studies and discussions or teaching and advocacy in the realm of ideas." He further charged that it was not unlawful "to conduct in an American college and university a course explaining the philosophical theories set forth in the books which have been placed in evidence." Such a charge is in strict accord with the statutory language, and illustrates the meaning to be placed on those words. Congress did not intend to eradicate the free discussion of political theories, to destroy the traditional rights of Americans to discuss and evaluate ideas without fear of governmental sanction. Rather Congress was concerned with the very kind of activity in which the evidence showed these petitioners engaged.

III.

But although the statute is not directed at the hypothetical cases which petitioners have conjured, its application in this case has resulted in convictions for the teaching and advocacy of the overthrow of the Government by force and violence, which, even though coupled with the intent to accomplish that overthrow, contains an element of speech. For this reason, we must pay special heed to the demands of the First Amendment marking out the boundaries of speech.

We [have] pointed out . . . that the basis of the First Amendment is the hypothesis that speech can rebut speech, propaganda will answer propaganda, free debate of ideas will result in the wisest governmental policies. It is for this reason that this Court has recognized the inherent value of free discourse. An analysis of the leading cases in this Court which have involved direct limitations on speech, however, will demonstrate that both the majority of the Court and the dissenters in particular cases have recognized that this is not an unlimited, unqualified right, but that the societal value of speech must, on occasion, be subordinated to other values and considerations.

[The opinion proceeds to review the Court's decisions in Schenck and other cases.]

The rule we deduce from these cases is that where an offense is specified by a statute in nonspeech or nonpress terms, a conviction relying upon speech or press as evidence of violation may be sustained only when the speech or publication created a "clear and present danger" of attempting or accomplishing the prohibited crime, e. g., interference with enlistment. The dissents . . . in emphasizing the value of speech, were addressed to the argument of the sufficiency of the evidence.

[The opinion continues to review prior decisions by discussing the Gitlow and Whitney cases.]

Although no case subsequent to Whitney and Gitlow has expressly overruled the majority opinions in those cases, there is little doubt that subsequent opinions have inclined toward the Holmes-Brandeis rationale. . . . [But] neither Justice Holmes nor Justice Brandeis ever envisioned that a shorthand phrase should be crystallized into a rigid rule to be applied inflexibly without regard to the circumstances of each case. Speech is not an absolute, above and beyond control by the legislature when its judgment, subject to review here, is that certain kinds of speech are so undesirable as to warrant criminal sanction. Nothing is more certain in modern society than the principle that there are no absolutes, that a name, a phrase, a standard has meaning only when associated with the considerations which gave birth to the nomenclature. To those who would paralyze our Government in the face of impending threat by encasing it in a semantic straitjacket we must reply that all concepts are relative.

In this case we are squarely presented with the application of the "clear and present danger" test, and must decide what that phrase imports. We first note that many of the cases in which this Court has reversed convictions by use of this or similar tests have been based on the fact that the interest which the State was attempting to protect was itself too insubstantial to warrant restriction of speech. . . . Overthrow of the Government by force and violence [however] is certainly a substantial enough interest for the Government to limit speech. Indeed, this is the ultimate value of any society, for if a society cannot protect its very structure from armed internal attack, it must follow that no subordinate value can be protected. If, then, this interest may be protected, the literal problem which is presented is what has been meant by the use of the phrase "clear and present danger" of the utterances bringing about the evil within the power of Congress to punish.

Obviously, the words cannot mean that before the Government may act, it must wait until the putsch is about to be executed, the plans have been laid and the signal is awaited. If Government is aware that a group aiming at its overthrow is attempting to indoctrinate its members and to commit them to a course whereby they will strike when the leaders feel the circumstances permit, action by the Government is required. The argument that there is no need for Government to concern itself, for Government is strong, it possesses ample powers to put down a rebellion, it may defeat the revolution with ease needs no answer. For that is not the question. Certainly an attempt to overthrow the Government by force, even though doomed from the outset because of inadequate numbers or power of the revolutionists, is a sufficient evil for Congress to prevent. The damage which such attempts create both physically and politically to a nation makes it impossible to measure the validity in terms of the probability of success, or the immediacy of a successful attempt. In the instant case the trial judge charged the jury that they could not convict unless they found that petitioners intended to overthrow the Government "as speedily as circumstances would permit." This does not mean, and could not properly mean, that they would not strike until there was certainty of success. What was meant was that the revolutionists would strike when they thought the time was ripe. We must therefore reject the contention that success or probability of success is the criterion.

The situation with which Justices Holmes and Brandeis were concerned in Gitlow was a comparatively isolated event, bearing little relation in their minds to any substantial threat to the safety of the community.... They were not confronted with any situation comparable to the instant one—the development of an apparatus designed and dedicated to the overthrow of the Government, in the context of world crisis after crisis.

Chief Judge Learned Hand, writing for the majority below, interpreted the phrase as follows: "In each case [courts] must ask whether the gravity of the 'evil,' discounted by its improbability, justifies such invasion of free speech as is necessary to avoid the danger." We adopt this statement of the rule. As articulated by Chief Judge Hand, it is as succinct and inclusive as any other we might devise at this time. It takes into consideration those factors which we deem relevant, and relates their significances. More we cannot expect from words.

Likewise, we are in accord with the court below, which affirmed the trial court's finding that the requisite danger existed. The mere fact that from the period 1945 to 1948 petitioners' activities did not result in an attempt to overthrow the Government by force and violence is of course no answer to the fact that there was a group that was ready to make the attempt. The formation by petitioners of such a highly organized conspiracy, with rigidly disciplined members subject to call when the leaders, these petitioners, felt that the time had come for action, coupled with the inflammable nature of world conditions, similar uprisings in other countries, and the touch-and-go nature of our relations with countries with whom petitioners were in the very least ideologically attuned, convince us that their convictions were justified on this score. And this analysis disposes of the contention that a conspiracy to advocate, as distinguished from the advocacy itself, cannot be constitutionally restrained, because it comprises only the preparation. It is the existence of the conspiracy which creates the danger. If the ingredients of the reaction are present, we cannot bind the Government to wait until the catalyst is added.

IV.

Although we have concluded that the finding that there was a sufficient danger to warrant the application of the statute was justified on the merits, there remains the problem of whether the trial judge's treatment of the issue was correct.

. . . The argument that the action of the trial court is erroneous, in declaring as a matter of law that such violation shows sufficient danger to justify the punishment despite the First Amendment, rests on the theory that a jury must decide a question of the application of the First Amendment. We do not agree.

When facts are found that establish the violation of a statute, the protection against conviction afforded by the First Amendment is a matter of law. The doctrine that there must be a clear and present danger of a substantive evil that Congress has a right to prevent is a judicial rule to be applied as a matter of law by the courts. The guilt is established by proof of facts. Whether the First Amendment protects the activity which constitutes the violation of the statute must depend upon a judicial determination of the scope of the First Amendment applied to the circumstances of the case. . . .

The question in this case is whether the statute which the legislature has enacted may be constitutionally applied. In other words, the Court must examine judicially the application of the statute to the particular situation, to ascertain if the Constitution prohibits the conviction. We hold that the statute may be applied where there is a "clear and present danger" of the substantive evil which the legislature had the right to prevent. Bearing, as it does, the marks of a "question of law," the issue is properly one for the judge to decide.

V.

There remains to be discussed the question of vagueness — whether the statute as we have interpreted it is too vague, not sufficiently advising those who would speak of the limitations upon their activity. . . .

We agree that the standard as defined is not a neat, mathematical formulary. Like all verbalizations it is subject to criticism on the score of indefiniteness. But petitioners themselves contend that the verbalization, "clear and present danger" is the proper standard. We see no difference from the standpoint of vagueness, whether the standard of "clear and present danger" is one contained in haec verba within the statute, or whether it is the judicial measure of constitutional applicability. We have shown the indeterminate standard the phrase necessarily connotes. We do not think we have rendered that standard any more indefinite by our attempt to sum up the factors which are included within its scope. We think it well serves to indicate to those who would advocate constitutionally prohibited conduct that there is a line beyond which they may not go — a line which they, in full knowledge of what they intend and the circumstances in which their activity takes place, will well appreciate and understand. . . .

We hold that §§ 2 (a) (1), (2) (a) (3) and 3 of the Smith Act, do not inherently, or as construed or applied in the instant case, violate the First Amendment and other provisions of the Bill of Rights, or the First and Fifth Amendments because of indefiniteness. Petitioners intended to overthrow the Government of the United States as speedily as the circumstances would permit. Their conspiracy to organize the Communist Party and to teach and advocate the overthrow of the Government of the United States by force and violence created a "clear and present danger" of an attempt to overthrow the Government by force and violence. They were properly and constitutionally convicted for violation of the Smith Act. The judgments of conviction are

Affirmed.

[Justices Burton, Minton, and Reed joined in the Chief Justice's opinion.]

   Mr. Justice Frankfurter, concurring:

   ... Viewed as a whole [the Court's prior decisions] express an attitude toward the judicial function and a standard of values which for me are decisive of the case before us.

   First. — Free-speech cases are not an exception to the principle that we are not legislators, that direct policy-making is not our province. How best to reconcile competing interests is the business of legislatures, and the balance they strike is a judgment not to be displaced by ours, but to be respected unless outside the pale of fair judgment....

   Second. — A survey of the relevant decisions indicates that the results which we have reached are on the whole those that would ensue from careful weighing of conflicting interests....

   Third. — Not every type of speech occupies the same position on the scale of values.... On any scale of values which we have hitherto recognized, speech of [the sort involved in this case] ranks low....

   It is not for us to decide how we would adjust the clash of interests which this case presents were the primary responsibility for reconciling it ours. Congress has determined that the danger created by advocacy of overthrow justifies the ensuing restriction on freedom of speech. The determination was made after due deliberation, and the seriousness of the congressional purpose is attested by the volume of legislation passed to effectuate the same ends.

   Can we then say that the judgment Congress exercised was denied it by the Constitution? Can we establish a constitutional doctrine which forbids the elected representatives of the people to make this choice? Can we hold that the First Amendment deprives Congress of what it deemed necessary for the Government's protection?...

   Civil liberties draw at best only limited strength from legal guaranties. Preoccupation by our people with the constitutionality, instead of with the wisdom, of legislation or of executive action is preoccupation with a false value. Even those who would most freely use the judicial brake on the democratic process by invalidating legislation that goes deeply against their grain, acknowledge, at least by paying lip service, that constitutionality does not exact a sense of proportion or the sanity of humor or an absence of fear. Focusing attention on constitutionality tends to make constitutionality synonymous with wisdom. When legislation touches freedom of thought and freedom of speech, such a tendency is a formidable enemy of the free spirit. Much that should be rejected as illiberal, because repressive and envenoming, may well be not unconstitutional. The ultimate reliance for the deepest needs of civilization must be found outside their vindication in courts of law ... A persistent, positive translation of the liberating faith into the feelings and thoughts and actions of men and women is the real protection against attempts to straitjacket the human mind. ...

Mr. Justice Jackson, concurring:

... The "clear and present danger" test was an innovation by Mr. Justice Holmes in the Schenck Case, reiterated and refined by him and Mr. Justice Brandeis in later cases, all arising before the era of World War II revealed the subtlety and efficacy of modernized revolutionary techniques used by totalitarian parties. In those cases, they were faced with convictions under so-called criminal syndicalism statutes aimed at anarchists but which, loosely construed, had been applied to punish socialism, pacifism, and left-wing ideologies, the charges often resting on far-fetched inferences which, if true, would establish only technical or trivial violations. They proposed "clear and present danger" as a test for the sufficiency of evidence in particular cases.

I would save it, unmodified, for application as a "rule of reason" in the kind of case for which it was devised. ...

The authors of the clear and present danger test never applied it to a case like this, nor would I. ...

The highest degree of constitutional protection is due to the individual acting without conspiracy. But even an individual cannot claim that the Constitution protects him in advocating or teaching overthrow of government by force or violence. I should suppose no one would doubt that Congress has power to make such attempted overthrow a crime. But the contention is that one has the constitutional right to work up a public desire and will to do what it is a crime to attempt. I think direct incitement by speech or writing can be made a crime, and I think there can be a conviction without also proving that the odds favored its success by 99 to 1, or some other extremely high ratio. ...

I do not suggest that Congress could punish conspiracy to advocate something, the doing of which it may not punish. ... But it is not forbidden to put down force or violence, it is not forbidden to punish its teaching or advocacy, and the end being punishable, there is no doubt of the power to punish conspiracy for the purpose. ...

While I think there was power in Congress to enact this statute and that, as applied in this case, it cannot be held unconstitutional, I add that I have little faith in the long-range effectiveness of this conviction to stop the rise of the Communist movement. Communism will not go to jail with these Communists. No decision by this Court can forestall revolution whenever the existing government fails to command the respect and loyalty of the people and sufficient distress and discontent is allowed to grow up among the masses. Many failures by fallen governments attest that no government can long prevent revolution by outlawry. Corruption, ineptitude, inflation, oppressive taxation, militarization, injustice, and loss of leadership capable of intellectual initiative in domestic or foreign affairs are allies on which the Communists count to bring opportunity knocking to their door. Sometimes I think they may be mistaken. But the Communists are not building just for today—the rest of us might profit by their example.

Mr. Justice Black, dissenting:

... At the outset I want to emphasize what the crime involved in this case is, and what it is not. These petitioners were not charged with an attempt to overthrow the Government. They were not charged with overt acts of any kind designed to overthrow the Government. They were not even charged with saying anything or writing anything designed to overthrow the Government. The charge was that they agreed to assemble and to talk and publish certain ideas at a later date: The indictment is that they conspired to organize the Communist Party and to use speech or newspapers and other publications in the future to teach and advocate the forcible overthrow of the Government. No matter how it is worded, this is a virulent form of prior censorship of speech and press, which I believe the First Amendment forbids. I would hold § 3 of the Smith Act authorizing this prior restraint unconstitutional on its face and as applied.

... I have always believed that the First Amendment is the keystone of our Government, that the freedoms it guarantees provide the best insurance against destruction of all freedom. At least as to speech in the realm of public matters, I believe that the "clear and present danger" test does not "mark the furthermost constitutional boundaries of protected expression" but does "not more than recognize a minimum compulsion of the Bill of Rights."

So long as this Court exercises the power of judicial review of legislation, I cannot agree that the First Amendment permits us to sustain laws suppressing freedom of speech and press on the basis of Congress' or our own notions of mere "reasonableness." Such a doctrine waters down the First Amendment so that it amounts to little more than an admonition to Congress. The Amendment as so construed is not likely to protect any but those "safe" or orthodox views which rarely need its protection. . . .

Public opinion being what it now is, few will protest the conviction of these Communist petitioners. There is hope, however, that in calmer times, when present pressures, passions and fears subside, this or some later Court will restore the First Amendment liberties to the high preferred place where they belong in a free society.

Mr. Justice Douglas, dissenting:

If this were a case where those who claimed protection under the First Amendment were teaching the techniques of sabotage, the assassination of the President, the filching of documents from public files, the planting of bombs, the art of street warfare, and the like, I would have no doubts. The freedom to speak is not absolute; the teaching of methods of terror and other seditious conduct should be beyond the pale along with obscenity and immorality. This case was argued as if those were the facts. The argument imported much seditious conduct into the record. That is easy and it has popular appeal, for the activities of Communists in plotting and scheming against the free world are common knowledge. But the fact is that no such evidence was introduced at the trial. . . .

So far as the present record is concerned, what petitioners did was to organize people to teach and themselves teach the Marxist-Leninist doctrine contained chiefly in four books: Foundations of Leninism by Stalin (1924), The Communist Manifesto by Marx and Engels (1848), State and Revolution by Lenin (1917), History of the Communist Party of the Soviet Union (B) (1939).

Those books are to Soviet Communism what Mein Kampf was to Nazism. If they are understood, the ugliness of Communism is revealed, its deceit and cunning are exposed, the nature of its activities becomes apparent, and the chances of its success less likely. That is not, of course, the reason why petitioners chose these books for their classrooms. They are fervent Communists to whom these volumes are gospel. They preached the creed with the hope that some day it would be acted upon.

The opinion of the Court does not outlaw these texts nor condemn them to the fire, as the Communists do literature offensive to their creed. But if the books themselves are not outlawed, if they can lawfully remain on library shelves, by what reasoning does their use in a classroom become a crime? It would not be a crime under the Act to introduce these books to a class, though that would be teaching what the creed of violent overthrow of the government is. The Act, as construed, requires the element of intent — that those who teach the creed believe in it. The crime then depends not on what is taught but on who the teacher is. That is to make freedom of speech turn not on *what is said,* but on the intent with which it is said. Once we start down that road we enter territory dangerous to the liberties of every citizen. . . .

We then start probing men's minds for motive and purpose; they become entangled in the law not for what they did but *for what they thought;* they get convicted not for what they said but for the purpose with which they said it. . . .

The vice of treating speech as the equivalent of overt acts of a treasonable or seditious character is emphasized by a concurring opinion, which by invoking the law of conspiracy makes speech do service for deeds which are dangerous to society. . . . But never until today has anyone seriously thought that the ancient law of conspiracy could constitutionally be used to turn speech into seditious conduct. . . .

Free speech has occupied an exalted position because of the high service it has given our society. Its protection is essential to the very existence of a democracy. The airing of ideas releases pressures which otherwise might become destructive. When ideas compete in the market for acceptance, full and free discussion exposes the false and they gain few adherents. Full and free discussion even of ideas we hate encourages the testing of our own prejudices and preconceptions. Full and free discussion keeps a society from becoming stagnant and unprepared for the stresses and strains that work to tear all civilizations apart.

Full and free discussion has indeed been the first article of our faith. We have founded our political system on it. It has been the safeguard of every religious, political, philosophical, economic, and racial group amongst us. We have counted on it to keep us from embracing what is cheap and false; we have trusted the common sense of our people to choose the doctrine true to our genius and to reject the rest. This has been the one single outstanding tenet that has made our institutions the symbol of freedom and equality. We have deemed it more costly to liberty to suppress a despised minority than to let them vent their spleen. We have above all else feared the political censor. We have wanted a land where our people can be exposed to all the diverse creeds and cultures of the world.

There comes a time when even speech loses its constitutional immunity. Speech innocuous one year may at another time fan such destructive flames that it must be halted in the interests of the safety of the Republic. That is the meaning of the clear and present danger test. When conditions are so critical that there will be no time to avoid the evil that the speech threatens, it is time to call a halt. Otherwise, free speech which is the strength of the Nation will be the cause of its destruction.

Yet free speech is the rule, not the exception. The restraint to be constitutional must be based on more than fear, on more than passionate opposition against the speech, on more than a revolted dislike for its contents. There must be some immediate injury to society that is likely if speech is allowed....

I had assumed that the question of the clear and present danger, being so critical an issue in the case, would be a matter for submission to the jury....

The nature of Communism as a force on the world scene would, of course, be relevant to the issue of clear and present danger of petitioners' advocacy within the United States. But the primary consideration is the strength and tactical position of petitioners and their converts in this country. On that there is no evidence in the record. If we are to take judicial notice of the threat of Communists within the nation, it should not be difficult to conclude that *as a political party* they are of little consequence.... Communism in the world scene is no bogey-man; but Communists as a political faction or party in this country plainly is. Communism has been so thoroughly exposed in this country that it has been crippled as a political force. Free speech has destroyed it as an effective political party....

How it can be said that there is a clear and present danger that this advocacy will succeed is, therefore, a mystery. Some nations less resilient than the United States, where illiteracy is high and where democratic traditions are only budding, might have to take drastic steps and jail these men for merely speaking their creed. But in America they are miserable merchants of unwanted ideas; their wares remain unsold. The fact that their ideas are abhorrent does not make them powerful.

The political impotence of the Communists in this country does not, of course, dispose of the problem. Their numbers; their positions in industry and government; the extent to which they have in fact infiltrated the police, the armed services, transportation, stevedoring, power plants, munitions works, and other critical places — these facts all bear on the likelihood that their advocacy of the Soviet theory of revolution will endanger the Republic. But the record is silent on these facts. If we are to proceed on the basis of judicial notice, it is impossible for me to say that the Communists in this country are so potent or so strategically deployed that they must be suppressed for their speech. I could not so hold unless I were willing to conclude that the activities in recent years of committees of Congress, of the Attorney General, of labor unions, of state legislatures, and of Loyalty Boards were so futile as to leave the country on the edge of grave peril. To believe that petitioners and their following are placed in such critical positions as to endanger the Nation is to believe the incredible. It is safe to say that the followers of the creed of Soviet Communism are known to the F. B. I.; that in case of war with Russia they will be picked up overnight as were all prospective saboteurs at the commencement of World War II; that the invisible army of petitioners is the best known, the most beset, and the least thriving of any fifth column in history. Only those held by fear and panic could think otherwise. . . .

The First Amendment reflects the philosophy of Jefferson "that it is time enough for the rightful purposes of civil government for its officers to interfere when principles break out into overt acts against peace and good order." The political censor has no place in our public debates. Unless and until extreme and necessitous circumstances are shown, our aim should be to keep speech unfettered and to allow the processes of law to be invoked only when the provocateurs among us move from speech to action.

Vishinsky wrote in 1948 in The Law of the Soviet State, "In our state, naturally there can be no place for freedom of speech, press, and so on for the foes of socialism."

Our concern should be that we accept no such standard for the United States. Our faith should be that our people will never give support to these advocates of revolution, so long as we remain loyal to the purposes for which our Nation was founded.

The Court and McCarthyism

The *Dennis* decision sustained the Smith Act and held that political expression might be proscribed if there was a reasonable possibility of its bringing about an attempt to overthrow the government under propitious circumstances at some future time. The danger need not be immediate and there need not be any definite acts of a subversive nature. That a "grave and probable" danger existed or might be created by the advocacy of Communist doctrine was sufficient. Essentially the Court had rejected the clear-and-present-danger test of *Schenck* and adopted in its place the

Gitlow bad-tendency test. Moreover, the decision implied that because of the nature of the problem the Court must accept any reasonable legislative determination of the need for curbing Communist activity.

This judicial acceptance of governmental policy had been evident at least a year before the *Dennis* case when the Court, although admitting that legislative action designed to influence a group's choice of its own leadership would normally be impermissible, upheld the Taft-Hartley Act provision denying the statute's benefits to any labor organization whose officers refused to file affidavits disclaiming membership in or affiliation with the Communist Party (*American Communications Association v. Douds,* 1950). But in its 1951 decision the Court went much further, allowing the exercise of broad restrictive power by government and virtually committing itself to acquiescence in the internal security policies of the federal and state legislatures.

The pressure on the Court to accept those restrictive policies was increased to a high pitch in the early 1950s by the emergence of "McCarthyism," which drew its support from the fears and frustrations of the cold war and ignored the Constitution in its overzealous pursuit of all who refused to accept its conformist dogma. And the result was that judicial protection of civil liberties became almost illusory during the next few years, as cases challenging a whole range of internal security measures and other forms of governmental action came before the Bench.

Thus the Court refused, for example, to define the limits of the authority which could be exercised by legislative investigating committees, despite the evident abuse of that authority on the part of certain congressional bodies. The Justices had long been wary of discussing the investigatory power, and as early as 1947 had denied certiorari in two cases (*Barsky v. United States* and *United States v. Josephson*) in which federal appellate courts had divided 2-1 on the issues of whether the House Un-American Activities Committee was engaged in a proper legislative purpose, whether its questions were within the scope of the committee's authorizing resolution, and whether it was violating rights protected by the First Amendment. By refusing to grant certiorari in those instances, the Court had implicitly approved the lower decisions upholding the committee procedures, and by continuing in later cases to avoid the major issues which had been raised, it allowed the House committee (as well as Senator McCarthy's Government Operations Committee and others) to abuse their powers and invade the rights of citizens who were called to testify before them.

In more positive, though no more protective, fashion the Court also upheld various state programs requiring public employees to take "loyalty oaths" or to file affidavits disclaiming past or present membership in Communist or other subversive organizations. "In the context of our time," said Justice Frankfurter, "such membership is sufficiently relevant to effective and dependable government, and to confidence of the electorate in its government" to allow for measures of this nature (*Garner v. Los Angeles Board of Public Works*, 1951). Indeed, membership in an organization found by the state to be subversive could be taken as "prima facie evidence" for disqualification from teaching and similarly "sensitive" public positions (*Adler v. New York City Board of Education*, 1952).

Yet another kind of state loyalty program was upheld when the Court refused to review a case in which an attorney had been denied admission to the bar because he objected to answering Bar Examiners' questions concerning his political beliefs (*In re Anastaplo*, 1955). And by a 4-4 vote, the federal loyalty-security program, instituted in 1947 by President Truman and somewhat modified in 1953 by President Eisenhower, was allowed to stand, although accused persons were not permitted to confront the anonymous informants whose unsworn statements were the source of the charges against them (*Bailey v. Richardson*, 1951).

Throughout this period the Court did make some effort to restrain the exercise of governmental power, and it often admonished Congress and the state legislatures against arbitrary action even while upholding their restrictive policies. In 1951, for example, it held that the Attorney General had acted improperly in listing various organizations as subversive "without notice, without disclosure of any reasons justifying it, without opportunity to meet the undisclosed evidence or suspicion on which designation may have been based, and without opportunity to establish affirmatively that the aims and acts of the organization are innocent" *(Joint Anti-Fascist Refugee Committee v. McGrath)*. In 1952 it invalidated an Oklahoma loyalty-oath statute which excluded from state employment all persons who were or had been members of proscribed organizations, regardless of whether their association was innocent or with knowledge of the organizations' purposes *(Wieman v. Updegraff)*. In 1953 it found that a congressional investigating committee had exceeded the power granted by its authorizing resolution *(United States v. Rumely)*. And by 1955, as the tide of judicial passivity began to turn, the Court not only upheld a government employee in a case involving the federal loyalty-security program *(Peters v. Hobby)*, but was even prepared to defend the constitutional right against self-incrimination and to denounce the McCarthyite method of branding uncooperative committee witnesses as "Fifth Amendment Communists" *(Emspak v. United States* and *Quinn v. United States)*.

The Development of a More Protective Policy

It was not until 1956-57, however, that the Court undertook to reassert the constitutional protection of political thought and expression and to reorient national policy in the field of internal security. A number of events, both at home and abroad, underlay this change of attitude. The election and re-election of Dwight Eisenhower in 1952 and 1956 helped to remove the Communist issue from the arena of partisan politics, and this political change also spelled the beginning of the end of rampant McCarthyism (the Senator was finally censured by his colleagues in 1954). In foreign affairs the Korean armistice and the death of Stalin in 1953 had brought a new and seemingly less aggressive regime to the Soviet Union. By the mid-1950s, therefore, the tensions which had been so high during the initial cold war period had abated. Moreover, Soviet advances in technology and the problem of "peaceful competition" in the world's under-developed areas had begun to appear as a greater threat to national security than the possibility of internal subversion. Finally, there had been a significant change in the Court itself, as several new members had come to the Bench.

That a judicial attitude more protective of civil liberty had at last emerged became evident when the Court, in *Pennsylvania v. Nelson* (1956), negated state anti-sedition efforts by holding that the federal government, through the Smith and other Acts, had "occupied the field" in protecting the nation against subversion and that all state laws in this field were therefore superseded.

This important decision was followed by another of equal significance, *Watkins v. United States* (1957), in which the petitioner's conviction for contempt of Congress—he had refused to answer questions related to other persons suspected of being Communists—was set aside. Restating the pre-cold war rules regarding the investigatory power, the Court decided 6-1 that a committee has "no general authority to expose the private affairs of individuals without justification in terms of the functions of Congress," and that Congress cannot "expose for the sake of exposure." No legislative inquiry "is an end in itself; it must be related to and in furtherance of a legitimate task of Congress." Nor is the legislature a law enforcement or trial agency, since these are functions of the executive and judicial branches of government. Moreover, "investigations conducted solely for the personal aggrandizement of the investigators or to 'punish' those investigated are indefensible."

Having thus unburdened itself, the Court held that a committee's authorizing resolution must spell out its jurisdiction and purpose "with sufficient particularity" so that a witness may have some basis for determining whether the questions he is asked are pertinent to the committee's legislative purpose. Simultaneously, the Court invalidated a conviction for contempt of a one-man state investigating committee because the committee's authority could not be determined by reference to the broad and general legislative act creating it (*Sweezy v. New Hampshire,* 1957).

In addition to these major decisions, the Court in 1956-57 also held: that in determining a teacher's fitness and loyalty local educational authorities could not regard as a "conclusive presumption of guilt" a refusal, based on the Fifth Amendment privilege against self-incrimination, to answer investigating committee questions about membership in allegedly subversive organizations (*Slochower v. New York City Board of Higher Education,* 1956); that a person holding a "non-sensitive" government position could not be summarily dismissed on suspicion of "sympathetic association" with Communists, since the Summary Suspension Act did not apply to such positions (*Cole v. Young,* 1956); that government employees were entitled to the protection of the procedural safeguards provided by their departments (*Service v. Dulles,* 1957); that a state in determining fitness for admission to the bar could not automatically infer that all former Communists had shared the party's evil purposes or participated in its illegal conduct, nor could it ignore a "lifetime of good citizenship" and deny admission on inconclusive evidence of past Communist associations or refusal to answer questions regarding one's political beliefs (*Schware v. New Mexico Board of Examiners* and *Konigsberg v. State Bar of California,* 1957); and that a person accused of filing a false non-Communist affidavit was entitled to inspect the FBI reports on which the charges against him were based, since "the Government which prosecutes an accused also has the duty to see that justice is done" and cannot invoke its privileges to deprive him of information which might be material to his defense (*Jencks v. United States,* 1957). During the same period, the Court also remanded a case involving the registration of the Communist Party as a subversive organization and thus postponed determining the constitutionality of the Subversive Activities Control Act of 1950 (*Communist Party v. Subversive Activities Control Board,* 1956).

Reappraisal of the Smith Act

This series of decisions set the stage for a second judicial look at the Smith Act. The *Dennis* case in 1951 had ostensibly opened the way to prosecutions under the Act of all persons connected with the Communist Party, and as a result of that decision the government had proceeded against "second string" party leaders throughout the country. It had been consistently successful in the lower courts, and by 1957, 89 convictions and 145 indictments had been secured.

Among these were the convictions of fourteen California Communist Party members for "conspiring 1) to advocate and teach the duty and necessity of overthrowing the Government of the United States by force and violence, and 2) to organize, as the Communist Party of the United States, a society of persons who so advocate and teach, all with the intent of causing the overthrow of the Government by force and violence as speedily as circumstances would permit." In 1955 the Court granted certiorari to review these cases, and its decision was handed down in 1957. That decision capped the development of the more protective policy which the Court had adopted in relation to political expression. Although only six years had passed since the *Dennis* case, the vote was 6-1 against upholding the convictions.

Yates v. United States
354 U.S. 298 (1957)

Mr. Justice Harlan delivered the opinion of the Court:

We brought these cases here to consider certain questions arising under the Smith Act which have not heretofore been passed upon by this Court, and otherwise to review the convictions of these petitioners for conspiracy to violate that Act. . . .

I. *The Term "Organize."*

. . . Petitioners claim that "organize" means to "establish," "found," or "bring into existence," and that in this sense the Communist Party was organized by 1945 at the latest. On this basis petitioners contend that this part of the indictment, returned in 1951, was barred by the three-year statute of limitations. The Government, on the other hand, says that "organize" connotes a continuing process which goes on throughout the life of an organization, and that, in the words of the trial court's instructions to the jury, the term includes such things as "the recruiting of new members and the forming of new units, and the regrouping or expansion of existing clubs, classes and other units of any society, party, group or other organization." The two courts below accepted the Government's position. We think, however, that petitioners' position must prevail.

[*The Court proceeds to discuss the meaning of the word "organize" as used in the Act. It finds no congressional intention to use the word in the broad sense urged by the prosecution.*]

... In these circumstances we should follow the familiar rule that criminal statutes are to be strictly construed and give to "organize" its narrow meaning, that is, that the word refers only to acts entering into the creation of a new organization, and not to acts thereafter performed in carrying on its activities, even though such acts may loosely be termed "organizational." ...

We conclude, therefore, that since the Communist Party came into being in 1945, and the indictment was not returned until 1951, the three-year statute of limitations had run on the "organizing" charge, and required the withdrawal of that part of the indictment from the jury's consideration.

II. *Instructions to the Jury.*

Petitioners contend that the instructions to the jury were fatally defective in that the trial court refused to charge that, in order to convict, the jury must find that the advocacy which the defendants conspired to promote was of a kind calculated to "incite" persons to action for the forcible overthrow of the Government. It is argued that advocacy of forcible overthrow as mere *abstract doctrine* is within the free speech protection of the First Amendment; that the Smith Act, consistently with that constitutional provision, must be taken as proscribing only the sort of advocacy which incites to illegal *action;* and that the trial court's charge, by permitting conviction for mere advocacy, unrelated to its tendency to produce forcible action, resulted in an unconstitutional application of the Smith Act. ...

We are thus faced with the question whether the Smith Act prohibits advocacy and teaching of forcible overthrow as an abstract principle, divorced from any effort to instigate action to that end, so long as such advocacy or teaching is engaged in with evil intent. We hold that it does not.

The distinction between advocacy of abstract doctrine and advocacy directed at promoting unlawful action is one that has been

consistently recognized in the opinions of this Court, beginning
with Fox v. Washington, and Schenck v. United States. This distinction was heavily underscored in Gitlow v. New York, in which
the statute involved was nearly identical with the one now
before us. . . .

We need not, however, decide the issue before us in terms of
constitutional compulsion, for our first duty is to construe this
statute. In doing so we should not assume that Congress chose to
disregard a constitutional danger zone so clearly marked, or that
it used the words "advocate" and "teach" in their ordinary diction-
ary meanings when they had already been construed as terms of
art carrying a special and limited connotation. . . . The legislative
history of the Smith Act and related bills shows beyond all question
that Congress was aware of the distinction between the advocacy
or teaching of abstract doctrine and the advocacy or teaching of
action, and that it did not intend to disregard it. The statute was
aimed at the advocacy and teaching of concrete action for the forcible overthrow of the Government, and not of principles divorced
from action.

The Government's reliance on this Court's decision in Dennis
is misplaced. The jury instructions which were refused here were
given there, and were referred to by this Court as requiring "the
jury to find the facts *essential* to establish the substantive crime."
(emphasis added). It is true that at one point in the late Chief
Justice's opinion it is stated that the Smith Act "is directed at advocacy, not discussion," but it is clear that the reference was to
advocacy of action, not ideas, for in the very next sentence the
opinion emphasizes that the jury was properly instructed that there
could be no conviction for "advocacy in the realm of ideas." The
two concurring opinions in that case likewise emphasize the distinction with which we are concerned.

In failing to distinguish between advocacy of forcible overthrow
as an abstract doctrine and advocacy of action to that end, the District Court appears to have been led astray by the holding in Dennis
that advocacy of violent action to be taken at some future time was
enough. It seems to have considered that, since "inciting" speech
is usually thought of as something calculated to induce immediate
action, and since Dennis held advocacy of action for future overthrow sufficient, this meant that advocacy, irrespective of its tendency to generate action, is punishable, provided only that it is uttered
with a specific intent to accomplish overthrow. In other words, the
District Court apparently thought that Dennis obliterated the tra-

ditional dividing line between advocacy of abstract doctrine and advocacy of action.

This misconceives the situation confronting the Court in Dennis and what was held there. Although the jury's verdict, interpreted in light of the trial court's instructions, did not justify the conclusion that the defendants' advocacy was directed at, or created any danger of, immediate overthrow, it did establish that the advocacy was aimed at building up a seditious group and maintaining it in readiness for action at a propitious time. In such circumstances, said Chief Justice Vinson, the Government need not hold its hand "until the *putsch* is about to be executed, the plans have been laid and the signal is awaited. If Government is aware that a group aiming at its overthrow is attempting to indoctrinate its members and commit them to a course whereby they will strike when the leaders feel the circumstances permit, action by the Government is required." The essence of the Dennis holding was that indoctrination of a group in preparation for future violent action, as well as exhortation to immediate action, by advocacy found to be directed to "action for the accomplishment" of forcible overthrow, to violence "as a rule or principle of action," and employing "language of incitement," is not constitutionally protected when the group is of sufficient size and cohesiveness, is sufficiently oriented towards action, and other circumstances are such as reasonably to justify apprehension that action will occur. This is quite a different thing from the view of the District Court here that mere doctrinal justification of forcible overthrow, if engaged in with the intent to accomplish overthrow, is punishable per se under the Smith Act. That sort of advocacy, even though uttered with the hope that it may ultimately lead to violent revolution, is too remote from concrete action to be regarded as the kind of indoctrination preparatory to action which was condemned in Dennis. As one of the concurring opinions in Dennis put it: "Throughout our decisions there has recurred a distinction between the statement of an idea which may prompt its hearers to take unlawful action, and advocacy that such action be taken." There is nothing in Dennis which makes that historic distinction obsolete. . . .

In light of the foregoing we are unable to regard the District Court's charge upon this aspect of the case as adequate. The jury was never told that the Smith Act does not denounce advocacy in the sense of preaching abstractly the forcible overthrow of the Government. We think that the trial court's statement that the proscribed advocacy must include the "urging," "necessity," and "duty" of forcible overthrow, and not merely its "desirability" and "propriety," may not be regarded as a sufficient substitute for charging that the Smith Act reaches only advocacy of action for the overthrow of government by force and violence. The essential distinction is that those to whom the advocacy is addressed must be urged to *do* something, now or in the future, rather than merely to *believe* in something. At best the expressions used by the trial court were equivocal, since in the absence of any instructions differentiating advocacy of abstract doctrine from advocacy of action, they were as consistent with the former as they were with the latter. Nor do we regard their ambiguity as lessened by what the trial court had to say as to the right of the defendants to announce their beliefs as to the inevitability of violent revolution, or to advocate other unpopular opinions. Especially when it is unmistakable that the court did not consider the urging of action for forcible overthrow as being a necessary element of the proscribed advocacy, but rather considered the crucial question to be whether the advocacy was uttered with specific intent to accomplish such overthrow, we would not be warranted in assuming that the jury drew from these instructions more than the court itself intended them to convey.

We recognize that distinctions between advocacy or teaching of abstract doctrines, with evil intent, and that which is directed to stirring people to action, are often subtle and difficult to grasp, for in a broad sense, as Mr. Justice Holmes said in his dissenting opinion in Gitlow, supra: "Every idea is an incitement." But the very subtlety of these distinctions required the most clear and explicit instructions with reference to them, for they concerned an issue which went to the very heart of the charges against these petitioners. The need for precise and understandable instructions on this issue is further emphasized by the equivocal character of the evidence in this record, with which we deal in Part III of this opinion. Instances of speech that could be considered to amount to "advocacy of action" are so few and far between as to be almost completely overshadowed by the hundreds of instances in the record in which overthrow, if mentioned at all, occurs in the course of doctrinal disputation so remote from action as to be almost wholly lacking in probative value. Vague references to "revolutionary" or "militant" action of an unspecified character, which are found in the evidence, might in addition be given too great weight by the jury in the absence of more precise instructions. Particularly in light of this record, we must regard the trial court's charge in this respect as furnishing wholly inadequate guidance to the jury on this central point in the case. We cannot allow a conviction to stand on such "an equivocal direction to the jury on a basic issue."

III. *The Evidence.*

The determinations already made require a reversal of these convictions. Nevertheless, in the exercise of our power under 28 USC § 2106 to "direct the entry of such appropriate judgment ... as may be just under the circumstances," we have conceived it to be our duty to scrutinize this lengthy record with care, in order to determine whether the way should be left open for a new trial of all or some of these petitioners. Such a judgment, we think, should, on the one hand, foreclose further proceedings against those of the petitioners as to whom the evidence in this record would be palpably insufficient upon a new trial, and should, on the other hand, leave the Government free to retry the other petitioners under proper legal standards, especially since it is by no means clear that certain aspects of the evidence against them could not have been clarified to the advantage of the Government had it not been under a misapprehension as to the burden cast upon it by the Smith Act.

[*The Court proceeds to review the evidence.*]

On this basis we have concluded that the evidence against petitioners Connelly, Kusnitz, Richmond, Spector, and Steinberg is so clearly insufficient that their acquittal should be ordered, but that as to petitioners Carlson, Dobbs, Fox, Healey (Mrs. Connelly), Lambert, Lima, Schneiderman, Stack, and Yates, we would not be justified in closing the way to their retrial. ...

IV. *Collateral Estoppel.*

There remains to be dealt with petitioner Schneiderman's claim based on the doctrine of collateral estoppel by judgment. Petitioner urges that in Schneiderman v. United States, a denaturalization proceeding in which he was the prevailing party, this Court made determinations favorable to him which are conclusive in this proceeding under the doctrine of collateral estoppel. Specifically, petitioner contends that the Schneiderman decision determined, for purposes of this proceeding, (1) that the teaching of Marxism-Leninism by the Communist Party was not necessarily the advocacy of violent overthrow of government; (2) that at least one tenable conclusion to be drawn from the evidence was that the Communist Party desired to achieve its goal of socialism through peaceful means; (3) that it could not be presumed, merely because of his membership or officership in the Communist Party, that Schneiderman adopted an illegal interpretation of Marxist doctrine; and finally, (4) that absent proof of overt acts indicating that Schneiderman per-

sonally adopted a reprehensible interpretation, the Government had
failed to establish its burden by the clear and unequivocal evidence
necessary in a denaturalization case. In the courts below, petitioner
urged unsuccessfully that these determinations were conclusive
in this proceeding under the doctrine of collateral estoppel, and entitled him either to an acquittal or to special instructions to the jury.
He makes the same contentions here.

... As we read the Schneiderman opinion, the only determination
essential to the decision was that Schneiderman had not, prior to
1927, adopted an interpretation of the Communist Party's teachings
featuring "agitation and exhortation calling for present violent action." ... The Court in Schneiderman certainly did not purport to determine what the doctrinal content of "Marxism-Leninism"
might be at all times and in all places.... It is therefore apparent that
determinations made by this Court in Schneiderman could not operate as a complete bar to this proceeding....

Since there must be a new trial, we have not found it necessary
to deal with the contentions of the petitioners as to the fairness of
the trial already held. The judgment of the Court of Appeals is
reversed, and the case remanded to the District Court for further
proceedings consistent with this opinion.

It is so ordered.

[*Although they concurred in the result in this case, Justices Black
and Douglas argued—as in Dennis—that the Smith Act violated
the First Amendment.*]

Conclusion: Limited Retreat Under Attack

Although Mr. Justice Harlan tried to reconcile the Court's
new policy of greater protection for political belief and expression with the restrictive doctrine of the *Dennis* case,
his opinion in *Yates* rejected the "probable danger" notion
of the previous decision by distinguishing between the permissible advocacy of abstract doctrine and the impermissible advocacy of or incitement to action. It should be noted,
however, that the Court did not rely on the *Schenck* rule in
this case, thus raising a question as to whether some broad
constitutional principle, rather than the clear-and-present-
danger test, is now being applied in this area of civil liberty.

The immediate effect of the *Yates* decision was to make
more difficult federal prosecutions for heretical political
opinions, a result which soon became apparent as lower

courts dismissed indictments or reversed convictions in a number of subversion cases and as the government gave up its prosecutions in others. But that decision, and the others manifesting a judicial attempt to reorient the nation's internal security policy, also resulted in attacks on the Court from powerful forces criticizing and condemning both its specific rulings and its general attitude.

In 1958, for example, the Conference of State Chief Justices issued an unusual statement regarding the effect of judicial pronouncements and the proper function of the judiciary.[1] Concerned about the impact of Supreme Court decisions on the distribution of power between the state and national governments, the Conference admonished the Court for its "policy-making" activity and called for the exercise of greater self-restraint on the part of its members. The Court's assumption of "primarily legislative powers," said the state judges, was incompatible with the traditional system of checks and balances.

The American Bar Association also expressed its concern in a series of Resolutions adopted in 1959. Although the ABA avowed that it had no intention of censuring the Court or attacking the independence of the judiciary, and while it opposed any congressional attempt to limit the Court's jurisdiction, it nonetheless noted that the recent decisions dealing with national and state security and Communist activity had been "severely criticized and deemed unsound by many responsible authorities." The Association recommended that Congress clarify its policies in the field of internal security, study recent judicial decisions with a view to reframing internal security legislation, and define the authority and procedures of its investigating committes.[2]

The most serious of these attacks on the Court came in Congress itself, however, where a coalition of civil-liberty and civil-rights restrictionists joined forces in an attempt

[1] Conference of Chief Justices, *Report of the Committee on Federal-State Relationships as Affected by Judicial Decisions* (Chicago: The Council of State Governments, 1958).

[2] American Bar Association, *Resolutions of the Special Committee on Communist Tactics, Strategy, and Objectives* (Chicago: American Bar Association, 1959).

to limit the Court's appellate jurisdiction over controversial matters—an approach to judicial regulation which Congress had used only once since the Civil War. About a month after the *Yates* and *Watkins* decisions, Senator Jenner introduced a bill to withdraw from the Court's jurisdiction cases involving the functions and practices of congressional investigating committees, state subversive activities measures, the executive loyalty-security program, educational subversive activities regulation, and state bar admission practices. This bill was amended by Senator Butler to deprive the Court of jurisdiction with regard to the last subject only, providing different legislative remedies for the others, and in this form it was approved by the Senate Judiciary Committee in 1958.

Meanwhile other Court-curbing proposals had been introduced in Congress, and a number had already been passed by the House as the legislative session entered its final week. The Jenner-Butler bill embodied the most serious attack on judicial power, however, and it was debated at great length before the vote was called. The measure was finally defeated 49-41, and before Congress adjourned every other proposal directed against the Court was also rejected, in one instance a motion for recommittal being passed by only one vote.

Thus the latest assault on the Court had been turned back. But the pressure generated by that effort was sufficient to bring about a modification of the more protective judicial policy so recently announced. This limited retreat was evident as early as 1958 when the Court upheld the discharge for "incompetence" and "doubtful trust and reliability" of employees who had declined to answer local officials' questions regarding their political associations *(Beilan v. Philadelphia Board of Education* and *Lerner v. Casey).* It was further revealed in several decisions minimizing the protections against congressional investigating committees which had been established in the *Watkins* case *(Barenblatt v. U.S.,* 1959; *Wilkinson v. U.S.* and *Braden v. U.S.,* 1961), as well as in a decision upholding state investigative power which had a similar effect *(Uphaus v. Wyman, 1960).* And, finally, it was manifest in the Court's most recent internal security decisions—one of which upheld an order requiring the Communist Party, as a Communist-action organization "substantially directed, dominated, or controlled by the foreign government . . . controlling the world Communist movement," to comply with the registration provisions of the Subversive Activities Control Act; and another of which declared constitutional the Smith Act provision which makes it a crime to be a "knowing, active, and purposive" member of a party illegally advocating violent overthrow of the government (*Communist Party v. Subversive Activities Control Board,* 1961; *Scales v. United States,* 1961).

Despite these recent decisions, however, the Court's attitude toward the First Amendment guarantee of free political belief and expression has remained more libertarian than it was at the height of the cold war. (In the 1961 membership clause case, for example, Mr. Justice Harlan reiterated the Court's adherence to the *Yates* rule protecting discussion of "abstract doctrine.") And this is significant, since serious civil liberties issues will inevitably continue to arise in the years ahead, and the Court will have to continue searching for the proper balance between national security and individual liberty.

Such issues are never easily resolved—as demonstrated by the fact that many of the cases discussed above resulted in 5-4 decisions—but as the experience of the past decade has shown, they are peculiarly troublesome under conditions of unrelenting global tension and recurrent crises. These conditions have added a new and complicating dimension to the problem of freedom versus authority with which the Supreme Court has wrestled on many occasions since World War I. That the Court has not come up with a final solution or developed an acceptable formula for dealing with that problem, that it has sometimes seemed confused and often vacillated, is not an indication of judicial failure, but only a measure of the difficulty involved in preserving *both* the existence of the nation and the liberty of its people.

CHAPTER IV

GOVERNMENT IN TIME OF WAR

The Problem of Presidential Emergency Power

The Constitution Under Wartime Conditions

Since the end of World War II, the United States has been engaged in a cold war which constantly threatens to turn "hot," as it did in 1950 in Korea, or to end in the cataclysmic holocaust of thermonuclear destruction. This protracted period of crisis has focused national attention on a host of important problems, ranging from foreign policy to military preparedness to economic stability. It has also made necessary an appraisal of the impact which wartime conditions have on the organization and operation of American government itself, for military crises test the basic conceptions of our constitutional system.

Which agency of government is primarily responsible for determining the existence of an emergency and for taking action to meet it? Are there any limits on the powers of government in time of war? What is the scope of judicial review during emergency periods? How does war affect the citizen's constitutionally guaranteed liberties? These questions go to the heart of America's ability to maintain its system of constitutional democratic government while meeting the challenges of an age in which the specter of war is always present. Next to the issue of war or peace itself, they raise the most serious problems of our time.

The nation's experience with wartime regimes is relatively limited. Yet during the past century the United States has faced four major war emergencies—the Civil War, the two World Wars, and the Korean War—and from this experience have emerged a number of "principles" of wartime government involving both the form and the substance of the constitutional system. Those principles are:

(1) In time of war the power of the national government is expanded to whatever extent the political branches deem necessary for a successful response to the crisis. There are no limits on the power of the government to assure the nation's survival.

(2) This vast emergency power is largely concentrated in the executive branch of the government. War crises require unity, leadership, and action. Only the President can fill these needs, and he is inevitably the focus of any emergency regime. Wartime government is essentially executive government.

(3) The expansion and concentration of governmental power under war conditions results in suspension of the Constitution's basic structural principles. Federalism has virtually no effect, for the nation must act as a single entity in meeting the challenge; the separation of powers is bridged, as Congress must accept the Commander-in-Chief's determinations of the nation's needs.

(4) Judicial review of governmental actions is largely nullified in time of war, as the "law of necessity" supersedes the law of the Constitution. With the nation's survival at stake, the Supreme Court cannot substitute its judgment of what is permissible for the political branches' determination of what is necessary. As a result, the Court must acquiesce in assertions of power which under normal conditions it could not consider constitutional.

(5) With the Constitution suspended and the Court neutralized, individual liberty is subject to restriction by governmental authority. Personal freedom may be circumscribed to whatever extent the war effort de-

mands. The preservation of the nation which gives
life and meaning to the Constitution takes precedence
over the rights which that Constitution was established to protect.

As stated here, these principles apply only to conditions
of "total war"; and, reflecting the limited nature of past
American wars (as compared with the experience of other
nations or with possible future situations), their full effect
has never been felt in the United States. But to the extent
which the gravity of each particular crisis requires their
application, these are the basic rules of governmental organization and operation in periods of grave national emergency.
They make it clear that wartime government is, in essence
and often in fact, "extraconstitutional" government.

The materials that follow deal with the Supreme Court's
interpretation of the basic law to allow for such government.
Illustrating various problems engendered by emergency
regimes, they demonstrate the peculiar difficulties which
the Court must face in time of war.

The Development of the "Wartime Constitution"

The problem of applying the Constitution to conditions
of serious military emergency first arose a century ago during the Civil War. After the attack on Fort Sumter, President
Lincoln instituted a "dictatorial" regime to meet the Rebellion. Acting on his own initiative, as Chief Executive and
Commander-in-Chief, he blockaded Confederate ports,
expanded the armed forces, appropriated funds from the
federal treasury, closed the mails to treasonable correspond-
ence, offered to pledge the credit of the United States for a
quarter-billion dollars, and — most controversial of all —
suspended the privilege of the writ of habeas corpus. All of
these actions raised serious questions of constitutionality,
although only the blockade and the habeas corpus suspension were ultimately tested in the Supreme Court.

When Congress, at Lincoln's call, finally convened on
July 4, 1861 — eleven weeks after the beginning of hostilities — the pattern of governmental response to the crisis had

already been established by the President. He sought, and received, retroactive approval of all the measures he had taken, but in reality Congress had been presented with a *fait accompli*. In his Message to the legislators, Lincoln defended his extraordinary actions and expounded a bold conception of presidential power in time of crisis. "These measures," said the President, "whether strictly legal or not, were ventured upon under what appeared to be a popular demand and a public necessity"; in the circumstances, the executive had found "the duty of employing the war power in defense of the government forced upon him."[1] According to Lincoln, necessity could legitimize actions which transcended the limits of constitutional authority, and the executive was the judge of that necessity. Upon his own determination that an emergency existed, the full powers of the government devolved upon him, and he was responsible — as sole representative of the entire people — for the nation's defense.

By admitting that Congress might have to ratify some of his actions the President included the legislature in his crisis regime. But at least theoretically, he regarded secession as rebellion or insurrection rather than war, and believed that he had inherent power as Chief Executive and Commander-in-Chief to assure that the law of the United States was obeyed throughout the Union. Lincoln clung to this theory despite the conflict's magnitude and duration, acting independently (as he did, for example, in issuing the Emancipation Proclamation) throughout the crisis period. He had declared the existence of the emergency, he had taken initial measures to meet it, and he continued to prosecute it to a successful conclusion.

The problem of determining what the nature of the conflict was and where the power to meet it resided arose in the first important wartime case to come before the Supreme Court, and it demonstrated the difficulties which confront the Court under crisis conditions. At issue was the propriety

---

[1] From the *Message to Congress* of July 4, 1861. See James Richardson, ed., *Messages and Papers of the Presidents,* 10 vols. (Washington: Government Printing Office, 1896-1899), VI, pp. 20-31, *passim.*

of treating as "enemy property" four neutral ships which had been captured by the Navy under the President's blockade proclamations. To uphold this seizure of prizes the Court would have to accept the validity of the presidential proclamations, and since a blockade was tantamount to recognition of belligerent status under international law, this would mean that the United States and the Confederacy were at war. Such a ruling would not only embarrass and endanger the government by providing foreign nations with grounds for establishing relations with the rebels, it would also imply that the President could institute war measures without a congressional declaration as required by the Constitution. On the other hand, if the Court stood firmly by the letter of the basic law and invalidated the seizures because there had been no declaration of war by Congress, the whole conduct of the government (that is, of the President) during the initial period of crisis would stand condemned.

It was this dilemma that the Court was called upon to resolve in *The Prize Cases*. The Justices disagreed sharply on the issue of presidential warmaking, but a bare majority — including all three of Lincoln's appointees — supported the crisis leader and thereby established an important precedent for future assertions of executive emergency power.

The Prize Cases
2 Black 635 (1863)

Mr. Justice Grier delivered the opinion of the Court:

There are certain propositions of law which must necessarily affect the ultimate decision of these cases, and many others, which it will be proper to discuss and decide before we notice the special facts peculiar to each.

They are, 1st. Had the President a right to institute a blockade of ports in possession of persons in armed rebellion against the Government, on the principles of international law, as known and acknowledged among civilized States?

2d. Was the property of persons domiciled or residing within those States a proper subject of capture on the sea as "enemies' property?"

I. Neutrals have a right . . . to enter the ports of a friendly nation for the purposes of trade and commerce, but are bound to recognize the rights of a belligerent engaged in actual war, to use this mode of coercion, for the purpose of subduing the enemy.

That a blockade *de facto* actually existed, and was formally declared and notified by the President on the 27th and 30th of April, 1861, is an admitted fact in these cases.

That the President, as the Executive Chief of the Government and Commander-in-chief of the Army and Navy, was the proper person to make such notification, has not been, and cannot be disputed.

The right of prize and capture has its origin in the *"jus belli,"* and is governed and adjudged under the law of nations. To legitimate the capture of a neutral vessel or property on the high seas, a war must exist *de facto*, and the neutral must have a knowledge or notice of the intention of one of the parties belligerent to use this mode of coercion against a port, city, or territory, in possession of the other.

Let us enquire whether, at the time this blockade was instituted, a state of war existed which would justify a resort to these means of subduing the hostile force.

War has been well defined to be, "That state in which a nation prosecutes its right by force."

The parties belligerent in a public war are independent nations. But it is not necessary to constitute war, that both parties should be acknowledged as independent nations or sovereign States. A war may exist where one of the belligerents claims sovereign rights as against the other.

Insurrection against a government may or may not culminate in an organized rebellion, but a civil war always begins by insurrection against the lawful authority of the Government. A civil war is never solemnly declared; it becomes such by its accidents—the number, power, and organization of the persons who originate and carry it on. When the party in rebellion occupy and hold in a hostile manner a certain portion of territory; have declared their independence; have cast off their allegiance; have organized armies; have commenced hostilities against their former sovereign, the world acknowledges them as belligerents, and the contest a *war*. *They* claim to be in arms to establish their liberty and independence, in order to become a sovereign State, while the sovereign party treats them as insurgents and rebels who owe allegiance, and who should be punished with death for their treason. . . .

As a civil war is never publicly proclaimed, *eo nomine* against insurgents, its actual existence is a fact in our domestic history which the Court is bound to notice and to know.

The true test of its existence, as found in the writing of the sages of the common law, may be thus summarily stated: "When the regular course of justice is interrupted by revolt, rebellion, or insurrection, so that the Courts of Justice cannot be kept open, *civil war exists* and hostilities may be prosecuted on the same footing as if those opposing the Government were foreign enemies invading the land."

By the Constitution, Congress alone has the power to declare a national or foreign war. It cannot declare war against a State, or any number of States, by virtue of any clause in the Constitution. The Constitution confers on the President the whole Executive power. He is bound to take care that the laws be faithfully executed. He is Commander-in-chief of the Army and Navy of the United States, and of the militia of the several States when called into the actual service of the United States. He has no power to initiate or declare a war either against a foreign nation or a domestic State. But by the Acts of Congress of February 28th, 1795, and 3d of March, 1807, he is authorized to call out the militia and use the military and naval forces of the United States in case of invasion by foreign nations, and to suppress insurrection against the government of a State or of the United States.

If a war be made by invasion of a foreign nation, the President is not only authorized but bound to resist force by force. He does not initiate the war, but is bound to accept the challenge without waiting for any special legislative authority. And whether the hostile party be a foreign invader, or States organized in rebellion, it is none the less a war, although the declaration of it be *"unilateral."*. . .

The battles of Palo Alto and Resaca de la Palma had been fought before the passage of the Act of Congress of May 13th, 1846, which recognized *"a state of war as existing by the act of the Republic of Mexico."* This act not only provided for the future prosecution of the war, but was itself a vindication and ratification of the Act of the President in accepting the challenge without a previous formal declaration of war by Congress.

This greatest of civil wars was not gradually developed by popular commotion, tumultuous assemblies, or local unorganized insurrections. However long may have been its previous conception, it nevertheless sprung forth suddenly from the parent brain, a Minerva in the full panoply of *war*. The President was bound to meet it in the shape it presented itself, without waiting for Congress to baptize it with a name; and no name given to it by him or them could change the fact. . . .

Whether the President in fulfilling his duties, as Commander-in-chief, in suppressing an insurrection, has met with such armed hostile resistance, and a civil war of such alarming proportions as will compel him to accord to them the character of belligerents, is a question to be decided *by him,* and this Court must be governed by the decisions and acts of the political department of the Government to which this power was entrusted. "He must determine what degree of force the crisis demands." The proclamation of blockade is itself official and conclusive evidence to the Court that a state of war existed which demanded and authorized a recourse to such a measure, under the circumstances peculiar to the case....

If it were necessary to the technical existence of a war, that it should have a legislative sanction, we find it in almost every act passed at the extraordinary session of the Legislature of 1861, which was wholly employed in enacting laws to enable the Government to prosecute the war with vigor and efficiency. And finally, in 1861, we find Congress *"ex majore cautela"* and in anticipation of such astute objections, passing an act "approving, legalizing, and making valid all the acts, proclamations, and orders of the President, &c., as if they had been *issued and done under the previous express authority* and direction of the Congress of the United States."

Without admitting that such an act was necessary under the circumstances, it is plain that if the President had in any manner assumed powers which it was necessary should have the authority or sanction of Congress, that on the well known principle of law, *"omnis ratihabitio retrotrahitur et mandato equiparatur,"* this ratification has operated to perfectly cure the defect....

On this first question therefore we are of the opinion that the President had a right, *jure belli,* to institute a blockade of ports in possession of the States in rebellion, which neutrals are bound to regard.

II. We come now to the consideration of the second question. What is included in the term *"enemies' property?"*

Is the property of all persons residing within the territory of the States now in rebellion, captured on the high seas, to be treated as "enemies' property" whether the owner be in arms against the Government or not?

The right of one belligerent not only to coerce the other by direct force, but also to cripple his resources by the seizure or destruction of his property, is a necessary result of a state of war. Money and wealth, the products of agriculture and commerce, are said to be the sinews of war, and as necessary in its conduct as numbers and physical force. Hence it is, that the laws of war recognize the right of a belligerent to cut these sinews of the power of the enemy, by capturing his property on the high seas....

Whether property be liable to capture as "enemies' property" does not in any manner depend on the personal allegiance of the owner. . . .

The produce of the soil of the hostile territory, as well as other property engaged in the commerce of the hostile power, as the source of its wealth and strength, are always regarded as legitimate prize, without regard to the domicile of the owner, and much more so if he reside and trade within their territory. . . .

Judgments affirmed [except as to certain property in one of the cases].

Mr. Justice Nelson, dissenting:

. . . In the case of a rebellion or resistance of a portion of the people of a country against the established government, there is no doubt, if in its progress and enlargement the government thus sought to be overthrown sees fit, it may by the competent power recognize or declare the existence of a state of civil war, which will draw after it all the consequences and rights of war between the contending parties. . . . But before this insurrection against the established Government can be dealt with on the footing of a civil war, within the meaning of the law of nations and the Constitution of the United States, and which will draw after it belligerent rights, it must be recognized or declared by the war-making power of the Government.

. . . Instead, therefore, of inquiring after armies and navies, and victories lost and won, or organized rebellion against the general Government, the inquiry should be into the law of nations and into the municipal fundamental laws of the Government. For we find there that to constitute a civil war in the sense in which we are speaking, before it can exist, in contemplation of law, it must be recognized or declared by the sovereign power of the State, and which sovereign power by our Constitution is lodged in the Congress of the United States — civil war, therefore, under our system of government, can exist only by an act of Congress, which requires the assent of two of the great departments of the Government, the Executive and Legislative.

We have thus far been speaking of the war power under the Constitution of the United States, and as known and recognized by the law of nations. But we are asked, what would become of the peace and integrity of the Union in case of an insurrection at home or invasion from abroad if this power could not be exercised by the President in the recess of Congress, and until that body could be assembled?

[*The opinion proceeds to note the power of the President (under various Acts of Congress) to call forth the militia in times of emergency.*]

It will be seen, therefore, that ample provision has been made under the Constitution and laws against any sudden and unexpected disturbance of the public peace from insurrection at home or invasion from abroad....

[But the Acts referred to] did not, and could not under the Constitution, confer on the President the power of declaring war against a State of this Union, or of deciding that war existed, and upon that ground authorize the capture and confiscation of the property of every citizen of the State whenever it was found on the waters. The laws of war, whether the war be civil or *inter gentes,* as we have seen, convert every citizen of the hostile State into a public enemy, and treat him accordingly, whatever may have been his previous conduct. This great power over the business and property of the citizen is reserved to the legislative department by the express words of the Constitution. It cannot be delegated or surrendered to the Executive. Congress alone can determine whether war exists or should be declared; and until they have acted, no citizen of the State can be punished in his person or property, unless he has committed some offence against a law of Congress passed before the act was committed, which made it a crime, and defined the punishment. The penalty of confiscation for the acts of others with which he had no concern cannot lawfully be inflicted....

So the war carried on by the President against the insurrectionary districts in the Southern States, as in the case of the King of Great Britain in the American Revolution, was a personal war against those in rebellion, and with encouragement and support of loyal citizens with a view to their co-operation and aid in suppressing the insurgents, with this difference, as the war-making power belonged to the King, he might have recognized or declared the war at the beginning to be a civil war which would draw after it all the rights of a belligerent, but in the case of the President no such power existed: the war therefore from necessity was a personal war, until Congress assembled and acted upon this state of things....

Upon the whole, after the most careful consideration of this case which the pressure of other duties has admitted, I am compelled to the conclusion that no civil war existed between this Government and the States in insurrection till recognized by the Act of Congress 13th of July, 1861; that the President does not possess the power under the Constitution to declare war or recognize its existence within the meaning of the law of nations, which carries with it belligerent rights, and thus change the country and all its citizens from a state of peace to a state of war; that this power belongs exclusively to the Congress of the United States, and, consequently, that the President had no power to set on foot a blockade under the law of nations, and that the capture of the vessel and cargo in this case, and in all cases before us in which the capture occurred before the 13th of July, 1861, for breach of blockade, or as enemies' property, are illegal and void, and that the decrees of condemnation should be reversed and the vessel and cargo restored.

Inter Arma Silent Leges

The *Prize Cases* answered two of the most important questions regarding crisis government, as the judiciary accepted the view that presidential authority encompassed both the determination of an emergency's existence and the initiation of measures to combat it. The President could not "declare war" in the legal or constitutional sense, but as Commander-in-Chief he could nonetheless commit the nation to military action without congressional approval. He had independent constitutional authority, in other words, to make "defensive war."

In this first major test of executive power under crisis conditions, therefore, the Court had acquiesced in the extraordinary actions taken by the President. And during the remainder of the war it displayed an almost unanimous reluctance to erect constitutional barriers against political determinations of crisis necessity, a reluctance which was most evident in its approach to the President's suspension of the habeas corpus privilege.

Suspension of the "Great Writ"—designed to guarantee investigation of the charges on which one's liberty has been restrained and historically the citizen's most important protection against unwarranted detention by executive authorities—is a hallmark of the establishment of martial rule, allowing for the transfer of law enforcement and judicial power from civil to military jurisdiction. It had been suspended by the President initially on April 27, 1861, to safeguard the Washington-Baltimore-Philadelphia railway line against disloyal persons in the area, and a year later the suspension had been extended throughout the theatre of war.

Interestingly enough, in the first test of the President's order, it was struck down. But the decision was not made by the Supreme Court, and the case never reached that tribunal. The occasion for this event was the arrest and imprisonment by military authorities of a Maryland secessionist leader. He directed his petition for a writ of habeas corpus to Chief Justice Taney, whose circuit included that state. With a speed which betrayed rather unjudicial eagerness, Taney issued the writ; but it was not honored by the area's commanding general, who based his refusal on the President's suspension proclamation. Taney held the general in contempt of court, the general barred the gates of Fort McHenry to the marshal attempting to serve the contempt papers, and the Chief Justice retired to file his opinion in *Ex parte Merryman*.

That circuit court opinion strongly denounced the President's action. Arguing that under the law of England only Parliament could suspend the writ of habeas corpus, that the constitutional provision allowing for suspension is found in Article I, which deals with legislative and not executive power, and that outstanding commentators like Marshall and Story accorded to Congress alone the power of suspension, the Chief Justice left no doubt that in his view Lincoln had violated the Constitution. The decision had little practical effect, however. Three months later Congress ratified the President's action, and in 1862 he proclaimed a broader suspension of the writ without any reference to the *Merryman* decision or to Congress. No further legislative attempt to settle this matter was made until 1863, and even then the Habeas Corpus Act's language was equivocal with regard to the source of presidential power.

The habeas corpus problem first reached the Supreme Court itself in *Ex parte Vallandigham* (1863). Along with his 1862 proclamation Lincoln had ordered that persons engaged in disloyal activities be tried by military commission. Clement Vallandigham, a well-known "copperhead," was arrested for making an anti-war speech, tried, found guilty, and sentenced to imprisonment for the war's duration by such a commission. His petition for a writ of habeas corpus was refused by the circuit court, and he was forced to take the case directly to the Supreme Court, which agreed to review the sentence. The petitioner argued that the military commission had no jurisdiction in his case because, as a civilian in an area where the courts were open and functioning, he was entitled to the normal guarantees of due process of law. Furthermore, he contended that the charge on which he was tried—"committing acts for the benefit of the enemy"—was unknown to the Constitution and the laws of the United States.

The validity of the President's institution of martial rule was thus challenged, but the Court avoided the issue. Adopting the government's technical argument as their own opinion, the Justices found that the failure of the circuit court to act in this matter constituted a fatal flaw in the proceedings. Under both their original jurisdiction (derived from the Constitution) and their appellate jurisdiction (derived from the Judiciary Act of 1789) they could review only the proceedings of a "court," and a military commission was not such a body. As a result, the executive retained the power to dispense justice in those areas which he had designated as war theatres, and on no occasion during the war did the Supreme Court attempt to subordinate military to civil authority or to rebuke the President for relying on martial rule rather than on procedures established by the Constitution or by congressional acts.

Only after both the crisis and the crisis leader had passed away was the Court prepared to speak the language of limitation. Then, in *Ex parte Milligan,* the Justices reconsidered and condemned those presidential actions which had been accepted throughout the war. The central figure in this case, a citizen of Indiana, had been convicted by a military commission in 1864 for conspiring to organize an expedition of rebel forces against the United States. Sentenced to be hanged, he petitioned the circuit court for a writ of habeas corpus. That court entertained the petition, but on a division of opinion, the case was brought before the Supreme Court early in 1866.

The issue presented was strikingly reminiscent of

Vallandigham's case, except that the circuit court action removed the jurisdictional technicality under which the Court had sought cover in 1864. Milligan's petition argued that as a civilian residing in a non-rebel state in which the regular courts were open and functioning, he was entitled under both the Constitution and the Habeas Corpus Act of 1863 to the normal guarantees of due process, including indictment and trial by jury. The main question, as the Court framed it, was whether "upon the facts stated in Milligan's petition . . . the military commission mentioned in it [had] jurisdiction, legally, to try and sentence him?"

The Court unanimously agreed that the military, that is the executive, had exceeded its authority by ignoring the procedure established by Congress and instituting military trial of civilians in areas where the regular courts were ready and able to conduct their normal business. All the Justices rejected the proposition that the military commander in a crisis period has the power, if in his opinion the exigencies of the situation demand it, to suspend citizens' rights in any area and subject civilians as well as soldiers to the "rule of his will." Said Justice Davis for the Court:

> The Constitution of the United States is a law for rulers and people, equally in war and in peace, and covers with the shield of its protection all classes of men, at all times, and under all circumstances. No doctrine involving more pernicious consequences was ever invented by the wit of man than that any of its provisions can be suspended during any of the great exigencies of government. Such a doctrine leads directly to anarchy or despotism, but the theory of necessity on which it is based is false; for the government, within the Constitution, has all the powers granted to it which are necessary to preserve its existence; as has been happily proved by the result of the great effort to throw off its just authority.

Martial law based on an extraconstitutional conception of crisis government, declared Davis, "destroys every guarantee of the Constitution, and effectually 'renders the military independent of and superior to the civil power'. . . . Civil liberty and this kind of martial law cannot endure together; the antagonism is irreconcilable; and in the conflict, one or the other must perish."

The Justices admitted that when "war exists in a community and the courts and civil authorities are overthrown" the institution of military rule is proper, but carried away by their desire to impose strict limitations on a regime which had already passed from the scene they insisted that martial law could not arise from a "threatened invasion."

> The necessity must be actual and present; the invasion real, such as effectually closes the courts and deposes the civil administration. . . . Martial rule can never exist where the courts are open, and in the proper and unobstructed exercise of their jurisdiction.

Since the conditions necessary to justify military government had not existed in Indiana when Milligan was arrested, the Commander-in-Chief's imposition of martial law on that area had been *ultra vires.* Indeed five of the Justices were prepared to go even further, declaring that as to military trial of civilians outside the actual theatre of war, even Congress "could grant no such power."

Thus, with the crisis over, the Court was at last prepared to speak about constitutional limitations. Without impugning the martyred war President personally—by this time five of the Court's members were Lincoln appointees—its decision nonetheless branded as unconstitutional a most important aspect of his crisis rule. For the decision in effect condemned the presidential suspension of habeas corpus and the institution of executive justice. But these limits had been imposed *ex post facto,* as Justice Davis virtually admitted in pointing out, with remarkable candor, that during the war

> the temper of the times did not allow that calmness in deliberation and discussion so necessary to a correct conclusion of a purely judicial question. *Then* considerations of safety were mingled with the exercise of power; and feelings and interests prevailed which are happily terminated. *Now* that the public safety is assured, this question, as well as all others, can be discussed and decided without passion or the admixture of any element not required to form a legal judgment.

The *Milligan* decision was a forceful rejection of the doctrine that wartime government is unlimited and an eloquent defense of the Constitution's sanctity. But its declaration that constitutional provisions cannot be suspended "during any of the great exigencies of government" had a hollow ring in view of the myriad extraordinary actions which Lincoln took, and which the Court either upheld or ignored, throughout the war. Coming, as it did, over a year after the emergency's end and the President's martyrdom, the decision was more quotable than applicable. It was, in the final analysis, more significant as an admission of judicial ineffectiveness and as an example of the fact that "the laws are silent" during war periods than as a condemnation of the vast power which had been assumed by the crisis government.

That government had, in effect, been a "presidential dictatorship" — though its impact on both individual citizens and the society as a whole was very mild in comparison with modern dictatorial regimes — and the Supreme Court, compelled to accept the judgments of those primarily responsible for the nation's defense, had acquiesced in its institution. The Court thereby established the precedent which it would follow in all subsequent war periods.

The Principles of Crisis Government Formalized and Extended

The next major war emergency — World War I — did not arise for a half century, but the policy of judicial acquiescence had not weakened during the interim. This was particularly interesting because of the Court's negative attitude toward the exercise of governmental power throughout the intervening period, and because the immediate threat to the nation was less serious in 1917-19 than it had been in 1861-65. But despite all this the judiciary was even less inclined than before to impose restraints on the war government.

While its philosophy of power was the same, the form of that second crisis government differed from its Civil War counterpart in at least one important respect. Lincoln's regime was based almost exclusively on the President's independent authority under the Constitution. Aside from ratifying the executive's more extraordinary actions, appropriating money, and engaging in an abortive (albeit harassing) attempt to investigate the conduct of the war, Congress had not played an active role in the regime. On only two occasions had the President requested, and received, delegations of power from the legislature.

President Wilson was no less convinced than Lincoln of the broad scope of executive power, but reflecting his proclivity to the British parliamentary system and the different circumstances surrounding the crisis, his emergency government was based primarily on authority delegated to the executive by a Congress operating under his direction. In other words, where Lincoln had broken down the separation of powers by assuming legislative authority on his own initiative, Wilson accomplished the same purpose by fusing the two political branches into a single organ of government under his domination.

The Supreme Court not only accepted this pattern but welcomed it, since the inclusion of Congress in the crisis regime removed many of the problems which had arisen during the Civil War. Indeed the Justices were relieved of many burdens during the emergency because of the methods adopted to meet it. Thus the fact that war had been declared in the constitutionally prescribed manner relieved them of a problem which the Civil War Court had been forced to resolve. And even though broad economic controls were introduced during this second crisis, the Court was able to avoid many of the problems created thereby because the executive's policies were often effectuated through resort to the extralegal (and non-justiciable) technique of applying "indirect sanctions" to secure compliance with his directives. Finally, insofar as military and foreign policy were concerned, the Court took the first opportunity to point out that both the responsibility and the power for the conduct of such affairs lies in the political departments, and therefore "the propriety of what may be done in the exercise of this political power is not subject to judicial inquiry or decision." *(Oetjen v. Central Leather Company.)*

With no question regarding the constitutionality of the regime's existence to be decided, and with the way in which the executive acquired his power to prosecute the emergency not seriously disputed, the most important matters presented for judicial determination during World War I involved "only" the government's exercises of power in mobilizing the economic resources of the nation and in circumscribing the liberties of its citizens.

In relation to these very serious problems Civil War precedents were not directly in point, since the World War I regime operated almost entirely under statutory authority, and therefore the power being tested was the "war power" of the combined political organs of American government rather than the authority of the President alone. But insofar as the judicial attitude toward the exercise of that power is concerned, the second crisis experience did not differ from the first. For the Supreme Court again gave the political branches a wide berth and adopted a "theory of relativity" in distinguishing between the wartime and the peacetime Constitution.

Incursions on economic rights resulted primarily from broad legislative acts empowering the President to regulate and control the war economy. The concept of "drafting" industry in meeting an emergency was new, and during the post-Civil War period the judicial branch had been strongly opposed to economic regulation.[1] But the wartime Court defended the government's contention that its emergency power encompassed control over economic affairs, and upheld all of its major assumptions of authority in this area.

Interestingly enough, the Court did not even have the opportunity to review certain aspects of this control over the economy because the power exercised was based on "directives" issued by agencies established under presidential authority rather than on statutes, and since compliance with these agency orders could usually be secured through subtle forms of executive coercion or "indirect sanctions" rather than through the judicial process. Thus in a labor-management dispute, for example, the company might be threatened with loss of war contracts and the workers with review of their draft status unless they obeyed the

[1]The problem of governmental control over economic affairs is discussed in Chapter I.

directives of the War Labor Board, but such extralegal actions could not be challenged in the courts.

Although this unusual method of controlling economic activity was not subjected to judicial scrutiny, the Supreme Court did review and uphold all of the government's legally based assertions of authority, including seizure of the railroad and communications systems, as valid exercises of the "war power." In all, only one insignificant provision of a major wartime statute was struck down, and the Court's permissive attitude toward economic regulation under war conditions was never in doubt. Long after the emergency's termination the reasons underlying that attitude were clearly expressed, when the Court pointed out that if the power of the government is great enough to draft men for battle service, "its power to draft business organizations to support the fighting men who risk their lives can be no less." *(United States v. Bethlehem Steel Corp.)*

The Court's approval of economic control measures was a striking example of the different constitutional standards applied under war conditions. But even more significant was its complete acceptance of governmental incursions on individual rights. This was evident in the doctrine which Justice Holmes enunciated in the *Schenck* case. "In many places and in ordinary times," he said, "the acts on which the defendants' convictions for violating the Espionage Act of 1917 were based would have been within their constitutional rights. . . . But the character of every act depends upon the circumstances in which it is done. . . . When a nation is at war many things that might be said in time of peace are such a hindrance to its effort that their utterance will not be endured so long as men fight and that no Court could regard them as protected by any constitutional right."

Justice Holmes, joined by Justice Brandeis, dissented from the later decisions of the Court which used similar reasoning to uphold restrictive wartime legislation, but in no case arising out of the emergency did a majority of the Court attempt to restrain, or even criticize, the government's unprecedented (and sometimes unnecessarily arbitrary) denial of rights traditionally protected by the Constitution.[1] The World War I Court, like its Civil War counterpart, accepted the proposition that during crisis periods the basic law is subject to suspension and acquiesced in the exercise of whatever power the government deemed necessary to meet the crisis successfuly. Its attitude was summed up, and the constitutional guarantees which had been circumscribed during the war were catalogued, by Justice Sutherland in one of the last cases related to the emergency:

> To the end that war may not result in defeat, freedom of speech may, by act of Congress, be curtailed or denied so that the morale of the people and the spirit of the army may not be broken by seditious utterances; freedom of the press curtailed to preserve our military plans and movements from the knowledge of the enemy; deserters and spies put to death without indictment or trial by jury; ships and supplies requisitioned; property of alien enemies, theretofore under the protection of the Constitution, seized without process and converted to the public use without compensation and without due process of law in the ordinary sense of that term; prices of food and other necessities of life fixed or regulated; railways taken over and operated by the government; and other drastic power, wholly inadmissible in time of peace, exercised to meet the emergencies of war. (*United States v. Macintosh.*)

In short, there were no significant limitations which the Court would presume to impose on the war government with regard to its power over either personal or property rights.

As a result of World War I, the extraordinary aspects of wartime government were formalized by giving them an aura of legality and extended by including within the purview of governmental authority all aspects of the nation's life. Wilson had adapted the Lincolnian conception of emergency rule to the circumstances of modern society, and the Supreme Court had quickly and wholeheartedly accepted the result. The next crisis President would borrow from both of his wartime predecessors in meeting the emergency which confronted him, and the Court would also accept his regime.

[1]The cases dealing with restrictions on fundamental freedoms during World War I are discussed more fully in the preceding chapter.

Crisis Government and "Total War"

The World War II Court, with seven Roosevelt appointees and a Chief Justice who had supported an emergency approach to economic depression, was well attuned to the language of power and quite prepared to acquiesce in the crisis decisions of the political branches. Like the earlier wartime Courts, it raised no constitutional barriers against the exercise of whatever authority the government considered necessary to meet the emergency, although in at least one instance that authority was used with flagrant disregard for the rights of American citizens. This was "total war" and the government had total power.

The Court had no occasion to comment on a number of extraordinary actions—like the destroyers-for-bases deal of 1940—which President Roosevelt had taken before Pearl Harbor, since they involved non-justiciable issues or came under the doctrine of "political questions." But the government's policies limiting economic rights and individual liberties during the war were quickly challenged in the courts.

Although Roosevelt had followed Wilson's lead in establishing his crisis government primarily on statutory delegations of power, the scope of the World War II delegations related to economic affairs was so broad that new issues were raised. Some of the most important problems in this area involved the Emergency Price Control Act of 1942, which gave the price administrator wide discretionary authority to halt inflation and set up an Emergency Court of Appeals with exclusive jurisdiction to determine the validity of orders issued by the Office of Price Administration. It was attacked as an improper delegation of legislative power, a violation of the Fifth Amendment "due process" and "just compensation" provisions, and as an unconstitutional incursion on the Court's own authority. All of these attacks failed, as even Justice Rutledge, while dissenting in *Yakus v. United States,* agreed that

> War such as we now fight calls into play the full power of government in extreme emergency. It compels invention of legal, as of martial tools adequate for the times' necessity. Inevitably some will be strange, if also lifesaving, instruments for a people

accustomed to peace and the normal working of constitutional limitations. Citizens must surrender or forego exercising rights which in other times could not be impaired.

And in another price control case, Justice Douglas pointed out that "a nation which can demand the lives of its men and women in the waging of war is under no constitutional necessity of providing a system of price control on the domestic front which will assure each landlord a 'fair return' on his property." *(Bowles v. Willingham.)*

As in 1917-19, most of the agencies charged with administering the World War II emergency program were established by the executive. Congress, in 1940, had authorized the creation of an Office for Emergency Management within the Executive Office of the President, but before the war's end the President, without specific congressional approval, had created 29 major agencies (plus their manifold alphabetical progeny) under the OEM. These agencies drew on executive power in enforcing their orders, and "indirect sanctions" again became a major weapon of crisis government. Thus strikes were prevented by placing the Selective Service System under the War Manpower Commission, which issued a "work or fight" order in February 1942. And employer cooperation with government directives was achieved by threats of publicity, deprivation of raw materials, and denial of war contracts. Moreover, President Roosevelt resorted to outright seizure of industrial facilities on 28 occasions between 1942 and 1945, eleven of these coming before passage of the War Labor Disputes Act which authorized such action; and after VE day, President Truman, citing that Act and his power as Commander-in-Chief, used the seizure method more than 40 times.

The executive's resort to extralegal techniques was not fully reviewed by the Supreme Court. But in 1944, in *Steuart and Brothers Inc. v. Bowles,* it upheld a lower court decision sustaining a penalty which OPA had imposed under the President's power to allocate defense materials rather than under the agency's own statutory authority. And during the same year there was a decision of the District of Columbia Court of Appeals, which refused to enjoin a directive of the

National War Labor Board on the ground that the orders
were "in reality" mere declarations of the equities of industrial disputes; they were only an appeal to the "moral
obligation" of workers and employers to abide by their
agreements and to carry out the directives of agencies
created under those agreements by the Commander-in-
Chief. In that court's rather naive view, the NWLB was simply an advisory body whose orders were "judicially unen-
forceable and unreviewable." *(Employers Group of Motor
Freight Carriers v. National War Labor Board.)* This was
one way of allowing the use of indirect sanctions, but the
litigation did not get to the Supreme Court for final approval.

No case involving statutorily unauthorized seizure was
reviewed during the war either. However, the validity of
such action was upheld by implication in a postwar case,
as the Court, in sustaining a lower decision which awarded
damages to a coal company for losses suffered while its
property had been under government control, said that
private properties "may be subjected to public operation
only for a short time to meet war or emergency needs, and
can then be returned to their owners." *(United States v.
Peewee Coal Corp.)*

Of final significance in relation to government's wartime
authority over economic affairs was the Court's acceptance
of the congressional delegation of that authority to the President. In *Lichter v. United States,* a decision upholding contract renegotiation as a valid means by which the government could recapture excess profits made on war contracts,
the Court declared that a constitutional power "implies a
power of delegation of authority under it sufficient to effect
its purposes" and that "broad discretion as to the methods
to be employed may be essential to an effective use of its
war powers by Congress." Moreover, the degree to which
the legislature must specify its policies and standards to
guide executive-administrative officials "is not capable of
precise definition." In war as in peace, said the Court, "it
is essential that the Constitution be scrupulously obeyed,
and particularly that the respective branches of the Government keep within the powers assigned to each," but "while

the constitutional structure and controls of our Government are our guides equally in war and in peace, they must be read with the realistic purposes of the entire instrument fully in mind."

The political branches had no difficulty with the judiciary, therefore, in applying the Constitution to a wartime economy. Whatever controls were necessary could be imposed "constitutionally." The President himself, however, was quite prepared to transcend the basic law if in his judgment necessity demanded, as he made clear in a 1942 speech to Congress concerning repeal of an inflationary provision of the Price Control Act:

> I ask the Congress to take this action by the first of October. Inaction on your part by that date will leave me with an inescapable responsibility to the people of this country to see to it that the war effort is no longer imperiled by threat of economic chaos.
>
> In the event that the Congress should fail to act, and act adequately, I shall accept the responsibility, and I will act....
>
> The American people can be sure that I will use my powers with a full sense of my responsibility to the Constitution and to my country....
>
> When the war is won, the powers under which I act automatically revert to the people—to whom they belong.[1]

A test of the President's threatened action never arose, since Congress bowed to his peremptory demand. But in this remarkable address, Roosevelt assumed Lincoln's position, claiming to represent the will of the people and asserting his power to dispense with the Constitution itself if the people's needs required. In most respects, including economic controls, the World War II government was in the Wilsonian rather than the Lincolnian tradition, but there can be little doubt that Franklin Roosevelt would have established a "presidential dictatorship" if the necessity had arisen. Indeed in connection with the major wartime problem involving individual liberty, his regime went further in the exercise of emergency power than the Civil War

---

[1] See Samuel Rosenman, ed., *The Public Papers and Addresses of Franklin D. Roosevelt,* 13 vols. (New York: Random House, 1938-1950), 1942 volume, 356, 364-365.

leader had ever gone. And it was this issue which presented the Supreme Court with its most difficult decisions of the war period.

Individual Rights Under Conditions of "Total War"

Judicial acceptance and approval of pervasive wartime controls over the national economy during World War II extended the concept of crisis government far beyond its previous frontiers. But more important was the Supreme Court's acquiescence in the unprecedented invasion of personal liberty with regard to American citizens of Japanese descent. This was especially noteworthy because the 1941-45 Court comprised a majority which had already given evidence of a protective attitude toward individual rights. And it was particularly striking because the war's impact on the civil liberties of the nation as a whole was in fact much milder than during World War I. But the single exception to this welcome difference was also the most flagrant denial of constitutional rights in American history.

The action giving rise to this unfortunate result was the issuance on February 19, 1942, of Executive Order 9066, which read in part:

> Whereas the successful prosecution of the war requires every possible protection against espionage and against sabotage . . .
>
> Now, therefore, by virtue of the authority vested in me as President of the United States, and Commander-in-Chief of the Army and Navy, I hereby authorize and direct the Secretary of War and the military commanders whom he may from time to time designate, whenever he or any designated commander deems such action necessary or desirable, to prescribe military areas in such places and of such extent as he or the appropriate military commander may determine, from which any or all persons may be excluded, and with respect to which, the right of any person to enter, remain in, or leave shall be subject to whatever restrictions the Secretary of War or the appropriate military commander may impose in his discretion.[1]

The Order further directed that all persons excluded from "military areas" be provided with food, shelter, transporta-

[1] Executive Order 9066, 7 *Federal Register* 1407 (1942).

tion, and other accommodations "until other arrangements are made." Such arrangements were made by another Executive Order of March 18, 1942, establishing the War Relocation Authority. On March 21, by voice vote in both Houses, Congress in effect ratified the President's orders by establishing penalties for their violation.

Under the directives, Secretary of War Stimson authorized the Western Defense Commander, General DeWitt, first to impose curfews and other restrictions, then to evacuate from their homes in California, Oregon, Washington, and parts of Arizona, and finally to transport to relocation centers in the interior, 112,000 persons of Japanese ancestry, of whom over 70,000 were American citizens. The reason given for these drastic actions was "military necessity," that is, the alleged danger of espionage, sabotage, or other "fifth column" operations in the event of an invasion of the West Coast by Japan. Significantly, the exclusion order was not promulgated until May 1942, and all Japanese were not removed from the designated areas until October. But at no time during this period, or later, was any procedure adopted to determine the loyalty or disloyalty of either citizen or alien Japanese; the sole and sufficient criterion for subjection to the restrictions was racial descent.

The first case challenging the constitutionality of this emergency program to reach the Supreme Court was *Hirabayashi v. United States,* decided on July 21, 1943. The plaintiff, a University of Washington student, had been tried and convicted for violation of both a military order directing him to report to a "civil control station" before being evacuated, and a curfew regulation; he had then been sentenced under the Act of Congress to three months' imprisonment on each count, the sentences to run concurrently.

Taking advantage of this latter fact, the Court proceeded to avoid the broad issue of constitutionality involved in the exclusion program and confined itself to examining the validity of the curfew regulation alone. That regulation it held valid by unanimous vote. "We have no occasion," declared Chief Justice Stone, "to consider whether the President, acting alone, could lawfully have made the curfew order in question or have authorized others to make it." Nor, he said, was the issue "one of Congressional power to delegate to the President the promulgation of the Executive Order." Rather, it was: "Whether, acting in cooperation, Congress and the Executive have constitutional [power] . . . to impose the curfew restriction here complained of." Such power the combined political branches certainly did possess, in the Court's opinion, and to the objection that it had been used discriminatorily against persons of Japanese ancestry, Stone replied that "the actions taken must be appraised in the light of the conditions with which the President and Congress were confronted in the early months of 1942."

> We cannot close our eyes to the fact, demonstrated by ex-perience, that in time of war residents having ethnic affiliations with an invading enemy may be a greater source of danger than those of different ancestry. Nor can we deny that Congress, and the military authorities acting with its authorization, have con-stitutional power to appraise the danger in the light of facts of public notoriety. We need not now attempt to define the ultimate boundaries of the war power. We decide only the issue as we have defined it — we decide only that the curfew order as applied, and at the time it was applied, was within the boundaries of the war power.

It was sufficient, the Chief Justice concluded, that "circum-stances within the knowledge of those charged with the re-sponsibility for maintaining the national defense afforded a rational basis for the decision which they made. Whether we would have made it is irrelevant."

This last comment indicated that the Court was sorely troubled by the government's Japanese-American policy. But it had nonetheless dodged the major issue in the case, and it had attempted to avoid future problems by basing the validity of an executive action on the combined "war powers of the government." Congress had indeed provided penalties for violation of military orders, but the evacuation program, and the curfew as well, were presidentially instituted on the ground of military exigency; they were, in fact, emergency actions based on the President's power as Commander-in-Chief in time of war. Thus, by its attempt to sidestep the issue of constitutional propriety in Hirabayashi's case, the Court revealed that it was unprepared, even in matters dealing with fundamental personal rights, to contradict the executive's determinations of "crisis necessity."

The crucial issue left unresolved in 1943 had finally to be considered eighteen months later, however. The case involved a citizen who refused to obey a military order directing him to report at an evacuation station for removal from his home in California. He challenged the validity of the order, and thus of the entire evacuation program, but was convicted. The conviction was affirmed, and the Supreme Court granted certiorari to review the case. By the time its decision was handed down, the danger of a West Coast invasion was long past and the end of the war with Japan was only nine months off, but a majority of the Court still refused to question the executive's judgment or strike down the emergency regime's extraordinary actions.

Korematsu v. United States
323 U.S. 214 (1944)

Mr. Justice Black delivered the opinion of the Court:

. . . In the light of the principles we announced in the Hirabayashi Case, we are unable to conclude that it was beyond the war power of Congress and the Executive to exclude those of Japanese ancestry from the West Coast war area at the time they did. True, exclusion from the area in which one's home is located is a far greater deprivation than constant confinement to the home from 8 p. m. to 6 a. m. Nothing short of apprehension by the proper military authorities of the gravest imminent danger to the public safety can constitutionally justify either. But exclusion from a threatened area, no less than curfew, has a definite and close relationship to the prevention of espionage and sabotage. The military authorities, charged with the primary responsibility of defending our shores, concluded that curfew provided inadequate protection and ordered exclusion. They did so, as pointed out in our Hirabayashi opinion, in accordance with congressional authority to the military to say who should, and who should not, remain in the threatened areas. . . .

Here, as in the Hirabayashi Case, supra, "we cannot reject as unfounded the judgment of the military authorities and of Congress that there were disloyal members of that population, whose number and strength could not be precisely and quickly ascertained. We cannot say that the war-making branches of the Government did not have ground for believing that in a critical hour such persons could not readily be isolated and separately dealt with, and constituted a menace to the national defense and safety, which demanded that prompt and adequate measures by taken to guard against it."

Like curfew, exclusion of those of Japanese origin was deemed necessary because of the presence of an unascertained number of disloyal members of the group, most of whom we have no doubt were loyal to this country. It was because we could not reject the finding of the military authorities that it was impossible to bring about an immediate segregation of the disloyal from the loyal that we sustained the validity of the curfew order as applying to the whole group. In the instant case, temporary exclusion of the entire group was rested by the military on the same ground. The judgment that exclusion of the whole group was for the same reason a military imperative answers the contention that the exclusion was in the nature of group punishment based on antagonism to those of Japanese origin. That there were members of the group who retained loyalties to Japan has been confirmed by investigations made subsequent to the exclusion. Approximately five thousand American citizens of Japanese ancestry refused to swear unqualified allegiance to the United States and to renounce allegiance to the Japanese Emperor, and several thousand evacuees requested repatriation to Japan.

We uphold the exclusion order as of the time it was made and when the petitioner violated it. In doing so, we are not unmindful of the hardships imposed by it upon a large group of American citizens. But hardships are part of war, and war is an aggregation of hardships. All citizens alike, both in and out of uniform, feel the impact of war in greater or lesser measure. Citizenship has its responsibilities as well as its privileges, and in time of war the burden is always heavier. Compulsory exclusion of large groups of citizens from their homes, except under circumstances of direst emergency and peril, is inconsistent with our basic governmental institutions. But when under conditions of modern warfare our shores are threatened by hostile forces, the power to protect must be commensurate with the threatened danger....

It is·said that we are dealing here with the case of imprisonment of a citizen in a concentration camp solely because of his ancestry, without evidence or inquiry concerning his loyalty and good disposition towards the United States. Our task would be simple, our duty clear, were this a case involving the imprisonment of a loyal citizen in a concentration camp because of racial prejudice. Regardless of the true nature of the assembly and relocation centers — and we deem it unjustifiable to call them concentration camps with all the ugly connotations that term implies — we are dealing specifically with nothing but an exclusion order. To cast this case into outlines of racial prejudice, without reference to the real military dangers which were presented, merely confuses the issue. Korematsu was not excluded from the Military Area because of hostility to him or his race. He *was* excluded because we are at war with the Japanese Empire, because the properly constituted military authorities feared an invasion of our West Coast and felt constrained to take proper security measures, because they decided that the military urgency of the situation demanded that all citizens of Japanese ancestry be segregated from the West Coast temporarily, and finally, because Congress, reposing its confidence in this time of war in our military leaders — as inevitably it must — determined that they should have the power to do just this. There was evidence of disloyalty on the part of some, the military authorities considered that the need for action was great, and time was short. We cannot — by availing ourselves of the calm perspective of hindsight — now say that at that time these actions were unjustified.

Affirmed.

Mr. Justice Frankfurter, concurring:

... The provisions of the Constitution which confer on the Congress and the President powers to enable this country to wage war are as much part of the Constitution as provisions looking to a nation at peace. And we have had recent occasion to quote approvingly the statement of former Chief Justice Hughes that the war power of the Government is "the power to wage war successfully." Therefore, the validity of action under the war power must be judged wholly in the context of war. That action is not to be stigmatized as lawless because like action in times of peace would be lawless. To talk about a military order that expresses an allowable judgment of war needs by those entrusted with the duty of conducting war as "an unconstitutional order" is to suffuse a part of the Constitution with an atmosphere of unconstitutionality. The respective spheres of action of military authorities and of judges are of course very different. But within their sphere, military authorities are no more outside the bounds of obedience to the Constitution than are judges within theirs. "The war power of the United States, like its other powers ... is subject to applicable constitutional limitations." To recognize that military orders are "reasonably expedient military precautions" in time of war and yet to deny them constitutional legitimacy makes of the Constitution an instrument for dialectic subtleties not reasonably to be attributed to the hard-headed Framers, of whom a majority had had actual participation in war. If a military order such as that under review does not transcend the means appropriate for conducting war, such action by the military is as constitutional as would be any authorized action by the Interstate Commerce Commission within the limits of the constitutional power to regulate commerce. And being an exercise of the war power explicitly granted by the Constitution for safe-guarding the national life by prosecuting war effectively, I find nothing in the Constitution which denies to Congress the power to enforce such a valid military order by making its violation an offense triable in the civil courts. To find that the Constitution does not forbid the military measures now complained of does not carry with it approval of that which Congress and the Executive did. That is their business, not ours.

Mr. Justice Roberts, dissenting:

I dissent, because I think the indisputable facts exhibit a clear violation of Constitutional rights.

This is not a case of keeping people off the streets at night as was Hirabayashi v. United States, nor a case of temporary exclusion of a citizen from an area for his own safety or that of the community, nor a case of offering him an opportunity to go temporarily out of an area where his presence might cause danger to himself or to his fellows. On the contrary, it is the case of convicting a citizen as a punishment for not submitting to imprisonment in a concentration camp, based on his ancestry, and solely because of his ancestry, without evidence or inquiry concerning his loyalty and good disposition towards the United States. If this be a correct statement of the facts disclosed by this record, and facts of which we take judicial notice, I need hardly labor the conclusion that constitutional rights have been violated. . . .

Mr. Justice Murphy, dissenting:

This exclusion of "all persons of Japanese ancestry, both alien and non-alien," from the Pacific Coast area on a plea of military necessity in the absence of martial law ought not to be approved. Such exclusion goes over "the very brink of constitutional power" and falls into the ugly abyss of racism. . . .

The judicial test of whether the Government, on a plea of military necessity, can validly deprive an individual of any of his constitutional rights is whether the deprivation is reasonably related to a public danger that is so "immediate, imminent, and impending" as not to admit of delay and not to permit the intervention of ordinary constitutional processes to alleviate the danger. Civilian Exclusion Order No. 34, banishing from a prescribed area of the Pacific Coast "all persons of Japanese ancestry, both alien and non-alien," clearly does not meet that test. Being an obvious racial discrimination, the order deprives all those within its scope of the equal protection of the laws as guaranteed by the Fifth Amendment. It further deprives these individuals of their constitutional rights to live and work where they will, to establish a home where they choose and to move about freely. In excommunicating them without benefit of hearings, this order also deprives them of all their constitutional rights to procedural due process. Yet no reasonable relation to an "immediate, imminent, and impending" public danger is evident to support this racial restriction which is one of the most sweeping and complete deprivations of constitutional rights in the history of this nation in the absence of martial law. . . .

The main reasons relied upon by those responsible for the forced evacuation . . . do not prove a reasonable relation between the group characteristics of Japanese Americans and the dangers of invasion, sabotage and espionage. The reasons appear, instead, to be largely an accumulation of much of the misinformation, half-truths and insinuations that for years have been directed against Japanese Americans by people with racial and economic prejudices—the same people who have been among the foremost advocates of the evacuation. A military judgment based upon such racial and sociological considerations is not entitled to the great weight ordinarily given the judgments based upon strictly military considerations. Especially is this so when every charge relative to race, religion, culture, geographical location, and legal and economic status has been substantially discredited by independent studies made by experts in these matters. . . .

No adequate reason is given for the failure to treat these Japanese Americans on an individual basis by holding investigations and hearings to separate the loyal from the disloyal, as was done in the case of persons of German and Italian ancestry. It is asserted merely that the loyalties of this group "were unknown and time was of the essence." Yet nearly four months elapsed after Pearl Harbor before the first exclusion order was issued; nearly eight months went by until the last order was issued; and the last of these "subversive" persons was not actually removed until almost eleven months had elapsed. Leisure and deliberation seem to have been more of the essence than speed. And the fact that conditions were not such as to warrant a declaration of martial law adds strength to the belief that the factors of time and military necessity were not as urgent as they have been represented to be. . . .

I dissent, therefore, from this legalization of racism. Racial discrimination in any form and in any degree has no justifiable part whatever in our democratic way of life. It is unattractive in any setting but it is utterly revolting among a free people who have embraced the principles set forth in the Constitution of the United States. All residents of this nation are kin in some way by blood or culture to a foreign land. Yet they are primarily and necessarily a part of the new and distinct civilization of the United States. They must accordingly be treated at all times as the heirs of the American experiment and as entitled to all the rights and freedoms guaranteed by the Constitution.

Mr. Justice Jackson, dissenting:

. . . [It] is said that if the military commander had reasonable military grounds for promulgating the orders, they are constitutional and become law, and the Court is required to enforce them. There are several reasons why I cannot subscribe to this doctrine.

It would be impracticable and dangerous idealism to expect or insist that each specific military command in an area of probable operations will conform to conventional tests of constitutionality. When an area is so beset that it must be put under military control at all, the paramount consideration is that its measures be successful, rather than legal. The armed services must protect a society, not merely its Constitution. The very essence of the military job is to marshal physical force, to remove every obstacle to its effectiveness, to give it every strategic advantage. Defense measures will not, and often should not, be held within the limits that bind civil authority in peace. No court can require such a commander in such circumstances to act as a reasonable man; he may be unreasonably cautious and exacting. Perhaps he should be. But a commander in temporarily focusing the life of a community on defense is carrying out a military program; he is not making law in the sense the courts know the term. He issues orders, and they may have a certain authority as military commands, although they may be very bad as constitutional law.

But if we cannot confine military expedients by the Constitution, neither would I distort the Constitution to approve all that the military may deem expedient. . . .

In the very nature of things military decisions are not susceptible of intelligent judicial appraisal. They do not pretend to rest on evidence, but are made on information that often would not be admissible and on assumptions that could not be proved. Information in support of an order could not be disclosed to courts without danger that it would reach the enemy. Neither can courts act on communications made in confidence. Hence courts can never have any real alternative to accepting the mere declaration of the authority that issued the order that it was reasonably necessary from a military viewpoint.

Much is said of the danger to liberty from the Army program for deporting and detaining these citizens of Japanese extraction. But a judicial construction of the due process clause that will sustain this order is a far more subtle blow to liberty than the promulgation of the order itself. A military order, however unconstitutional, is not apt to last longer than the military emergency. Even during that period a succeeding commander may revoke it all. But once a judicial opinion rationalizes such an order to show that it conforms to the Constitution, or rather rationalizes the Constitution to show that the Constitution sanctions such an order, the Court for all time has validated the principle of racial discrimination in criminal procedure and of transplanting American citizens. The principle then lies about like a loaded weapon ready for the hand of any authority that can bring forward a plausible claim of an urgent need. Every repetition imbeds that principle more deeply in our law and thinking and expands it to new purposes. . . . A military commander may overstep the bounds of constitutionality, and it is an incident. But if we review and approve, that passing incident becomes the doctrine of the Constitution. There it has a generative power of its own, and all that it creates will be in its own image. . . .

I should hold that a civil court cannot be made to enforce an order which violates constitutional limitations even if it is a reasonable exercise of military authority. The courts can exercise only the judicial power, can apply only law, and must abide by the Constitution, or they cease to be civil courts and become instruments of military policy.

Of course the existence of a military power resting on force, so vagrant, so centralized, so necessarily heedless of the individual, is an inherent threat to liberty. But I would not lead people to rely on this Court for a review that seems to me wholly delusive. The military reasonableness of these orders can only be determined by military superiors. If the people ever let command of the war power fall into irresponsible and unscrupulous hands, the courts wield no power equal to its restraint. The chief restraint upon those who command the physical forces of the country, in the future as in the past, must be their responsibility to the political judgments of their contemporaries and to the moral judgments of history....

Postwar Limitations on the Crisis Government

On the same day that the *Korematsu* decision was handed down, the Supreme Court, with its conscience obviously troubled, also held that a Japanese-American girl of proven loyalty was entitled to a writ of habeas corpus releasing her unconditionally from the custody of the War Relocation Authority. The young lady, Mitsuye Endo, was already free by the time her case was decided (the relocation centers were then being disestablished) but she now had the satisfaction of knowing that her detention had been improper all along. The Court did not refer to her prior release, however, nor did it mention that her case had been in the judicial mill for two and a half years. As for the issue of evacuation of a loyal citizen, it was avoided; and by inference the Court conceded the WRA's power to detain further those evacuees whose loyalty had not as yet been proved. *(Ex parte Endo.)*

In all, the Japanese-American cases demonstrated more clearly than ever before that in time of war the "law of necessity" is superior to the law of the Constitution. The Court, lacking even a declaration of martial rule by which to rationalize the drastic actions of the executive, and hardly saved by Congress's tardy participation in the matter, found it difficult to uphold what appeared to be a blatant denial of due process. But uphold the exclusion program it did, thereby institutionalizing the crisis principle that in time of war the laws are silent.

As it had after the nation's first major war (and under strikingly similar circumstances) the Court spoke the language of limitation only when the emergency was over. Six months after hostilities had ceased, a year after President Roosevelt's death, and four years after Pearl Harbor, it reviewed and found unconstitutional the President's imposition of martial law in Hawaii. The citizens of the Islands had been denied the privilege of the writ of habeas corpus and subjected to the summary procedures of military justice from December 7, 1941, through October 1944. However, a civil-military agreement in 1943 allowed for appeals to the regular courts, and on this basis two civilians convicted by military tribunals petitioned the territorial district court for writs of habeas corpus. That court ruled that the military trials were improper, the circuit court reversed its decision, and the Supreme Court granted certiorari.

A full year later, in 1946, it gave its opinion, relying heavily on *Ex parte Milligan,* but attempting to avoid the constitutional issue by referring instead to the Hawaiian Organic Act. "The phrase 'martial law' as employed in the Act," said Justice Black in *Duncan v. Kahanamoku,* "while intended to authorize the military to act vigorously for the maintenance of an orderly civil government and for the defense of the islands against actual or threatened rebellion or invasion, was not intended to authorize the supplanting of courts by military tribunals." Concurring, Chief Justice Stone said that "Executive action is not proof of its own necessity." But he should have added "now that the war is over," for the Court had not adopted this view in the Japanese cases or in any others involving presidential or executive-legislative determinations during the existence of the crisis.

World War II was America's fullest experience with crisis government, and it demonstrated most clearly the operation of all the principles on which such a regime is based: the assumption of plenary power by the national government, the concentration of that power in the executive, the suspension of the traditional Constitution, and the neutralization of the Supreme Court. All of this raised disturbing problems for American society, but even more disturbing was the fact that while in every former period of emergency these extraordinary alterations in the constitutional system could be viewed as temporary, events in the wake of World War II created the threat that to a large degree they might have to be adopted on a permanent basis. For there was no return to "peaceful normalcy" this time. Within little more than a year, the victors were divided into two opposing camps and the cold war was on.

The Constitution in Time of Cold War

For the United States the cold war began in earnest with the decision to assume leadership of the free world against the threat of Communist expansionism. This decision, impelled by a realization that postwar economic and political instability in the non-Communist nations might open the door to Soviet domination, was manifested first in President Truman's proposal of the Greek-Turkish aid program in 1947, and then in the two major programs for Western European economic and military defense—the Marshall Plan and the NATO Alliance. These initial moves were followed quickly by the development of a "containment policy" and the creation of a system of alliances encircling the globe. The Soviets, who had penetrated deep into Central Europe at the end of World War II, pushed deeper still as a result of the Czech coup in 1948. Their Asian counterparts established a Communist regime in China in 1949. By 1950 a counter-alliance system had been created, and the world was divided into two hostile blocs.

Tension between the free and Communist worlds was highest at those points where they confronted each other across a common border. The 38th parallel in Korea was such a point, and it was there that the antagonism exploded in armed conflict on June 25, 1950, as Communist aggression against the Republic of South Korea turned the cold war "hot."

President Truman responded to this challenge on his own initiative by ordering American forces to defend the invaded country. The President characterized this move as a "police action" designed to uphold the rule of international law, and it was quickly given international sanction through a United Nations resolution. But in fact he had committed the United States, and its allies, to war. Indeed, for America, it was to be the fourth greatest war in the nation's history.

In all of this Truman had acted in the Lincolnian tradition, projecting the Civil War leader's crisis approach onto a global stage. Viewing the American Presidency as the focal position of the free world alliance, and American military power as the principal instrument for preserving Western security and global peace, he had acted as both American and Western chief executive and commander-in-chief to meet the national and international emergency. America's new position of global responsibility had expanded the President's authority into new and uncharted areas of action.

Although the manner in which the nation entered the Korean War raised very real constitutional problems, they were not of a nature to be reviewed by the Supreme Court. But since that conflict was and continued to be viewed by Mr. Truman as a presidentially directed "police action," the Court ultimately was presented with an important issue of executive power under cold war conditions.

The President had not declared the existence of a "national emergency" after the Communist attack, nor had he requested Congress to ratify his initial actions. He did address the legislators on July 10, however, at which time, in addition to a request for funds, he asked for the delegation of limited powers to allocate and determine priorities for scarce materials, to stabilize wages and prices, and to requisition property essential to the war effort. He also asked Congress to consider tax increases and other measures to prevent inflation, and he hinted at the possible need for price control and rationing. But, reflecting both a recognition of hostility to his domestic policies in the Republican-dominated legislature and a desire to limit the emergency's impact on American society, the President did not seek the delegation of vast war power. Nor did Congress insist on greater participation in the crisis regime. The conflict had begun as a "presidential war" and so it would remain.

In any event, as the winter of 1950 approached, it looked as though that war would soon be concluded victoriously. Having stopped the initial Red thrust, the UN force began a steady march northward and by November had occupied most of the Korean peninsula up to the Manchurian border. Then, with the successful end of the operation in sight, Communist China entered the conflict, and the crisis became even more serious than before.

Although President Truman decided to maintain the policy of limited war in Korea despite this change in cir-

cumstances, the Chinese intervention led him to proclaim
the formal existence of a national emergency on December
16, 1950. The proclamation was designed to accomplish
two purposes: it automatically activated over sixty statutes
applicable to emergency periods as well as laying the base
for resort to other forms of presidential authority, and it
emphasized for both Congress and the nation the dangers
of the new situation. The President's action was attacked by
his opponents in Congress as an unnecessary and "dictatorial" move to expand executive power, but the popular
reaction was not unfavorable, and Congress did not attempt
to repeal any of the measures which had been reactivated
or to impose limitations on the exercise of presidential
power.

Nonetheless, the emergency proclamation was the first
step in a series of events leading to the most definite judicial
rebuff ever suffered by a wartime President. For it was on
the ground that a national emergency existed that Truman,
in 1952, seized the steel industry, and it was this action in
turn which impelled the Supreme Court, for the first time
under such circumstances in American history, to declare
an exercise of presidential power unconstitutional.

The "Steel Case" arose out of a long and bitter labor-
management dispute resulting in the issuance of a strike
notice by the United Steelworkers in December 1951. Attempts by federal mediation agencies failed to achieve a settlement, and President Truman refused to invoke the
"cooling-off period" provisions of the Taft-Hartley Act,
which he regarded as an anti-labor measure and which had
been repassed by Congress over his veto in 1947. The union
postponed its first strike call at the President's request, but
when the settlement efforts failed, it set a nationwide walkout
for April 9, 1952.

To avert this strike Mr. Truman, on April 8, issued an
Executive Order directing Secretary of Commerce Sawyer
to seize and operate the country's major steel plants. Citing
the existence of a national emergency, and asserting that a
work stoppage in the steel industry would jeopardize and
imperil the national defense, the President based the seizure

order on his "inherent power" under "the Constitution and laws of the United States, and as President of the United States and Commander-in-Chief of the armed forces."[1]

The next day Truman informed Congress of his action and, in effect, requested its approval and support. But neither then nor two weeks later when he again asked for congressional participation in the affair did the legislature enter the controversy. Meanwhile, however, the steel companies had sought a temporary restraining order from the District of Columbia district court. Their request was denied on the ground that no evidence of irreparable injury had been presented and that "to issue a restraining order . . . and in effect to nullify an order of the President of the United States, promulgated by him to meet a nationwide emergency problem is something that the court should not do, unless there is some very vital reason for the court stepping in."

But on a second try in the same court, a different judge, noting that the issue which had been raised "requires a discussion of the fundamental principles of constitutional government," denounced the President's action as unconstitutional and granted a preliminary injunction. This injunction was stayed by the Court of Appeals because five of its nine members considered the issue to be of such importance that the Supreme Court should make the determination, and on May 3 the high court granted certiorari. One month later— and only nine weeks after the seizure order had been issued —a "majority" opinion, five concurrences, and a three-man dissent were announced.

Youngstown Sheet & Tube Company v. Sawyer
343 U.S. 579 (1952)

Mr. Justice Black delivered the opinion of the Court:

We are asked to decide whether the President was acting within his constitutional power when he issued an order directing the Secretary of Commerce to take possession of and operate most of the Nation's steel mills. The mill owners argue that the President's order amounts to lawmaking, a legislative function which the Constitution has expressly confided to the Congress and not to the President. The

[1]Executive Order 10340, 17 *Federal Register* 3139 (1952).

Government's position is that the order was made on findings of the President that his action was necessary to avert a national catastrophe which would inevitably result from a stoppage of steel production, and that in meeting this grave emergency the President was acting within the aggregate of his constitutional powers as the Nation's Chief Executive and the Commander in Chief of the Armed Forces of the United States. . . .

Two crucial issues have developed: *First.* Should final determination of the constitutional validity of the President's order be made in this case which has proceeded no further than the preliminary injunction stage? *Second.* If so, is the seizure order within the constitutional power of the President?

I.

It is urged that there were non-constitutional grounds upon which the District Court could have denied the preliminary injunction and thus have followed the customary judicial practice of declining to reach and decide constitutional questions until compelled to do so. . . . [But] in the light of the facts presented, the District Court saw no reason for delaying decision of the constitutional validity of the orders. We agree with the District Court and can see no reason why that question was not ripe for determination on the record presented. We shall therefore consider and determine that question now.

II.

The President's power, if any, to issue the order must stem either from an act of Congress or from the Constitution itself. There is no statute that expressly authorizes the President to take possession of property as he did here. Nor is there any act of Congress to which our attention has been directed from which such a power can fairly be implied. . . .

Moreover, the use of the seizure technique to solve labor disputes in order to prevent work stoppages was not only unauthorized by any congressional enactment; prior to this controversy, Congress had refused to adopt that method of settling labor disputes. When the Taft-Hartley Act was under consideration in 1947, Congress rejected an amendment which would have authorized such governmental seizures in cases of emergency. . . .

It is clear that if the President had authority to issue the order he did, it must be found in some provision of the Constitution. And it is not claimed that express constitutional language grants this power to the President. The contention is that presidential power should be implied from the aggregate of his powers under the Constitution. Particular reliance is placed on provisions in Article II which say that "The executive Power shall be vested in a President...."; that "he shall take Care that the Laws be faithfully executed"; and that he "shall be Commander in Chief of the Army and Navy of the United States."

The order cannot properly be sustained as an exercise of the President's military power as Commander in Chief of the Armed Forces. The Government attempts to do so by citing a number of cases upholding broad powers in military commanders engaged in day-to-day fighting in a theater of war. Such cases need not concern us here. Even though "theater of war" be an expanding concept, we cannot with faithfulness to our constitutional system hold that the Commander in Chief of the Armed Forces has the ultimate power as such to take possession of private property in order to keep labor disputes from stopping production. This is a job for the Nation's lawmakers, not for its military authorities.

Nor can the seizure order be sustained because of the several constitutional provisions that grant executive power to the President. In the framework for our Constitution, the President's power to see that laws are faithfully executed refutes the idea that he is to be a lawmaker. The Constitution limits his functions in the lawmaking process to the recommending of laws he thinks wise and the vetoing of laws he thinks bad. And the Constitution is neither silent nor equivocal about who shall make laws which the President is to execute. The first section of the first article says that "All legislative Powers herein granted shall be vested in a Congress of the United States...." After granting many powers to the Congress, Article I goes on to provide that Congress may "make all Laws which shall be necessary and proper for carrying into Execution the foregoing Powers, and all other Powers vested by this Constitution in the Government of the United States, or in any Department or Officer thereof."

The President's order does not direct that a congressional policy be executed in a manner prescribed by Congress—it directs that a presidential policy be executed in a manner prescribed by the President. The preamble of the order itself, like that of many statutes, sets out reasons why the President believes certain policies should be adopted, proclaims these policies as rules of conduct to be followed, and again, like a statute, authorizes a government official to promulgate additional rules and regulations consistent with the policy proclaimed and needed to carry that policy into execution. The power of Congress to adopt such public policies as those proclaimed by the order is beyond question. It can authorize the taking of private property for public use. It can make laws regulating the relationships between employers and employees, prescribing rules designed to settle labor disputes, and fixing wages and working conditions in certain fields of our economy. The Constitution does not subject this lawmaking power of Congress to presidential or military supervision or control.

It is said that other Presidents without congressional authority have taken possession of private business enterprises in order to settle labor disputes. But even if this be true, Congress has not thereby lost its exclusive constitutional authority to make laws necessary and proper to carry out the powers vested by the Constitution "in the Government of the United States, or any Department or Officer thereof."

The Founders of this Nation entrusted the lawmaking power to the Congress alone in both good and bad times. It would do no good to recall the historical events, the fears of power and the hopes for freedom that lay behind their choice. Such a review would but confirm our holding that this seizure order cannot stand.

The judgment of the District Court is

Affirmed.

Mr. Justice Frankfurter, concurring:

... The issue before us can be met, and therefore should be, without attempting to define the President's powers comprehensively.

... We must therefore put to one side consideration of what powers the President would have had if there had been no legislation whatever bearing on the authority asserted by the seizure, or if the seizure had been only for a short, explicitly temporary period, to be terminated automatically unless Congressional approval were given. These and other questions, like or unlike, are not now here. I would exceed my authority were I to say anything about them.

The question before the Court comes in this setting. Congress has frequently — at least 16 times since 1916 — specifically provided for executive seizure of production, transportation, communications, or storage facilities. In every case it has qualified this grant of power with limitations and safeguards. This body of enactments demonstrates that Congress deemed seizure so drastic a power as to require that it be carefully circumscribed whenever the President was vested with this extraordinary authority.

Congress in 1947 was again called upon to consider whether governmental seizure should be used to avoid serious industrial shutdowns. Congress decided against conferring such power generally and in advance, without special Congressional enactment to meet each particular need. Under the urgency of telephone and coal strikes in the winter of 1946, Congress addressed itself to the problems raised by "national emergency" strikes and lockouts. The termination of wartime seizure powers on December 31, 1946, brought these matters to the attention of Congress with vivid impact. A proposal that the President be given powers to seize plants to avert a shutdown where the "health or safety" of the nation was endangered, was thoroughly canvassed by Congress and rejected. No room for doubt remains that the proponents as well as the opponents of the bill which became the Labor Management Relations Act of 1947 clearly understood that as a result of that legislation the only recourse for preventing a shutdown in any basic industry, after failure of mediation, was Congress. Authorization for seizure as an available remedy for potential dangers was unequivocally put aside.... In any event, nothing can be plainer than that Congress made a conscious choice of policy in a field full of perplexity and peculiarly within legislative responsibility for choice.

... Previous seizure legislation had subjected the powers granted to the President to restrictions of varying degrees of stringency. Instead of giving him even limited powers, Congress in 1947 deemed it wise to require the President, upon failure of attempts to reach a voluntary settlement, to report to Congress if he deemed the power of seizure a needed shot for his locker. The President could not ignore the specific limitations of prior seizure statutes. No more could he act in disregard of the limitation put upon seizure by the 1947 Act.

It cannot be contended that the President would have had power to issue this order had Congress explicitly negated such authority in formal legislation. Congress has expressed its will to withhold this power from the President as though it had said so in so many words.

... But it is now claimed that the President has seizure power by virtue of the Defense Production Act of 1950 and its Amendments. And the claim is based on the occurrence of new events — Korea and the need for stabilization, etc. — although it was well known that seizure power was withheld by the Act of 1947, and although the President, whose specific requests for other authority were in the main granted by Congress, never suggested that in view of the new events he needed the power of seizure which Congress in its judgment had decided to withhold from him. The utmost that the Korean conflict may imply is that it may have been desirable to have given the President further authority, a freer hand in these matters. Absence of authority in the President to deal with a crisis does not imply want of power in the Government. Conversely the fact that power exists in the Government does not vest it in the President. The need for new legislation does not enact it. Nor does it repeal or amend existing law.

No authority that has since been given to the President can by any fair process of statutory construction be deemed to withdraw the restriction or change the will of Congress as expressed by a body of enactments, culminating in the Labor Management Relations Act of 1947.

... The powers of the President are not as particularized as are those of Congress. But unenumerated powers do not mean undefined powers. The separation of powers built into our Constitution gives essential content to undefined provisions in the frame of our government.

To be sure, the content of the three authorities of government is not to be derived from an abstract analysis.... In short, a systematic, unbroken, executive practice, long pursued to the knowledge of the Congress and never before questioned, engaged in by Presidents who have also sworn to uphold the Constitution, making as it were such exercise of power part of the structure of our government, may be treated as a gloss on "executive Power" vested in the President by § 1 of Art. 2.... [But no such] practice can be vouched for executive seizure of property at a time when this country was not at war, in the only constitutional way in which it can be at war....

A scheme of government like ours no doubt at times feels the lack of power to act with complete, all-embracing, swiftly moving authority. No doubt a government with distributed authority, subject to be challenged in the courts of law, at least long enough to consider and adjudicate the challenge, labors under restrictions from which other governments are free. It has not been our tradition to envy such governments. In any event our government was designed to have such restrictions. The price was deemed not too high in view of the safeguards which these restrictions afford. I know no more impressive words on this subject than those of Mr. Justice Brandeis:

"The doctrine of the separation of powers was adopted by the Convention of 1787, not to promote efficiency but to preclude the exercise of arbitrary power. The purpose was, not to avoid friction, but, by means of the inevitable friction incident to the distribution of the governmental powers among three departments, to save the people from autocracy." ...

Mr. Justice Douglas, concurring:

There can be no doubt that the emergency which caused the President to seize these steel plants was one that bore heavily on the country. But the emergency did not create power; it merely marked an occasion when power should be exercised. And the fact that it was necessary that measures be taken to keep steel in production does not mean that the President, rather than the Congress, had the constitutional authority to act. The Congress, as well as the President, is trustee of the national welfare. . . . The legislative nature of the action taken by the President seems to me to be clear. . . . [Thus] we could not sanction the seizures and condemnations of the steel plants in this case without reading Article II as giving the President not only the power to execute the laws but to make some. Such a step would most assuredly alter the pattern of the Constitution.

We pay a price for our system of checks and balances, for the distribution of power among the three branches of government. It is a price that today may seem exorbitant to many. Today a kindly President uses the seizure power to effect a wage increase and to keep the steel furnaces in production. Yet tomorrow another President might use the same power to prevent a wage increase, to curb trade unionists, to regiment labor as oppressively as industry thinks it has been regimented by this seizure.

Mr. Justice Jackson, concurring:

. . . We may well begin by a somewhat over-simplified grouping of practical situations in which a President may doubt, or others may challenge, his powers, and by distinguishing roughly the legal consequences of this factor of relativity.

1. When the President acts pursuant to an express or implied authorization of Congress, his authority is at its maximum, for it includes all that he possesses in his own right plus all that Congress can delegate. In these circumstances, and in these only, may he be said (for what it may be worth), to personify the federal sovereignty. If his act is held unconstitutional under these circumstances, it usually means that the Federal Government as an undivided whole lacks power. A seizure executed by the President pursuant to an Act of Congress would be supported by the strongest of presumptions and the widest latitude of judicial interpretation, and the burden of persuasion would rest heavily upon any who might attack it.

2. When the President acts in absence of either a congressional grant or denial of authority, he can only rely upon his own independ-

ent powers, but there is a zone of twilight in which he and Congress may have concurrent authority, or in which its distribution is uncertain. Therefore, congressional inertia, indifference or quiescence may sometimes, at least as a practical matter, enable, if not invite, measures on independent presidential responsibility. In this area, any actual test of power is likely to depend on the imperatives of events and contemporary imponderables rather than on abstract theories of law.

3. When the President takes measures incompatible with the expressed or implied will of Congress, his power is at its lowest ebb, for then he can rely only upon his own constitutional powers minus any constitutional powers of Congress over the matter. Courts can sustain exclusive Presidential control in such a case only by disabling the Congress from acting upon the subject. Presidential claim to a power at once so conclusive and preclusive must be scrutinized with caution, for what is at stake is the equilibrium established by our constitutional system.

Into which of these classifications does this executive seizure of the steel industry fit? It is eliminated from the first by admission, for it is conceded that no congressional authorization exists for this seizure....

Can it then be defended under flexible tests available to the second category? It seems clearly eliminated from that class because Congress has not left seizure of private property an open field but has covered it by three statutory policies inconsistent with this seizure....

This leaves the current seizure to be justified only by the severe tests under the third grouping, where it can be supported only by any remainder of executive power after subtraction of such powers as Congress may have over the subject. In short, we can sustain the President only by holding that seizure of such strike-bound industries is within his domain and beyond control by Congress....

The Solicitor General seeks the power of seizure in three clauses of the Executive Article, the first reading, "The Executive Power shall be vested in a President of the United States of America."... I cannot accept the view that this clause is a grant in bulk of all conceivable executive power but regard it as an allocation to the presidential office of generic powers thereafter stated.

The clause on which the Government next relies is that "The President shall be Commander in Chief of the Army and Navy of the United States...."

We should not use this occasion to circumscribe, much less to contract, the lawful role of the President as Commander-in-Chief.

I should indulge the widest latitude of interpretation to sustain his exclusive function to command the instruments of national force, at least when turned against the outside world for the security of our society. But, when it is turned inward, not because of rebellion but because of a lawful economic struggle between industry and labor, it should have no such indulgence....

The third clause in which the Solicitor General finds seizure powers is that "he shall take Care that the Laws be faithfully executed...." That authority must be matched against words of the Fifth Amendment that "No person shall be ... deprived of life, liberty or property, without due process of law...." One gives a governmental authority that reaches so far as there is law, the other gives a private right that authority shall go no farther. These signify about all there is of the principle that ours is a government of laws, not of men, and that we submit ourselves to rulers only if under rules.

The Solicitor General lastly grounds support of the seizure upon nebulous, inherent powers never expressly granted but said to have accrued to the office from the customs and claims of preceding administrations. The plea is for a resulting power to deal with a crisis or an emergency according to the necessities of the case, the unarticulated assumption being that necessity knows no law....

The appeal, however, that we declare the existence of inherent powers *ex necessitate* to meet an emergency asks us to do what many think would be wise, although it is something the forefathers omitted. They knew what emergencies were, knew the pressures they engender for authoritative action, knew, too, how they afford a ready pretext for usurpation. We may also suspect that they suspected that emergency powers would tend to kindle emergencies....

In the practical working of our Government we already have evolved a technique within the framework of the Constitution by which normal executive powers may be considerably expanded to meet an emergency. Congress may and has granted extraordinary authorities which lie dormant in normal times but may be called into play by the Executive in war or upon proclamation of a national emergency....

In view of the ease, expedition and safety with which Congress can grant and has granted large emergency powers, certainly ample to embrace this crisis, I am quite unimpressed with the argument that we should affirm possession of them without statute. Such power either has no beginning or it has no end. If it exists, it need submit to no legal restraint. I am not alarmed that it would plunge us straightway into dictatorship, but it is at least a step in that wrong direction....

Mr. Justice Burton, concurring:

... The controlling fact here is that Congress, within its constitutionally delegated power, has prescribed for the President specific procedures, exclusive of seizure, for his use in meeting the present type of emergency. Congress has reserved to itself the right to determine where and when to authorize the seizure of property in meeting such an emergency. Under these circumstances, the President's order of April 8 invaded the jurisdiction of Congress. It violated the essence of the principle of the separation of governmental powers. Accordingly, the injunction against its effectiveness should be sustained.

Mr. Justice Clark, concurring:

... I conclude that where Congress has laid down specific procedures to deal with the type of crisis confronting the President, he must follow those procedures in meeting the crisis; but that in the absence of such action by Congress, the President's independent power to act depends upon the gravity of the situation confronting the nation. I cannot sustain the seizure in question because here, as in *Little v. Barreme,* Congress had prescribed methods to be followed by the President in meeting the emergency at hand....

Mr. Chief Justice Vinson, joined by Mr. Justice Reed and Mr. Justice Minton, dissenting:

Because we cannot agree that affirmance is proper on any ground, and because of the transcending importance of the questions presented not only in this critical litigation but also to the powers of the President and of future Presidents to act in time of crisis, we are compelled to register this dissent.

I.

In passing upon the question of Presidential powers in this case, we must first consider the context in which those powers were exercised.

Those who suggest that this is a case involving extraordinary powers should be mindful that these are extraordinary times.

[*The opinion proceeds to note the Korean action and the various legislative programs designed to support that action.*]

The President has the duty to execute the foregoing legislative programs. Their successful execution depends upon continued pro-

duction of steel and stabilized prices for steel. Accordingly, when . . .
a strike shutting down the entire basic steel industry was threatened,
the President acted to avert a complete shutdown of steel production. . . .

One is not here called upon even to consider the possibility of
executive seizure of a farm, a corner grocery store or even a single
industrial plant. Such considerations arise only when one ignores
the central fact of this case—that the Nation's entire basic steel
production would have shut down completely if there had been no
Government seizure. Even ignoring for the moment whatever con-
fidential information the President may possess as "the Nation's
organ for foreign affairs," the uncontroverted affidavits in this record
amply support the finding that "a work stoppage would immediately
jeopardize and imperil our national defense.". . .

Accordingly, if the President has any power under the Constitution to meet a critical situation in the absence of express statutory
authorization, there is no basis whatever for criticizing the exercise
of such power in this case.

II.

. . . Admitting that the Government could seize the mills, plaintiffs claim that the implied power of eminent domain can be exercised
only under an Act of Congress; under no circumstances, they say,
can that power be exercised by the President unless he can point
to an express provision in enabling legislation. . . .

Under this view, the President is left powerless at the very
moment when the need for action may be most pressing and when
no one, other than he, is immediately capable of action. Under this
view, he is left powerless because a power not expressly given to
Congress is nevertheless found to rest exclusively with Congress. . . .

III.

A review of executive action demonstrates that our Presidents
have on many occasions exhibited the leadership contemplated by
the Framers when they made the President Commander in Chief,
and imposed upon him the trust to "take Care that the Laws be
faithfully executed." With or without explicit statutory authorization, Presidents have at such times dealt with national emergencies
by acting promptly and resolutely to enforce legislative programs,
at least to save those programs until Congress could act. Congress
and the courts have responded to such executive initiative with consistent approval.

[The Chief Justice proceeds to review the occasions on which Presidents—from Washington to Roosevelt—exercised emergency power without congressional authorization.]

This is but a cursory summary of executive leadership. But it amply demonstrates that Presidents have taken prompt action to enforce the laws and protect the country whether or not Congress happened to provide in advance for the particular method of execution. At the minimum, the executive actions reviewed herein sustain the action of the President in this case. And many of the cited examples of Presidential practice go far beyond the extent of power necessary to sustain the President's order to seize the steel mills. The fact that temporary executive seizures of industrial plants to meet an emergency have not been directly tested in this Court furnishes not the slightest suggestion that such actions have been illegal. Rather, the fact that Congress and the courts have consistently recognized and given their support to such executive action indicates that such a power of seizure has been accepted throughout our history....

IV.

... Much of the argument in this case has been directed at straw men. We do not now have before us the case of a President acting solely on the basis of his own notions of the public welfare. Nor is there any question of unlimited executive power in this case. The President himself closed the door to any such claim when he sent his Message to Congress stating his purpose to abide by any action of Congress, whether approving or disapproving his seizure action. Here, the President immediately made sure that Congress was fully informed of the temporary action he had taken only to preserve the legislative programs from destruction until Congress could act.

The absence of a specific statute authorizing seizure of the steel mills as a mode of executing the laws—both the military procurement program and the anti-inflation program—has not until today been thought to prevent the President from executing the laws. Unlike an administrative commission confined to the enforcement of the statute under which it was created, or the head of a department when administering a particular statute, the President is a constitutional officer charged with taking care that a "mass of legislation" be executed. Flexibility as to mode of execution to meet critical situations is a matter of practical necessity....

V.

Plaintiffs place their primary emphasis on the Labor Management Relations Act of 1947, hereinafter referred to as the Taft-Hartley Act, but do not contend that that Act contains any provision prohibiting seizure.

... Plaintiffs admit that the emergency procedures of Taft-Hartley are not mandatory. Nevertheless, plaintiffs apparently argue that, since Congress did provide the 80-day injunction method for dealing with emergency strikes, the President cannot claim that an emergency exists until the procedures of Taft-Hartley have been exhausted. This argument was not the basis of the District Court's opinion and, whatever merit the argument might have had following the enactment of Taft-Hartley, it loses all force when viewed in light of the statutory pattern confronting the President in this case....

When the President acted on April 8, he had exhausted the procedures for settlement available to him.... Faced with immediate national peril through stoppage in steel production on the one hand and faced with destruction of the wage and price legislative programs on the other, the President took temporary possession of the steel mills as the only course open to him consistent with his duty to take care that the laws be faithfully executed....

VI.

The diversity of views expressed in the six opinions of the majority, the lack of reference to authoritative precedent, the repeated reliance upon prior dissenting opinions, the complete disregard of the uncontroverted facts showing the gravity of the emergency and the temporary nature of the taking all serve to demonstrate how far afield one must go to affirm the order of the District Court.

The broad executive power granted by Article II to an officer on duty 365 days a year cannot, it is said, be invoked to avert disaster. Instead, the President must confine himself to sending a message to Congress recommending action. Under this messenger-boy concept of the Office, the President cannot even act to preserve legislative programs from destruction so that Congress will have something left to act upon. There is no judicial finding that the executive action was unwarranted because there was in fact no basis for the President's finding of the existence of an emergency for, under this view, the gravity of the emergency and the immediacy of the threatened disaster are considered irrelevant as a matter of law.

... Presidents have been in the past, and any man worthy of the Office should be in the future, free to take at least interim action necessary to execute legislative programs essential to survival of the Nation. A sturdy judiciary should not be swayed by the unpleasantness or unpopularity of necessary executive action, but must independently determine for itself whether the President was acting, as required by the Constitution, "to take Care that the Laws be faithfully executed."...

As the District Judge stated, this is no time for "timorous" judicial action. But neither is this a time for timorous executive action. Faced with the duty of executing the defense programs which Congress had enacted and the disastrous effects that any stoppage in steel production would have on those programs, the President acted to preserve those programs by seizing the steel mills. There is no question that the possession was other than temporary in character and subject to congressional direction — either approving, disapproving or regulating the manner in which the mills were to be administered and returned to the owners. The President immediately informed Congress of his action and clearly stated his intention to abide by the legislative will. No basis for claims of arbitrary action, unlimited powers or dictatorial usurpation of congressional power appears from the facts of this case. On the contrary, judicial, legislative and executive precedents throughout our history demonstrate that in this case the President acted in full conformity with his duties under the Constitution. Accordingly, we would reverse the order of the District Court.

Conclusion: The Major Constitutional Problem of Our Time

Marking only the second time since the post-Civil War era that a presidential resort to emergency power had been struck down, and the first time that the Supreme Court had taken such action while a declared emergency was in existence, the steel seizure decision must be regarded as a significant commentary on American crisis government. But its importance as a limitation on presidential power should not be overestimated. For the opinion, or rather the "opinions," of the Court avoided the main issue and the case may have little relevance for the future.

Actually the decision reflected neither a deep division on the Bench, nor a significant departure from its previous position on emergency rule. There can be no doubt that the seizure would have been upheld if Congress and the President had agreed on its necessity; and there is every likelihood that even as an independent executive action it would have been upheld if legislation directly related to the situation had not existed. For four of the majority Justices the crux of the matter (and their principal point of disagreement with the minority) was that Congress had taken a definite stand against the use of the seizure technique in labor-management disputes and had thereby precluded the exercise of discretionary power by the President. But with the minority's basic contention that the President during critical periods possesses a residuum of authority in addition to, or as a consequence of, his specific constitutional powers, and that in the absence of explicitly restrictive legislation he is free to exercise such authority as he deems necessary for the national defense—on these crucial points, at least four of the majority indicated agreement. The minority, on the other hand, would probably have admitted that any domestic emergency action by the President is subject to congressional revision or recision.

Thus both the vote and the holding in the Steel Case were deceptive. There was a wide (though unstated) area of agreement on the fundamental issue, and in terms of limiting executive authority in time of crisis, the decision's applicability to future situations is doubtful. This is particularly true because of the variety of factors peculiar to the case, especially the absence of firm popular support for the President's action and the hostility to him in Congress. Moreover, by the time it was decided truce talks had long been under way in Korea and the emergency seemed to have passed its most critical stage. Had the circumstances been different or had the danger seemed more immediate, it is unlikely that the Justices would have written even the cautious opinions that they did. What is most significant about the decision, therefore, is that by 1952—after so long a period of recurrent national emergencies—the Supreme Court had again seized an opportunity to speak the language of constitutional limitation.

For it was by then evident that the United States had entered an era in which crisis would be the "normal" condition of the nation's life, and that a major casualty of this era might be the Constitution itself. The impact of the cold war on the Constitution had already been felt in the increasing activity of congressional investigating committees, in the executive's establishment of a loyalty-security program, in the emergence of McCarthyism, and in the Court's own decision (in the *Dennis* case) broadening the restrictive power of the government over freedom of political belief and expression.[1] If the Court had acquiesced in the President's resort to extraordinary power in 1952, it would have extended into an indefinite period of protracted emergency the wartime concept of unlimited governmental power, and thereby dealt another (and, in long-range terms, perhaps a vital) blow to the basic law.

The Steel Case, like the *Dennis* case, exemplified the new problems which would confront the Court under conditions of cold war, and it was a timely reminder that there is a need for serious appraisal of the effect which such conditions can have on the American system of constitutional government. The expansion and concentration of governmental authority is inevitable in time of crisis, and inevitably the result is a suspension of established constitutional principles and practices. This was disturbing but not disastrous so long as the society could be confident that alteration of the constitutional system was only temporary. But wartime government on a permanent basis can only mean the end of constitutional rule and the freedom which it guarantees. This fact is, in itself, sufficient cause for viewing the cold war with alarm. But it also means that the nation must find some way to meet the problems of an era characterized by crises without destroying the fundamental principles on which it is founded.

---

[1] The effect of the cold war on fundamental freedoms is discussed more fully in the preceding chapter.

CONCLUSION

THE COURT,
THE CONSTITUTION,
AND THE FUTURE

The Court's Role in American Government

It is in the nature of the American governmental system —and it is a unique feature of that system—that sooner or later, directly or indirectly, virtually all of the nation's major political, social, and economic problems become constitutional problems; and that the Supreme Court, through its power to interpret the meaning of the Constitution, ultimately determines the legitimacy of attempts to resolve them. Limited though it may be by external political forces and by its own sense of self-restraint, and notwithstanding the fact that many of its most important decisions consist only in accepting the necessary or the inevitable, it is still the Court which "constitutionalizes" efforts to adapt the fundamental law to the changing needs and aspirations of American society.

In short, the Constitution cannot be separated from the nation's development, and the Court cannot be separated from the Constitution. The basic law embodies the rules by which the American people are governed, but that law, as Charles Evans Hughes once remarked, "is what the judges say it is."

As a result of its interpretative function, the Supreme Court is a policymaking organ of government. Its role is

essentially supervisory, being related primarily to the ratification rather than to the formulation of public policy, but
while the Court does not ordinarily initiate or effectuate
policy, as do Congress, the President, or the state governments, it nonetheless "makes law" in three ways:

(1) positively, by extending the provisions of the Con-
    stitution into areas of individual or governmental ac-
    tivity where they did not formerly apply;

(2) negatively, by "vetoing" the policy determinations
    of other governmental agencies; and

(3) passively, by accepting the constitutional changes
    brought about by custom or practice.

The Court's enunciation over the past twenty-five years of
the doctrine of racial equality is an example of positive judicial action setting a new standard of conduct for American
society. Its rejection of the national government's attempts
at social and economic reform in the period before 1937 was
accomplished by resort to the judicial "veto." And passive
policymaking best describes its acceptance of the principles
and practices related to party politics, foreign affairs, and
war.

Judicial participation in the policymaking process has
often made the Supreme Court a center of political controversy, and dissatisfaction with its decisions has often raised
the charge that it is an institutional anomaly in a democratic
society. But while the Court has on occasion blocked pro-
gressive change temporarily, there have also been instances
— again judicial activity in the field of racial relations is the
best example — in which it has led the way for the people's
elected representatives in realizing the society's goals. On
the whole the Supreme Court has been a responsive organ
of democracy, and it has played a notable part in guaranteeing a dynamic system of government.

Equally important, the Court has helped to maintain the
kind of governmental stability which makes a continuing
democracy possible; indeed in certain respects its role has
been indispensable to the preservation of "a scheme of
ordered liberty." As umpire of the federal system, for example, it has performed a function which probably could not

have been performed by any other agency in defining the boundaries between state and national authority, in assuring the uniform application of national law throughout the country, and in holding the individual states to national standards of justice. It may well be, as Justice Holmes once wrote, that the nation would not come to an end if he and his brethren lost their power to declare an Act of Congress void, but that "the Union would be imperiled if we could not make that declaration as to the laws of the several states."

One need not even accept Holmes's qualification, however. For, if the basic tenet of American (and Western) political thought is valid, and democratic government can only operate successfully within a framework of constitutional rules, then the Court's power to impose limits on Congress and the President, and thus to safeguard individual liberty against national as well as state authority, has also been an essential element in preserving the nation. The representation of manifold interests in the political branches of government helps to protect minority rights, but "pluralistic politics" does not always provide a sufficient guarantee of freedom for citizens whose race or faith or ideas differ from those of the majority. By assuming the difficult task of reviewing political decisions which affect individual liberty, the Court has helped to maintain a vigorous system of constitutional democracy in the United States.

Finally, the Supreme Court has made a unique contribution to American government by its very existence. For the Court, like the Constitution, is not only an instrument of power—it is also a symbol of restraint. Even when it approves extraordinary exercises of governmental authority, the fact of judicial review is an important indication that American government is ultimately subject to limitations. And even though its decisions seldom satisfy all of the people, they are manifestations of the concept that all disputes must be resolved peacefully. Aside from its specific functions and powers, therefore, the Court has been a moral force, representing the institutionalization of the rule of law in American society.

The Court and the Defense of Constitutionalism

If the Supreme Court has thus far been an essential factor in the success of "the great experiment in free government," it also has an important role to play in maintaining the vitality of that experiment. Through the exercise of its interpretative power, it has helped to fashion a contemporary Constitution accurately reflecting the momentous changes which have taken place in American society since the turn of this century. Now it must face the problems which arise from the very nature of that Constitution.

The past fifty years have been characterized by a steady growth of democracy and by repeated responses to emergency, and the constitutional changes impelled by both have been incorporated into the basic law by the Court. Those changes have provided primarily for the expansion and concentration of governmental authority — authority to meet the popular demand for economic security and social equality, and authority to meet the need for more efficient government in a critical age — as democratic pressure has made government a positive instrument for effectuating the majority will, and necessity has given it pervasive control over most areas of the nation's life.

Under the impact of these forces, the Constitution has become a compendium of powers rather than a catalogue of limitations, and each of its basic principles has been affected: the growth of national feeling, the recognition of a need for national efforts in meeting problems which affect the entire society, and the establishment of an increasingly close relationship between the citizen and the national government have weakened federalism; the dominance of foreign affairs among the nation's problems, the constant threat or occurrence of war, and the evident need for centralized and effective leadership in an age of crisis have broken down the separation of powers; the challenge presented by contemporary international conditions and the need for unity of purpose in meeting that challenge have produced a national attitude favoring conformity and allowing for governmental action restrictive of individual freedom. The words of the Constitution have been changed hardly at all, but every element of the traditional system of constitutional government has been recast in terms of the revolutionary conditions of our time.

Whatever judgment one may make regarding the necessity or desirability of these changes, since the pressures which brought them about will probably continue or even become more intense in the years ahead, it is important to recognize that they raise serious questions regarding the future of the constitutional system. For there is a real danger that under conditions of protracted crisis the basic law may become *only* an instrument of power, an infinitely interpretable and therefore essentially meaningless Constitution allowing for total governmental authority over the nation's life.

Thus the great task of the Supreme Court in our time must be the defense of constitutionalism itself—the protection of individual liberty and human dignity under the "rule of law." And this will be a difficult task, not only because the fears and frustrations of an uncertain age create pressures which the judiciary may find it hard to withstand, but also because the Court today is neither institutionally nor politically strong, having by its own decisions been relegated largely to its original role as an instrument for strengthening the central government, and having been subjected in the same generation to attacks from both ends of the political spectrum.

But despite these difficulties, the Supreme Court can play a major role in defending the constitutional order so long as the nation's commitment to its political heritage remains firm, and so long as the American people continue to regard the Court as the special guardian of that heritage. In addition to its participation in the political process, therefore, the contemporary Court must also be an educator, constantly reminding the nation of the Constitution's meaning and purpose. For ultimately it is the people themselves—through their appreciation of and attachment to the values embodied in their basic law—who must determine whether or not the Constitution will endure "for ages to come."

APPENDIX A

THE CONSTITUTION
OF THE UNITED STATES

PREAMBLE

WE THE PEOPLE of the United States, in order to form a more perfect union, establish justice, insure domestic tranquility, provide for the common defense, promote the general welfare, and secure the blessings of liberty to ourselves and our posterity, do ordain and establish this Constitution for the United States of America.

ARTICLE I

SECTION 1. All legislative powers herein granted shall be vested in a Congress of the United States, which shall consist of a Senate and House of Representatives.

SECTION 2. (1). The House of Representatives shall be composed of members chosen every second year by the people of the several States, and the electors in each State shall have the qualifications requisite for electors of the most numerous branch of the State legislature.

(2). No person shall be a Representative who shall not have attained to the age of twenty-five years, and been seven years a citizen of the United States, and who shall not, when elected, be an inhabitant of that State in which he shall be chosen.

(3). Representatives and direct taxes[1] shall be apportioned among the several States which may be included within this Union, according to their respective numbers, which shall be determined by adding to the whole number of free persons, including those bound to service for a term of years, and excluding Indians not taxed, three fifths of all other persons.[2] The actual enumeration shall be made within three years after the first meeting of the Congress of the United States, and within every subsequent term of ten years, in such manner as they shall by law direct. The number of Representatives shall not exceed one for every thirty thousand, but each State shall have at least one Representative; and until such enumeration shall be made, the State of New Hampshire shall be entitled to choose three, Massachusetts eight, Rhode Island and Providence Plantations one, Connecticut five, New York six, New Jersey four, Pennsylvania eight, Delaware one, Maryland six, Virginia ten, North Carolina five, South Carolina five, and Georgia three.

(4). When vacancies happen in the representation from any State, the executive authority thereof shall issue writs of election to fill such vacancies.

(5). The House of Representatives shall choose their Speaker and other officers; and shall have the sole power of impeachment.

SECTION 3. (1). The Senate of the United States shall be composed of two Senators from each State, chosen by the legislature thereof,[3] for six years; and each Senator shall have one vote.

(2). Immediately after they shall be assembled in consequence of the first election, they shall be divided as equally as may be into three classes. The seats of the Senators of the first class shall be vacated at the expiration of the second year, of the second class at the expiration of the fourth year, and of the third class at the expiration of the sixth year, so that one third may be chosen every second year; and if va-

[1] Modified as to income taxes by the 16th Amendment.
[2] Replaced by the 14th Amendment.
[3] Modified by the 17th Amendment.

cancies happen by resignation, or otherwise, during the recess of the legislature of any State, the executive thereof may make temporary appointments until the next meeting of the legislature, which[1] shall then fill such vacancies.

(3). No person shall be a Senator who shall not have attained to the age of thirty years, and been nine years a citizen of the United States, and who shall not, when elected, be an inhabitant of that State for which he shall be chosen.

(4). The Vice President of the United States shall be president of the Senate, but shall have no vote, unless they be equally divided.

(5). The Senate shall choose their other officers, and also a president pro tempore, in the absence of the Vice President, or when he shall exercise the office of President of the United States.

(6). The Senate shall have the sole power to try all impeachments. When sitting for that purpose, they shall be on oath or affirmation. When the President of the United States is tried, the Chief Justice shall preside: and no person shall be convicted without the concurrence of two thirds of the members present.

(7). Judgment in cases of impeachment shall not extend further than to removal from office, and disqualification to hold and enjoy any office of honor, trust or profit under the United States: but the party convicted shall nevertheless be liable and subject to indictment, trial, judgment and punishment, according to law.

SECTION 4. (1). The times, places and manner of holding elections for Senators and Representatives, shall be prescribed in each State by the legislature thereof; but the Congress may at any time by law make or alter such regulations, except as to the places of choosing Senators.

(2). The Congress shall assemble at least once in every year, and such meeting shall be on the first Monday in December, unless they shall by law appoint a different day.

SECTION 5. (1). Each House shall be the judge of the elections, returns and qualifications of its own members, and a majority of each shall constitute a quorum to do

[1]Modified by the 17th Amendment.

business; but a smaller number may adjourn from day to day, and may be authorized to compel the attendance of absent members, in such manner, and under such penalties as each House may provide.

(2). Each House may determine the rules of its proceedings, punish its members for disorderly behavior, and, with the concurrence of two thirds, expel a member.

(3). Each House shall keep a journal of its proceedings, and from time to time publish the same, excepting such parts as may in their judgment require secrecy; and the yeas and nays of the members of either House on any question shall, at the desire of one fifth of those present, be entered on the journal.

(4). Neither House, during the session of Congress, shall, without the consent of the other, adjourn for more than three days, nor to any other place than that in which the two Houses shall be sitting.

SECTION 6. (1). The Senators and Representatives shall receive a compensation for their services, to be ascertained by law, and paid out of the Treasury of the United States. They shall in all cases, except treason, felony and breach of the peace, be privileged from arrest during their attendance at the session of their respective Houses, and in going to and returning from the same; and for any speech or debate in either House, they shall not be questioned in any other place.

(2). No Senator or Representative shall, during the time for which he was elected, be appointed to any civil office under the authority of the United States, which shall have been created, or the emoluments whereof shall have been increased during such time; and no person holding any office under the United States, shall be a member of either House during his continuance in office.

SECTION 7. (1). All bills for raising revenue shall originate in the House of Representatives; but the Senate may propose or concur with amendments as on other bills.

(2). Every bill which shall have passed the House of Representatives and the Senate, shall, before it become a law, be presented to the President of the United States; if he approve he shall sign it, but if not he shall return it, with his objections to that House in which it shall have originated, who shall enter the objections at large on their journal, and proceed to reconsider it. If after such reconsideration two thirds of that House shall agree to pass the bill, it shall be sent, together with the objections, to the other House, by which it shall likewise be reconsidered, and if approved by two thirds of that House, it shall become a law. But in all such cases the votes of both Houses shall be determined by yeas and nays, and the names of the persons voting for and against the bill shall be entered on the journal of each House respectively. If any bill shall not be returned by the President within ten days (Sundays excepted) after it shall have been presented to him, the same shall be a law, in like manner as if he had signed it, unless the Congress by their adjournment prevent its return, in which case it shall not be a law.

(3). Every order, resolution, or vote to which the concurrence of the Senate and House of Representatives may be necessary (except on a question of adjournment) shall be presented to the President of the United States; and before the same shall take effect, shall be approved by him, or being disapproved by him, shall be repassed by two thirds of the Senate and House of Representatives, according to the rules and limitations prescribed in the case of a bill.

SECTION 8. (1). The Congress shall have power to lay and collect taxes, duties, imposts and excises, to pay the debts and provide for the common defense and general welfare of the United States; but all duties, imposts and excises shall be uniform throughout the United States;

(2). To borrow money on the credit of the United States;

(3). To regulate commerce with foreign nations, and among the several States, and with the Indian tribes;

(4). To establish an uniform rule of naturalization, and uniform laws on the subject of bankruptcies throughout the United States;

(5). To coin money, regulate the value thereof, and of foreign coin, and fix the standard of weights and measures;

(6). To provide for the punishment of counterfeiting the securities and current coin of the United States;

(7). To establish post offices and post roads;

(8). To promote the progress of science and useful arts, by securing for limited times to authors and inventors the exclusive right to their respective writings and discoveries;

(9). To constitute tribunals inferior to the Supreme Court;

(10). To define and punish piracies and felonies committed on the high seas, and offenses against the law of nations;

(11). To declare war, grant letters of marque and reprisal, and make rules concerning captures on land and water;

(12). To raise and support armies, but no appropriation of money to that use shall be for a longer term than two years;

(13). To provide and maintain a navy;

(14). To make rules for the government and regulation of the land and naval forces;

(15). To provide for calling forth the militia to execute the laws of the Union, suppress insurrections and repel invasions;

(16). To provide for organizing, arming, and disciplining the militia, and for governing such part of them as may be employed in the service of the United States, reserving to the States respectively, the appointment of the officers, and the authority of training the militia according to the discipline prescribed by Congress;

(17). To exercise exclusive legislation in all cases whatsoever, over such district (not exceeding ten miles square) as may, by cession of particular States, and the acceptance of Congress, become the seat of the government of the United States, and to exercise like authority over all places purchased by the consent of the legislature of the State in which the same shall be, for the erection of forts, magazines, arsenals, dockyards, and other needful buildings; and

(18). To make all laws which shall be necessary and proper for carrying into execution the foregoing powers, and all other powers vested by this Constitution in the government of the United States, or in any department or officer thereof.

SECTION 9. (1). The migration or importation of such persons as any of the States now existing shall think proper to admit, shall not be prohibited by the Congress prior to the year one thousand eight hundred and eight, but a tax or duty may be imposed on such importation, not exceeding ten dollars for each person.

(2). The privilege of the writ of habeas corpus shall not be suspended, unless when in cases of rebellion or invasion the public safety may require it.

(3). No bill of attainder or ex post facto law shall be passed.

(4). No capitation, or other direct, tax shall be laid, unless in proportion to the census or enumeration herein before directed to be taken.[1]

(5). No tax or duty shall be laid on articles exported from any State.

(6). No preference shall be given by any regulation of commerce or revenue to the ports of one State over those of another: nor shall vessels bound to, or from, one State, be obliged to enter, clear, or pay duties in another.

(7). No money shall be drawn from the Treasury, but in consequence of appropriations made by law; and a regular statement and account of the receipts and expenditures of all public money shall be published from time to time.

(8). No title of nobility shall be granted by the United States: and no person holding any office of profit or trust under them, shall, without the consent of the Congress, accept of any present, emolument, office, or title, of any kind whatever, from any king, prince, or foreign State.

SECTION 10. (1). No State shall enter into any treaty, alliance, or confederation; grant letters of marque and reprisal; coin money; emit bills of credit; make anything but gold and silver coin a tender in payment of debts; pass any bill of attainder, ex post facto law, or law impairing the obligation of contracts, or grant any title of nobility.

(2). No State shall, without the consent of the Congress, lay any imposts or duties on imports or exports, except what may be absolutely necessary for executing its inspection

[1]Modified by the 16th Amendment.

laws; and the net produce of all duties and imposts, laid by any State on imports or exports, shall be for the use of the Treasury of the United States; and all such laws shall be subject to the revision and control of the Congress.

(3). No State shall, without the consent of Congress, lay any duty of tonnage, keep troops, or ships of war in time of peace, enter into any agreement or compact with another State, or with a foreign power, or engage in war, unless actually invaded, or in such imminent danger as will not admit of delay.

ARTICLE II

SECTION 1. (1). The executive power shall be vested in a President of the United States of America. He shall hold his office during the term of four years, and, together with the Vice President, chosen for the same term, be elected, as follows:

(2). Each State shall appoint, in such manner as the legislature thereof may direct, a number of electors, equal to the whole number of Senators and Representatives to which the State may be entitled in the Congress: but no Senator or Representative, or person holding an office of trust or profit under the United States, shall be appointed an elector.

The electors[1] shall meet in their respective States, and vote by ballot for two persons, of whom one at least shall not be an inhabitant of the same State with themselves. And they shall make a list of all the persons voted for, and of the number of votes for each; which list they shall sign and certify, and transmit sealed to the seat of the government of the United States, directed to the president of the Senate. The president of the Senate shall, in the presence of the Senate and House of Representatives, open all the certificates, and the votes shall then be counted. The person having the greatest number of votes shall be the President, if such number be a majority of the whole number of electors appointed; and if there be more than one who have such majority, and have an equal number of votes, then the House of Representatives

[1]This paragraph was replaced by the 12th Amendment.

shall immediately choose by ballot one of them for President; and if no person have a majority, then from the five highest on the list the said House shall in like manner choose the President. But in choosing the President, the votes shall be taken by States, the representation from each State having one vote; a quorum for this purpose shall consist of a member or members from two thirds of the States, and a majority of all the States shall be necessary to a choice. In every case, after the choice of the President, the person having the greatest number of votes of the electors shall be the Vice President. But if there should remain two or more who have equal votes, the Senate shall choose from them by ballot the Vice President.

(3). The Congress may determine the time of choosing the electors, and the day on which they shall give their votes; which day shall be the same throughout the United States.

(4). No person except a natural born citizen, or a citizen of the United States, at the time of the adoption of this Constitution, shall be eligible to the office of President; neither shall any person be eligible to that office who shall not have attained to the age of thirty five years, and been fourteen years a resident within the United States.

(5). In the case of the removal of the President from office, or of his death, resignation, or inability to discharge the powers and duties of the said office, the same shall devolve on the Vice President, and the Congress may by law provide for the case of removal, death, resignation, or inability, both of the President and Vice President, declaring what officer shall then act as President, and such officer shall act accordingly, until the disability be removed, or a President shall be elected.

(6). The President shall, at stated times, receive for his services, a compensation, which shall neither be increased nor diminished during the period for which he shall have been elected, and he shall not receive within that period any other emolument from the United States, or any of them.

(7). Before he enter on the execution of his office, he shall take the following oath or affirmations: — "I do solemnly swear (or affirm) that I will faithfully execute the office of

President of the United States, and will to the best of my ability, preserve, protect and defend the Constitution of the United States."

SECTION 2. (1). The President shall be commander in chief of the army and navy of the United States, and of the militia of the several States, when called into the actual service of the United States; he may require the opinion, in writing, of the principal officer in each of the executive departments, upon any subject relating to the duties of their respective offices, and he shall have power to grant reprieves and pardons for offenses against the United States, except in cases of impeachment.

(2). He shall have power, by and with the advice and consent of the Senate, to make treaties, provided two thirds of the Senators present concur; and he shall nominate, and by and with the advice and consent of the Senate, shall appoint ambassadors, other public ministers and consuls, judges of the Supreme Court, and all other officers of the United States, whose appointments are not herein otherwise provided for, and which shall be established by law: but the Congress may by law vest the appointment of such inferior officers, as they think proper, in the President alone, in the courts of law, or in the heads of departments.

(3). The President shall have power to fill up all vacancies that may happen during the recess of the Senate, by granting commissions which shall expire at the end of their next session.

SECTION 3. He shall from time to time give to the Congress information of the state of the Union, and recommend to their consideration such measures as he shall judge necessary and expedient; he may, on extraordinary occasions, convene both Houses, or either of them, and in case of disagreement between them, with respect to the time of adjournment, he may adjourn them to such time as he shall think proper; he shall receive ambassadors and other public ministers; he shall take care that the laws be faithfully executed, and shall commission all the officers of the United States.

SECTION 4. The President, Vice President and all civil

officers of the United States, shall be removed from office on impeachment for, and conviction of, treason, bribery, or other high crimes and misdemeanors.

ARTICLE III

SECTION 1. The judicial power of the United States, shall be vested in one Supreme Court, and in such inferior courts as the Congress may from time to time ordain and establish. The judges, both of the Supreme and inferior courts, shall hold their offices during good behavior, and shall, at stated times, receive for their services, a compensation, which shall not be diminished during their continuance in office.

SECTION 2. (1). The judicial power shall extend to all cases, in law and equity, arising under this Constitution, the laws of the United States, and treaties made, or which shall be made, under their authority;—to all cases affecting ambassadors, other public ministers and consuls;—to all cases of admiralty and maritime jurisdiction;—to controversies to which the United States shall be a party;—to controversies between two or more States;—between a State and citizens of another State;[1]—between citizens of different States,—between citizens of the same State claiming lands under grants of different States, and between a State, or the citizens thereof, and foreign States, citizens or subjects.

(2). In all cases affecting ambassadors, other public ministers and consuls, and those in which a State shall be party, the Supreme Court shall have original jurisdiction. In all the other cases before mentioned, the Supreme Court shall have appellate jurisdiction, both as to law and fact, with such exceptions, and under such regulations as the Congress shall make.

(3). The trial of all crimes, except in cases of impeachment, shall be by jury; and such trial shall be held in the State where the said crimes shall have been committed; but when not committed within any State, the trial shall be at such place or places as the Congress may by law have directed.

[1]Restricted by the 11th Amendment.

SECTION 3. (1). Treason against the United States, shall consist only in levying war against them, or in adhering to their enemies, giving them aid and comfort. No person shall be convicted of treason unless on the testimony of two witnesses to the same overt act, or on confession in open court.

(2). The Congress shall have power to declare the punishment of treason, but no attainder of treason shall work corruption of blood, or forfeiture except during the life of the person attainted.

ARTICLE IV

SECTION 1. Full faith and credit shall be given in each State to the public acts, records, and judicial proceedings of every other State. And the Congress may by general laws prescribe the manner in which such acts, records and proceedings shall be proved, and the effect thereof.

SECTION 2. (1). The citizens of each State shall be entitled to all privileges and immunities of citizens in the several States.

(2). A person charged in any State with treason, felony, or other crime, who shall flee from justice, and be found in another State, shall on demand of the executive authority of the State from which he fled, be delivered up, to be removed to the State having jurisdiction of the crime.

(3). No person held to service or labor in one State, under the laws thereof, escaping into another, shall, in consequence of any law or regulation therein, be discharged from such service or labor, but shall be delivered up on claim of the party to whom such service or labor may be due.

SECTION 3. (1). New States may be admitted by the Congress into this Union; but no new State shall be formed or erected within the jurisdiction of any other State; nor any State be formed by the junction of two or more States, or parts of States, without the consent of the legislatures of the States concerned as well as of the Congress.

(2). The Congress shall have power to dispose of and make all needful rules and regulations respecting the territory or other property belonging to the United States; and nothing in this Constitution shall be so construed as to prejudice any claims of the United States, or of any particular State.

SECTION 4. The United States shall guarantee to every State in this Union a republican form of government, and shall protect each of them against invasion; and on application of the legislature, or of the executive (when the legislature cannot be convened) against domestic violence.

ARTICLE V

The Congress, whenever two thirds of both Houses shall deem it necessary, shall propose amendments to this Constitution, or, on the application of the legislatures of two thirds of the several States, shall call a convention for proposing amendments, which, in either case, shall be valid to all intents and purposes, as part of this Constitution, when ratified by the legislatures of three fourths of the several States, or by conventions in three fourths thereof, as the one or the other mode of ratification may be proposed by the Congress; Provided that no amendment which may be made prior to the year one thousand eight hundred and eight shall in any manner affect the first and fourth clauses in the ninth section of the first article; and that no State, without its consent, shall be deprived of its equal suffrage in the Senate.

ARTICLE VI

SECTION 1. All debts contracted and engagements entered into, before the adoption of this Constitution, shall be as valid against the United States under this Constitution, as under the Confederation.

SECTION 2. This Constitution, and the laws of the United States which shall be made in pursuance thereof; and all treaties made, or which shall be made, under the authority of the United States, shall be the supreme law of the land; and the judges in every State shall be bound thereby, anything in the constitution or laws of any State to the contrary notwithstanding.

SECTION 3. The Senators and Representatives before mentioned, and the members of the several State legislatures, and all executive and judicial officers, both of the United States and of the several States, shall be bound by oath or affirmation to support this Constitution; but no religious test shall ever be required as a qualification to any office or public trust under the United States.

ARTICLE VII

The ratification of the conventions of nine States, shall be sufficient for the establishment of this Constitution between the States so ratifying the same.

Done in Convention by the unanimous consent of the States present the seventeenth day of September in the year of our Lord one thousand seven hundred and eight-seven, and of the independence of the United States of America the twelfth. In witness whereof we have hereunto subscribed our names.

GEORGE WASHINGTON,
President and Deputy from Virginia

AMENDMENTS TO THE CONSTITUTION

The first ten amendments, comprising the Bill of Rights, were adopted in 1791

ARTICLE I

Congress shall make no law respecting an establishment of religion, or prohibiting the free exercise thereof; or abridging the freedom of speech, or of the press; or the right of the people peaceably to assemble, and to petition the government for a redress of grievances.

ARTICLE II

A well regulated militia, being necessary to the security of a free State, the right of the people to keep and bear arms, shall not be infringed.

ARTICLE III

No soldier shall, in time of peace, be quartered in any house, without the consent of the owner, nor in time of war, but in a manner to be prescribed by law.

ARTICLE IV

The right of the people to be secure in their persons, houses, papers, and effects, against unreasonable searches and seizures, shall not be violated, and no warrants shall issue, but upon probable cause, supported by oath or affirmation, and particularly describing the place to be searched, and the persons or things to be seized.

ARTICLE V

No person shall be held to answer for a capital, or otherwise infamous crime, unless on a presentment or indictment of a grand jury, except in cases arising in the land or naval forces, or in the militia, when in actual service in time of war or public danger; nor shall any person be subject for the same offense to be twice put in jeopardy of life or limb; nor shall be compelled in any criminal case to be a witness against himself, nor be deprived of life, liberty, or property, without due process of law; nor shall private property be taken for public use, without just compensation.

ARTICLE VI

In all criminal prosecutions the accused shall enjoy the right to a speedy and public trial, by an impartial jury of the State and district wherein the crime shall have been committed, which district shall have been previously ascertained by law, and to be informed of the nature and cause of the accusation; to be confronted with the witnesses against him; to have compulsory process for obtaining witnesses in his favor, and to have the assistance of counsel for his defense.

ARTICLE VII

In suits at common law, where the value in controversy shall exceed twenty dollars, the right of trial by jury shall be preserved, and no fact tried by a jury shall be otherwise re-examined in any court of the United States, than according to the rules of the common law.

ARTICLE VIII

Excessive bail shall not be required, nor excessive fines imposed, nor cruel and unusual punishments inflicted.

ARTICLE IX

The enumeration in the Constitution, of certain rights, shall not be construed to deny or disparage others retained by the people.

ARTICLE X

The powers not delegated to the United States by the Constitution, nor prohibited by it to the States, are reserved to the States respectively, or to the people.

ARTICLE XI
(1798)

The judicial power of the United States shall not be construed to extend to any suit in law or equity, commenced or prosecuted against one of the United States by citizens of another State, or by citizens or subjects of any foreign State.

ARTICLE XII
(1804)

The electors shall meet in their respective States and vote by ballot for President and Vice-President, one of whom, at

least, shall not be an inhabitant of the same State with themselves; they shall name in their ballots the person voted for
as President, and in distinct ballots the person voted for as
Vice-President, and they shall make distinct lists of all persons voted for as President, and of all persons voted for as
Vice-President, and of the number of votes for each, which
lists they shall sign and certify, and transmit sealed to the
seat of the government of the United States, directed to the
president of the Senate; — The president of the Senate shall,
in the presence of the Senate and House of Representatives,
open all the certificates and the votes shall then be counted;
— The person having the greatest number of votes for President, shall be the President, if such number be a majority of
the whole number of electors appointed; and if no person
have such majority, then from the persons having the highest
numbers not exceeding three on the list of those voted for as
President, the House of Representatives shall choose immediately, by ballot, the President. But in choosing the
President, the votes shall be taken by States, the representation from each State having one vote; a quorum for this
purpose shall consist of a member or members from two
thirds of the States, and a majority of all the States shall be
necessary to a choice. And if the House of Representatives
shall not choose a President whenever the right of choice
shall devolve upon them, before the fourth day of March
next following, then the Vice-President shall act as President, as in the case of the death or other constitutional disability of the President. — The person having the greatest
number of votes as Vice-President, shall be the Vice-President, if such number be a majority of the whole number of
electors appointed, and if no person have a majority, then
from the two highest numbers on the list, the Senate shall
choose the Vice-President; a quorum for the purpose shall
consist of two thirds of the whole number of Senators, and a
majority of the whole number shall be necessary to a choice.
But no person constitutionally ineligible to the office
of President shall be eligible to that of Vice-President of the
United States.

ARTICLE XIII
(1865)

Section 1. Neither slavery nor involuntary servitude, except as a punishment for crime whereof the party shall have been duly convicted, shall exist within the United States, or any place subject to their jurisdiction.

Section 2. Congress shall have power to enforce this article by appropriate legislation.

ARTICLE XIV
(1868)

Section 1. All persons born or naturalized in the United States, and subject to the jurisdiction thereof, are citizens of the United States and of the State wherein they reside. No State shall make or enforce any law which shall abridge the privileges or immunities of citizens of the United States; nor shall any State deprive any person of life, liberty, or property, without due process of law; nor deny to any person within its jurisdiction the equal protection of the laws.

Section 2. Representatives shall be apportioned among the several States according to their respective numbers, counting the whole number of persons in each State, excluding Indians not taxed. But when the right to vote at any election for the choice of electors for President and Vice President of the United States, Representatives in Congress, the executive and judicial officers of a State, or the members of the legislature thereof, is denied to any of the male inhabitants of such State, being twenty-one years of age, and citizens of the United States, or in any way abridged, except for participation in rebellion, or other crime, the basis of representation therein shall be reduced in the proportion which the number of such male citizens shall bear to the whole number of male citizens twenty-one years of age in such State.

Section 3. No person shall be a Senator or Representative in Congress, or elector of President and Vice President, or hold any office, civil or military, under the United States, or under any State, who, having previously taken an oath, as a member of Congress, or as an officer of the United States, or as a member of any State legislature, or as an executive or judicial officer of any State, to support the Constitution of the United States, shall have engaged in insurrection or rebellion against the same, or given aid or comfort to the enemies thereof. But Congress may by a vote of two thirds of each House, remove such disability.

SECTION 4. The validity of the public debt of the United States, authorized by law, including debts incurred for payment of pensions and bounties for services in suppressing insurrection or rebellion, shall not be questioned. But neither the United States nor any State shall assume or pay any debt or obligation incurred in aid of insurrection or rebellion against the United States, or any claim for the loss or emancipation of any slave; but all such debts, obligations and claims shall be held illegal and void.

SECTION 5. The Congress shall have power to enforce, by appropriate legislation, the provisions of this article.

ARTICLE XV
(1870)

SECTION 1. The right of citizens of the United States to vote shall not be denied or abridged by the United States or by any State on account of race, color, or previous condition of servitude.

SECTION 2. The Congress shall have power to enforce this article by appropriate legislation.

ARTICLE XVI
(1913)

The Congress shall have power to lay and collect taxes on incomes, from whatever source derived, without apportionment among the several States, and without regard to any census or enumeration.

ARTICLE XVII
(1913)

The Senate of the United States shall be composed of two Senators from each State, elected by the people thereof, for six years; and each Senator shall have one vote. The electors in each State shall have the qualifications requisite for electors of the most numerous branch of the State legislatures.

When vacancies happen in the representation of any State in the Senate, the executive authority of such State shall issue writs of election to fill such vacancies: *Provided,* That the legislature of any State may empower the executive thereof to make temporary appointments until the people fill the vacancies by election as the legislature may direct.

This amendment shall not be so construed as to affect the election or term of any Senator chosen before it becomes valid as part of the Constitution.

ARTICLE XVIII[1]
(1919)

SECTION 1. After one year from the ratification of this article the manufacture, sale, or transportation of intoxicating liquors within, the importation thereof into, or the exportation thereof from the United States and all territory subject to the jurisdiction thereof for beverage purposes is hereby prohibited.

SECTION 2. The Congress and the several States shall have concurrent power to enforce this article by appropriate legislation.

SECTION 3. This article shall be inoperative unless it shall have been ratified as an amendment to the Constitution by the legislatures of the several States, as provided in the Constitution, within seven years from the date of the submission hereof to the States by the Congress.

[1]Repealed by Article XXI.

ARTICLE XIX
(1920)

The right of citizens of the United States to vote shall not be denied or abridged by the United States or by any State on account of sex.

The Congress shall have power to enforce this article by appropriate legislation.

ARTICLE XX
(1933)

SECTION 1. The terms of the President and Vice President shall end at noon on the 20th day of January, and the terms of Senators and Representatives at noon on the 3rd day of January, of the years in which such terms would have ended if this article had not been ratified; and the terms of their successors shall then begin.

SECTION 2. The Congress shall assemble at least once in every year, and such meeting shall begin at noon on the 3rd day of January, unless they shall by law appoint a different day.

SECTION 3. If, at the time fixed for the beginning of the term of the President, the President elect shall have died, the Vice President elect shall become President. If a President shall not have been chosen before the time fixed for the beginning of his term, or if the President elect shall have failed to qualify, then the Vice President elect shall act as President until a President shall have qualified; and the Congress may by law provide for the case wherein neither a President elect nor a Vice President elect shall have qualified, declaring who shall then act as President, or the manner in which one who is to act shall be selected, and such person shall act accordingly until a President or Vice President shall have qualified.

SECTION 4. The Congress may by law provide for the case of the death of any of the persons from whom the House of Representatives may choose a President whenever the right of choice shall have devolved upon them, and for the case of the death of any of the persons from whom the

Senate may choose a Vice President whenever the right of choice shall have devolved upon them.

SECTION 5. Sections 1 and 2 shall take effect on the 15th day of October following the ratification of this article.

SECTION 6. This article shall be inoperative unless it shall have been ratified as an amendment to the Constitution by the legislatures of three fourths of the several States within seven years from the date of its submission.

ARTICLE XXI
(1933)

SECTION 1. The Eighteenth Article of Amendment to the Constitution of the United States is hereby repealed.

SECTION 2. The transportation or importation into any State, Territory or Possession of the United States for delivery or use therein of intoxicating liquors in violation of the laws thereof is hereby prohibited.

SECTION 3. This article shall be inoperative unless it shall have been ratified as an amendment to the Constitution by conventions in the several States, as provided in the Constitution, within seven years from the date of submission hereof to the States by the Congress.

ARTICLE XXII
(1951)

SECTION 1. No person shall be elected to the office of the President more than twice, and no person who has held the office of President, or acted as President, for more than two years of a term to which some other person was elected President shall be elected to the office of the President more than once. But this Article shall not apply to any person holding the office of President when this Article was proposed by the Congress, and shall not prevent any person who may be holding the office of President, or acting as President, during the term within which this Article becomes operative from holding the office of President or acting as President during the remainder of such term.

SECTION 2. This article shall be inoperative unless it shall have been ratified as an amendment to the Constitution by the legislatures of three-fourths of the several States within seven years from the date of its submission to the States by the Congress.

ARTICLE XXIII
(1961)

SECTION 1. The district constituting the seat of government of the United States shall appoint in such manner as the Congress may direct:

A number of electors of President and Vice President equal to the whole number of Senators and Representatives in Congress to which the District would be entitled if it were a State, but in no event more than the least populous state; they shall be in addition to those appointed by the states, but they shall be considered, for the purposes of the election of President and Vice President, to be electors appointed by a state; and they shall meet in the District and perform such duties as provided by the twelfth article of amendment.

SECTION 2. The Congress shall have power to enforce this article by appropriate legislation.

ARTICLE XXIV
(1964)

SECTION 1. The right of citizens of the United States to vote in any primary or other election for President or Vice President, for electors for President or Vice President, or for Senator or Representative in Congress, shall not be denied or abridged by the United States or any state by reason of failure to pay any poll tax or other tax.

SECTION 2. The Congress shall have the power to enforce this article by appropriate legislation.

JUDICIAL STRUCTURE, JURISDICTION, AND PROCEDURE: THE TECHNICALITIES OF THE SUPREME COURT DECISION-PROCESS

Structure of the American Judicial System

The most striking feature of the American judicial system is its dual nature, reflecting the principle of federalism and characterized by two separate hierarchies of courts—state and national (or federal).

Each state has its own court system, generally composed of municipal and county courts which try both criminal and civil cases, and a final court of appeals, usually but not always called the supreme court, which is the state's highest judicial body. (In the larger states there are also intermediate appellate courts.) These courts are established by the constitutions and laws of the states, and have sole power to decide cases which are not within the jurisdiction granted to the national courts by the United States Constitution, as well as concurrent power with those courts over certain types of cases which Congress designates.

The national judicial system is divided into three levels of courts. At the lowest or trial level are 91 *district courts* (at least one in each state and territory, plus one for the District of Columbia) with jurisdiction to try cases involving federal crimes, issues of a federal nature where the amount in controversy exceeds $10,000, suits between citizens of different states or between American and foreign citizens where the amount in dispute exceeds $10,000, certain claims against the United States, and actions to enforce the laws of the United States.

At the next level are eleven *courts of appeal* (one for each of the ten judicial areas or "circuits" into which the nation is divided, plus one in the District of Columbia) with jurisdiction to hear appeals from decisions of the district courts, as well as from various federal administrative agencies. Both the district and the circuit courts are created by Congress, which is constitutionally empowered to "ordain and establish" the inferior national courts.

Only the Supreme Court of the United States is established by the Constitution itself. It is the highest court in the national judicial hierarchy, and it also joins together the two separate court systems in the United States, since its jurisdiction—determined both by the Constitution and by Congress—makes it the final court of appeal from decisions of the state as well as of the national courts.

In addition to the Supreme Court, the courts of appeal, and the district courts, the federal judicial system also includes a number of "legislative courts" (the Court of Claims, the Court of Customs and Patent Appeals, the Tax Court, and the Court of Military Appeals) established by Congress to deal with special types of litigation.

The federal courts are staffed by 308 judges in the district courts (63 new judgeships were created by Congress in 1961), 78 in the courts of appeal (including 10 added in 1961), and the nine Justices of the Supreme Court. All are appointed by the President, with the consent of the Senate, and all hold office for life "during good behavior."[1]

Jurisdiction of the Supreme Court

The Supreme Court is a "constitutional" tribunal not only in the sense that it is established by and draws its authority from the basic law, but also in the sense that it reviews only those cases or controversies "arising under this

[1] Since the turn of this century approximately 90 per cent of these judicial appointments have gone to members of the appointing President's political party.

Constitution," that is, disputes in which a final interpretation of statutes or treaties of the United States, or of the basic law itself, is required. Not all legal disputes, therefore, may be brought before the Court, but only those which involve issues of importance to the operation of the American governmental system.

A case may originate in the Supreme Court, that is the Court has *original jurisdiction* over the matter, if it affects ambassadors or other public ministers and consuls, or if one of the parties is a state. In all other constitutional cases, the Court has *appellate jurisdiction*, the case originating in a lower court (state or federal) and coming to the high bench as the result of an appeal against the decision below.

If the lower court decision involved a question of state or federal power—for example, if a state court has declared a federal law invalid or if a federal court has held a state law to be in conflict with the Constitution—the Supreme Court must hear the case, for it is the only tribunal which can determine the issue finally. This method of coming to the Court "by right" is called review *on appeal*.

The vast majority of cases (about 85 per cent) come to the Court by a different route, however. These are disputes involving issues of public concern and constitutional significance which are so compelling that the Court may be convinced of the need to rule on them—for example, a state court decision interpreting a federal law or a federal court decision interpreting the Constitution. Such cases the Justices review in their discretion by issuing a *writ of certiorari* to the lower court directing it to send up the record in the case so that a final decision may be made. The Court receives more than 1500 petitions for this kind of review every term, and grants about 150. Certiorari is granted if four Justices vote to hear the case. It is important to note that the Court does not take the initiative in deciding any issue; it only hears cases which litigants bring to its attention.

Procedure of the Supreme Court

Once an application for appeal or a petition for certiorari has been granted, the case is first presented to the Justices

in the form of written "briefs" submitted by the opposing
counsel. Each brief includes excerpts from the record of the
lower court, citations of relevant prior decisions, and arguments to support the contentions of the party submitting it.
Additional briefs may also be submitted, with the Court's
permission, by non-litigants who are particularly interested
in the dispute. Such a party is regarded as a "friend of the
court" or *amicus curiae*. Before a case is formally presented
in court, each Justice, assisted by his law clerks, reads the
briefs and consults any other materials which may be helpful
in understanding the problems which are involved.

The annual term of the Court runs from October through
June (on rare occasions the Justices will also sit in special
session to decide a pressing matter). This term is divided
into alternating two-week periods during which the Court
first hears various counsel in oral arguments based on the
briefs they have already submitted, and then retires to pre-
pare its opinions on the cases which have been presented.
The oral arguments are made before the Bench daily from
Monday through Thursday during these two-week periods,
beginning (as of 1961) at 10:00 A.M. and ending at 2:30
P.M., with a half hour for lunch at noon. Each side in the
dispute—the appellant and the respondent—has one hour
to state its case, and counsel may be questioned by the
Justices on any points of interest. The public may attend
these sessions.

Discussion of cases which have had oral argument is
held on Friday, "conference day," in a private session of the
Court with the Chief Justice presiding. Taking each case in
turn, he will ordinarily review the facts and give his opinion
as to the manner in which the case should be decided. Then,
in order of seniority on the Bench, each Justice will present
his view of the matter. After discussion is ended (there is
no limitation on discussion, and a case may be carried over
from one conference to the next), a vote is taken, the most
recently appointed Justice voting first and the Chief Justice
last. All cases are decided by majority vote.

Once a decision has been reached, assignments are made
for writing both the majority and minority opinions, with

the Chief Justice assigning for the group with which he voted, and the senior Associate Justice having the contrary point of view assigning for the other side. If the Court's decision is unanimous, the Chief Justice makes the assignment, often writing the opinion himself.

The Justice who has been charged with preparing an opinion proceeds in light of the discussion at the conference to express the views of his side. Aided by his clerks, he first writes the opinion and then circulates it among his colleagues for comment. An attempt is made, particularly if the assignment is to write the majority opinion—the "opinion of the Court"—to reflect the general position accurately, and thus to reduce the number of divergent views which will finally be expressed. However, any Justice may write his own separate opinion, concurring with or dissenting from the majority in whole or in part, and any Justice may change his mind and his vote on a case up until the decision is announced. In Chief Justice Marshall's time, there was an informal rule against separate opinions, since Marshall thought that by revealing divergent views, they weakened the Court's prestige and power. But dissenting opinions are often very important, since they may herald future changes in the Court's attitude.

When the deliberative process is completed, the opinions are announced in open court on a subsequent "decision Monday." The dispute between the litigants is then settled, and the decision—now "the law of the land"—becomes a rule for the lower courts to apply, a guide for the legal profession to follow, and a discourse on the basic law for the edification of all students of the Constitution.

Reporting of Supreme Court Decisions

The Court's opinions are reported in three different sets of volumes. The official edition is the *United States Reports* (cited "U.S." and published by the Government Printing Office in Washington, D. C.). Through 1962 there were 371 volumes of these reports, the first 90 of which (up to 1875) are known by the names of the Court reporters—Dallas, Cranch, Wheaton, Peters, Howard, Black, and Wallace—

and the subsequent volumes by number only. Another edition of the Court's decisions is the commercially published *United States Supreme Court Reports, Lawyers Edition* (cited "L.Ed." and published by the Lawyers' Cooperative Publishing Company, Rochester, New York). It includes, in addition to the opinions, material from the briefs of counsel, and notes and annotations on the issues in the cases. The third edition of the decisions, also published commercially, is the *Supreme Court Reporter* (cited "S.Ct." and published by the West Publishing Company, St. Paul, Minnesota), which is similar to the *Lawyers Edition*. In addition, complete texts of the opinions are published unbound about a week after the decision in the *United States Law Week* (Bureau of National Affairs) and the *Supreme Court Bulletin* (Commerce Clearing House). Preliminary reports or "advance sheets" are also published by the commercial houses well in advance of the bound volumes.

A uniform system of citation is used for all cases. Each citation includes the title of the case, the volume and edition of the reporters in which the opinions will be found, the page at which they begin, and the year of decision. Thus the desegregation case is cited in full: *Brown v. Board of Education of Topeka,* 347 U.S. 483, 74 S.Ct. 686, 98 L.Ed. 873 (1954).

APPENDIX C

HOW TO READ
A CONSTITUTIONAL
LAW CASE

The Importance of Case Study

Cases are the raw material of judicial interpretation and thus the vehicle for development of the basic law. For it is in the resolution of legal disputes between the citizen and his government, or between individuals, that the Supreme Court applies the Constitution to specific problems in American society and helps to determine the policies under which that society will be governed. Case analysis is therefore the key to an understanding of the Court's function in the American system of government.

The materials that follow demonstrate an effective method of constitutional law case study. Taking for purposes of illustration *McCulloch v. Maryland,* one of the most important cases ever decided by the Supreme Court (and a document which is generally regarded as Chief Justice Marshall's greatest state paper), these materials include: (1) a "headnote" giving the background of the case and placing it in its historical and political context, (2) a list of the major elements which form a framework for analysis of the case, (3) the text (slightly abbreviated) of the Supreme Court's opinion in the case, and (4) a "brief" or analytical outline of the case.

I. The Background of the Case

To comprehend the meaning and significance of a constitutional law case, it must be read in the context of the historical and political situation out of which it arose. What follows is a brief review of the events leading up to the *McCulloch* case:

In 1790 Secretary of the Treasury Alexander Hamilton proposed, and the Federalist-controlled Congress approved, the establishment of a national bank. President Washington then called upon his Cabinet for opinions regarding the constitutionality of the bank bill, and the response revealed deep division among his advisors.

Secretary of State Thomas Jefferson, consistently opposed to the formation of a strong and consolidated national government and to its domination by powerful financial interests, declared that the measure was unconstitutional. Taking a "strict-constructionist" view of the basic law, he argued that even though Congress had been specifically delegated a number of fiscal powers, and despite the fact that it had the authority to make all laws "necessary and proper" for carrying those powers into execution, it could not establish instrumentalities which were merely convenient for such execution. Unless a national bank was absolutely essential to effectuating the enumerated powers of Congress —and in Jefferson's view it was not—a law creating such an institution would violate the Constitution.

Hamilton, the principal advocate of a powerful and financially stable central government, countered with the "broad constructionist" argument that every power vested in the government included "a right to employ all the means requisite . . . to the attainment of the ends of such power."

> If the end be clearly comprehended within any of the specified powers, and if the measure have an obvious relation to that end, and is not forbidden by any particular provision of the Constitution, it may safely be deemed to come within the compass of the national authority.

A bank, Hamilton insisted, was sufficiently related to the specifically delegated congressional powers of collecting taxes, regulating commerce, and paying debts to justify its establishment by the legislature.

This dispute between the Hamiltonian Federalists and the Jeffersonian decentralists was reflected throughout the nation, with Northern mercantile and creditor interests supporting the former and Southern agrarian and debtor elements the latter. Hamilton's arguments were accepted by the President, however, and the first Bank of the United States came into existence with Washington's approval of the controversial measure in 1791.

The constitutionality of that Bank was not tested in the courts, and it operated until the expiration of its charter in 1811. There was no immediate pressure to reestablish the institution, but largely as a result of financial difficulties following the War of 1812 a proposal to create another national bank was introduced in Congress. This time there was less division in the legislature and the second Bank of the United States was chartered in 1816, with the government as its principal client and the holder of one-fifth of its stock, while much of the remaining stock was held by financial interests in the East and in England.

Despite accord in Congress, however, the issue again stirred up bitter controversy in a number of Southern and Western states, where the agrarian interests were now joined by frontier elements in branding the Bank of the United States a ruthless, conservative, and foreign-controlled "money trust" seeking to stifle prosperity and deprive the common man of economic opportunity. The pro-Bank forces regarded their opponents as reckless speculators, heedless of runaway inflation and the stability of the nation, but they were not able to overcome the popular pressure in several states to restrict the Bank's activities.

One such state was Maryland, which enacted a law in 1818 imposing a heavy tax on notes issued by any bank or branch not chartered by the state (i.e. the Bank of the United States), or in lieu of the tax a large annual fee. A substantial penalty was provided for each violation of the law. The issue of the Bank's constitutionality came before the Supreme Court when the cashier of the Bank's Baltimore branch,

McCulloch, refused to comply with this statute, and the state, having sued to recover the penalties, obtained a decision against McCulloch in Maryland's highest court. That decision was then appealed to the Supreme Court of the United States.

II. The Elements of the Case

As a framework of reference for analyzing and "briefing" a case, its major elements — in addition to the historical and political background of the litigation — should be noted. Those elements include:

Elements of identification

1. The *name* of the case.
2. The *citation* of the case (in the *Supreme Court Reports*).
3. The *year* in which the case was decided.

Elements of analysis

4. The *facts* of the case.
5. The *issues* or questions presented for determination by the Court (and the Court's answers).
6. The *decision* or judgment of the Court (its final disposition of the case).
7. The *opinion* of the Court (the reasons for its decision).
8. The *concurring* or *dissenting* opinions (points of disagreement with the majority and reasons).
9. The *general principle* of constitutional law established by the case.
10. The *significance* of the case in terms of the governmental system and the development of the Constitution.

Essentially, successful case study lies in recognizing the basic issue which the Court is attempting to resolve, in following the Court's intellectual process as it seeks to reach a decision on that issue, and in understanding the significance of the general principle established by that decision. None of this is easy to do. Mastery of constitutional law materials requires careful reading, as well as clear and incisive thinking, and there are no "short-cuts." But the use of an analytical outline is an indispensable aid in distinguishing and comprehending the most important features of a case.

III. The Text of the Court's Opinion in the Case

McCulloch v. Maryland
4 Wheaton 316 (1819)

Mr. Chief Justice Marshall delivered the opinion of the Court:

In the case now to be determined, the defendant, a sovereign State, denies the obligation of a law enacted by the legislature of the Union, and the plaintiff, on his part, contests the validity of an act which has been passed by the legislature of that State. The constitution of our country, in its most interesting and vital parts, is to be considered; the conflicting powers of the government of the Union and of its members, as marked in that constitution, are to be discussed; and an opinion given which may essentially influence the great operations of the government. . . . On the Supreme Court of the United States has the constitution of our country devolved this important duty.

The first question made in the cause is, has Congress power to incorporate a bank? . . .

The power now contested was exercised by the first Congress elected under the present constitution. The bill for incorporating the bank of the United States did not steal upon an unsuspecting legislature, and pass unobserved. Its principle was completely understood, and was opposed with equal zeal and ability. After being resisted, first in the fair and open field of debate, and afterwards in the executive cabinet, with as much persevering talent as any measure has ever experienced, and being supported by arguments which convinced minds as pure and as intelligent as this country can boast, it became a law. The original act was permitted to expire; but a short experience of the embarrassments to which the refusal to revive it exposed the government, convinced those who were most prejudiced against the measure of its necessity and induced the passage of the present law. It would require no ordinary share of intrepidity to assert that a measure adopted under these circumstances was a bold and plain usurpation, to which the constitution gave no countenance. . . .

In discussing this question, the counsel for the State of Maryland have deemed it of some importance, in the construction of the constitution, to consider that instrument not as emanating from the people, but as the act of sovereign and independent States. The powers of the general government, it has been said, are delegated by the States, who alone are truly sovereign; and must be exercised in subordination to the States, who alone possess supreme dominion.

It would be difficult to sustain this proposition. The Convention which framed the constitution was indeed elected by the state legislatures. But the instrument, when it came from their hands, was a mere proposal, without obligation, or pretensions to it. It was reported to the then existing Congress of the United States, with a request that it might "be submitted to a convention of delegates, chosen in each State by the people thereof, under the recommendation of its legislature, for their assent and ratification." This mode of proceeding was adopted; and by the convention, by Congress, and by the state legislatures, the instrument was submitted to the people. They acted upon it in the only manner in which they can act safely, effectively, and wisely, on such a subject, by assembling in convention. . . .

From these conventions the constitution derives its whole authority. The government proceeds directly from the people; is "ordained and established" in the name of the people; and is declared to be ordained, "in order to form a more perfect union, establish justice, insure domestic tranquillity, and secure the blessings of liberty, to themselves and to their posterity." The assent of the States, in their sovereign capacity, is implied in calling a convention, and thus submitting that instrument to the people. But the people were at perfect liberty to accept or reject it; and their act was final. It required not the affirmance, and could not be negatived, by the state governments. The constitution, when thus adopted, was of complete obligation, and bound the state sovereignties. . . .

The government of the Union, then (whatever may be the influence of this fact on the case) is emphatically and truly a government of the people. In form and in substance it emanates from them, its powers are granted by them, and are to be exercised directly on them, and for their benefit.

This government is acknowledged by all to be one of enumerated powers: The principle that it can exercise only the powers granted to it, would seem too apparent to have required to be enforced by all those arguments which its enlightened friends, while it was depending before the people, found it necessary to urge. That principle is now universally admitted. But the question respecting the extent of the powers actually granted, is perpetually arising, and will probably continue to arise, as long as our system shall exist.

In discussing these questions, the conflicting powers of the general and State governments must be brought into view, and the supremacy of their respective laws, when they are in opposition, must be settled.

If any one proposition could command the universal assent of mankind, we might expect it would be this: that the government of the Union, though limited in its powers, is supreme within its sphere of action. This would seem to result necessarily from its nature. It is the government of all; its powers are delegated by all; it represents all, and acts for all. Though any one State may be willing to control its operations, no State is willing to allow others to control them. The nation, on those subjects on which it can act, must necessarily bind its component parts. But this question is not left to mere reason: the people have, in express terms, decided it, by saying, "this Constitution, and the laws of the United States, which shall be made in pursuance thereof," "shall be the supreme law of the land," and by requiring that the members of the State legislatures, and the officers of the executive and judicial departments of the States, shall take the oath of fidelity to it.

The government of the United States, then, though limited in its powers, is supreme; and its laws, when made in pursuance of the Constitution, form the supreme law of the land, "anything in the Constitution or laws of any State to the contrary notwithstanding."

Among the enumerated powers, we do not find that of establishing a bank or creating a corporation. But there is no phrase in the instrument which, like the Articles of Confederation, excludes incidental or implied powers; and which requires that everything granted shall be expressly and minutely described. Even the Tenth Amendment, which was framed for the purpose of quieting the excessive jealousies which had been excited, omits the word "expressly," and declares only that the powers "not delegated to the United States, nor prohibited to the States, are reserved to the States or to the people"; thus leaving the question, whether the particular power which may become the subject of contest, has been delegated to the one government, or prohibited to the other, to depend on a fair construction of the whole instrument.... A constitution, to contain an accurate detail of all the subdivisions of which its great powers will admit, and of all the means by which they may be carried into execution, would partake of the prolixity of a legal code, and could scarcely be embraced by the human mind. It would probably never be understood by the public. Its nature, therefore, requires, that only its great outlines should be marked, its important objects designated, and the minor ingredients which compose those objects be deduced from the nature of the objects themselves.... In considering this question, then, we must never forget, that it is a *constitution* we are expounding.

Although, among the enumerated powers of government, we do not find the word "bank," or "incorporation," we find the great powers to lay and collect taxes; to borrow money; to regulate commerce; to declare and conduct a war; and to raise and support armies and navies. The sword and the purse, all the external relations, and no inconsiderable portion of the industry of the nation, are entrusted to its government.... [A] government, entrusted with such ample powers, on the due execution of which the happiness and prosperity of the nation so vitally depends, must also be entrusted with ample means for their execution. The power being given, it is the interest of the nation to facilitate its execution. It can never be their interest, and cannot be presumed to have been their intention, to clog and embarrass its execution by withholding the most appropriate means. Throughout this vast republic, from the St. Croix to the Gulf of Mexico, from the Atlantic to the Pacific, revenue is to be collected and expended, armies are to be marched and supported. The exigencies of the nation may require, that the treasure raised in the North should be transported to the South, that raised in the East conveyed to the West, or that this order should be reversed. Is that construction of the Constitution to be preferred which would render these operations difficult, hazardous, and expensive? Can we adopt that construction (unless the words imperiously require it) which would impute to the framers of that instrument, when granting these powers for the public good, the intention of impeding their exercise by withholding a choice of means? If, indeed, such be the mandate of the Constitution, we have only to obey; but that instrument does not profess to enumerate the means by which the powers it confers may be executed; nor does it prohibit the creation of a corporation, if the existence of such a being be essential to the beneficial exercise of those powers. It is, then, the subject of fair inquiry, how far such means may be employed.

It is not denied, that the powers given to the government imply the ordinary means of execution. That, for example, of raising revenue, and applying it to national purposes, is admitted to imply the power of conveying money from place to place, as the exigencies of the nation may require, and of employing the usual means of conveyance. But it is denied that the government has its choice of means; or, that it may employ the most convenient means, if, to employ them, it be necessary to erect a corporation. . . .

The power of creating a corporation, though appertaining to sovereignty, is not, like the power of making war, or levying taxes, or of regulating commerce, a great substantive and independent power, which cannot be implied as incidental to other powers, or used as a means of executing them. It is never the end for which other powers are exercised, but a means by which other objects are accomplished. . . . The power of creating a corporation is never used for its own sake, but for the purpose of effecting something else. No sufficient reason is, therefore, perceived, why it may not pass as incidental to those powers which are expressly given, if it be a direct mode of executing them.

But the Constitution of the United States has not left the right of Congress to employ the necessary means, for the execution of the powers conferred on the government, to general reasoning. To its enumeration of powers is added that of making "all laws which shall be necessary and proper, for carrying into execution the foregoing powers, and all other powers vested by this Constitution, in the government of the United States, or in any department thereof."

The counsel for the State of Maryland have urged various arguments, to prove that this clause, though in terms a grant of power, is not so in effect; but is really restrictive of the general right, which might otherwise be implied, of selecting means for executing the enumerated powers.

In support of this proposition, they have found it necessary to contend, that this clause was inserted for the purpose of conferring on Congress the power of making laws. That, without it, doubts might be entertained, whether Congress could exercise its powers in the form of legislation.

But could this be the object for which it was inserted? . . . That a legislature, endowed with legislative powers, can legislate is a proposition too self-evident to have been questioned.

But the argument on which most reliance is placed, is drawn from the peculiar language of this clause. Congress is not empowered by it to make all laws, which may have relation to the powers conferred on the government, but such only as may be "necessary and proper" for carrying them into execution. The word "necessary" is considered as controlling the whole sentence, and as limiting the right to pass laws for the execution of the granted powers, to such as are indispensable, and without which the power would be nugatory. That it excludes the choice of means, and leaves to Congress, in each case, that only which is most direct and simple.

Is it true, that this is the sense in which the word "necessary" is always used? Does it always import an absolute physical necessity, so strong, that one thing, to which another may be termed necessary, cannot exist without that other? We think it does not. If reference be had to its use, in the common affairs of the world, or in approved authors, we find that it frequently imports no more than that one thing is convenient, or useful, or essential to another. To employ the means necessary to an end, is generally understood as employing any means calculated to produce the end, and not as being confined to those single means, without which the end would be entirely unattainable. Such is the character of human language, that no word conveys to the mind in all situations one single definite idea; and nothing is more common than to use words in a figurative sense. . . . The word "necessary" is of this description. It has not a fixed character peculiar to itself. It admits of all degrees of comparison; and is often connected with other words, which increase or diminish the impression the mind receives of the urgency it imports. A thing may be necessary, very necessary, absolutely or indispensably necessary. To no mind would the same idea be conveyed by these several phrases. . . . This word, then, like others, is used in various senses; and, in its construction, the subject, the context, the intention of the person using them, are all to be taken into view.

Let this be done in the case under consideration. The subject is the execution of those great powers on which the welfare of a nation essentially depends. It must have been the intention of those who gave these powers, to insure, as far as human prudence could insure, their beneficial execution. This could not be done by confiding the choice of means to such narrow limits as not to leave it in the power of Congress to adopt any which might be appropriate, and which were conducive to the end. This provision is made in a constitution intended to endure for ages to come, and, consequently, to be adapted to the various crises of human affairs. To have prescribed the means by which government should, in all future time, execute its powers, would have been to change, entirely, the character of the instrument, and give it the properties of a legal code. It would have been an unwise attempt to provide, by immutable rules, for exigencies which, if foreseen at all, must have been seen dimly, and which can be best provided for as they occur. To have declared that the best means shall not be used, but those alone without which the power given would be nugatory, would have been to deprive the legislature of the capacity to avail itself of experience, to exercise its reason, and to accommodate its legislation to circumstances. . . .

In ascertaining the sense in which the word "necessary" is used in this clause of the constitution, we may derive some aid from that with which it is associated. Congress shall have power "to make all laws which shall be necessary and *proper* to carry into execution" the powers of the government. If the word "necessary" was used in that strict and rigorous sense for which the counsel for the State of Maryland contend, it would be an extraordinary departure from the usual course of the human mind, as exhibited in composition, to add a word, the only possible effect of which is to qualify that strict and rigorous meaning; to present to the mind the idea of some choice of means of legislation not straightened and compressed within the narrow limits for which gentlemen contend.

But the argument which most conclusively demonstrates the error of the construction contended for by the counsel for the State of Maryland, is founded on the intention of the convention, as manifested in the whole clause. . . . We think so for the following reasons:

1. The clause is placed among the powers of Congress, not among the limitations on those powers.

2. Its terms purport to enlarge, not to diminish the powers vested in the government. It purports to be an additional power not a restriction on those already granted. . . . If the Framers' intention had been, by this clause to restrain the free use of means which might otherwise have been implied, that intention would have been inserted in another place, and would have been expressed in terms resembling these: "In carrying into execution the foregoing powers and all others," etc., "no laws shall be passed but such as are necessary and proper." Had the intention been to make this clause restrictive, it would unquestionably have been so in form as well as in effect.

We admit, as all must admit, that the powers of the government are limited, and that its limits are not to be transcended. But we think the sound construction of the Constitution must allow to the national legislature that discretion, with respect to the means by which the powers it confers are to be carried into execution, which will enable that body to perform the high duties assigned to it, in the manner most beneficial to the people. Let the end be legitimate, let it be within the scope of the Constitution, and all means which are appropriate, which are plainly adapted to that end, which are not prohibited, but consist with the letter and spirit of the Constitution, are constitutional. . . .

If a corporation may be employed indiscriminately with other means to carry into execution the powers of the government, no particular reason can be assigned for excluding the use of a bank, if required for its fiscal operations. To use one, must be within the discretion of Congress, if it be an appropriate mode of executing the powers of government. That it is a convenient, a useful, and essential instrument in the prosecution of its fiscal operations, is not now a subject of controversy.

. . . Should Congress, in the execution of its powers, adopt measures which are prohibited by the constitution; or should Congress, under the pretext of executing its powers, pass laws for the accomplishment of objects not entrusted to the government; it would become the painful duty of this tribunal, should a case requiring such a decision come before it, to say that such an act was not the law of the land. But where the law is not prohibited, and is really calculated to effect any of the objects entrusted to the government, to undertake here to inquire into the degree of its necessity, would be to pass the line which circumscribes the judicial department, and to tread on legislative ground. This court disclaims all pretensions to such a power. . . .

After the most deliberate consideration, it is the unanimous and decided opinion of this court, that the Act to incorporate the Bank of the United States is a law made in pursuance of the Constitution, and is a part of the supreme law of the land. . . .

It being the opinion of the court that the act incorporating the bank is constitutional; and that the power of establishing a branch in the State of Maryland might be properly exercised by the bank itself, we proceed to inquire—

Whether the State of Maryland may, without violating the Constitution, tax that branch?

That the power of taxation is one of vital importance; that it is retained by the States; that it is not abridged by the grant of a similar power to the government of the Union; that it is to be concurrently exercised by the two governments; are truths which have never been denied. But, such is the paramount character of the Constitution, that its capacity to withdraw any subject from the action of even this power, is admitted. The States are expressly forbidden to lay any duties on imports or exports, except what may be absolutely necessary for executing their inspection laws. If the obligation of this prohibition must be conceded—if it may restrain a State from the exercise of its taxing power on imports and exports; the same paramount character would seem to restrain, as it certainly may restrain, a State from such other exercise of this power, as is in its nature incompatible with, and repugnant to, the constitutional laws of the Union. A law, absolutely repugnant to another, as entirely repeals that other as if express terms of repeal were used.

On this ground the counsel for the bank place its claim to be exempted from the power of a State to tax its operations. There is no express provision for the case, but the claim has been sustained on a principle which so entirely pervades the Constitution, is so intermixed with the materials which compose it, so interwoven with its web, so blended with its texture, as to be incapable of being separated from it, without rending it into shreds.

This great principle is, that the Constitution and the laws made in pursuance thereof are supreme; that they control the Constitution and laws of the respective States, and cannot be controlled by them. From this, which may be almost termed an axiom, other propositions are deduced as corollaries, on the truth or error of which, and on their application to this case, the cause has been supposed to depend. These are, 1st. That a power to create implies a power to preserve. 2d. That a power to destroy, if wielded by a different hand, is hostile to, and incompatible with, these powers to create and preserve. 3d. That where this repugnancy exists, that authority which is supreme must control, not yield to that over which it is supreme. . . .

The power of Congress to create, and of course to continue, the bank, was the subject of the preceding part of this opinion; and is no longer to be considered as questionable.

That the power of taxing it by the States may be exercised so as to destroy it, is too obvious to be denied. But taxation is said to be an absolute power, which acknowledges no other limits than those expressly prescribed in the Constitution, and like sovereign power of every other description, is trusted to the discretion of those who use it. . . .

The argument on the part of the State of Maryland, is, not that the States may directly resist a law of Congress, but that they may exercise their acknowledged powers upon it, and that the Constitution leaves them this right in the confidence that they will not abuse it. . . .

That the power to tax involves the power to destroy; that the power to destroy may defeat and render useless the power to create; that there is a plain repugnance, in conferring on one government a power to control the constitutional measures of another, which other, with respect to those very measures, is declared to be supreme over that which exerts the control, are propositions not to be denied But all inconsistencies are to be reconciled by the magic of the word "confidence." Taxation, it is said, does not necessarily and unavoidably destroy. To carry it to the excess of destruction would be an abuse, to presume which, would banish that confidence which is essential to all government.

But is this a case of confidence? Would the people of any one State trust those of another with a power to control the most insignificant operations of their State government? We know they would not. Why, then, should we suppose that the people of any one State should be willing to trust those of another with a power to control the operations of a government to which they have confided their most important and most valuable interests? In the legislature of the Union alone, are all represented. The legislature of the Union alone, therefore, can be trusted by the people with the power of controlling measures which concern all, in the confidence that it will not be abused. This, then, is not a case of confidence, and we must consider it as it really is.

If we apply the principle for which the State of Maryland contends, to the Constitution generally, we shall find it capable of changing totally the character of that instrument. We shall find it capable of arresting all the measures of the government, and of prostrating it at the foot of the States. The American people have declared their Constitution, and the laws made in pursuance thereof, to be supreme; but this principle would transfer the supremacy, in fact, to the States.

If the States may tax one instrument, employed by the government in the execution of its powers, they may tax any and every other instrument. They may tax the mail; they may tax the mint; they may tax patent rights; they may tax the papers of the custom-house; they may tax judicial process; they may tax all the means employed by the government, to an excess which would defeat all the ends of government. This was not intended by the American people. They did not design to make their government dependent on the States....

It has also been insisted, that, as the power of taxation in the general and State governments is acknowledged to be concurrent, every argument which would sustain the right of the general government to tax banks chartered by the States, will equally sustain the right of the States to tax banks chartered by the general government.

But the two cases are not on the same reason. The people of all the States have created the general government, and have conferred upon it 'the general power of taxation. The people of all States, and the States themselves, are represented in Congress, and, by their representatives, exercise this power. When they tax the chartered institutions of the States, they tax their constituents; and these taxes must be uniform. But when a State taxes the operations of the government of the United States, it acts upon institutions created, not by their own constituents, but by people over whom they claim no control. It acts upon the measures of a government created by others as well as themselves, for the benefit of others in common with themselves. The difference is that which always exists, and always must exist, between the action of the whole on a part, and the action of a part on the whole — between the laws of a government declared to be supreme, and those of a government which, when in opposition to those laws, is not supreme.

But if the full application of this argument could be admitted, it might bring into question the right of Congress to tax the State banks, and could not prove the right of the States to tax the Bank of the United States.

The court has bestowed on this subject its most deliberate consideration. The result is a conviction that the States have no power, by taxation or otherwise, to retard, impede, burden, or in any manner control, the operations of the constitutional laws enacted by Congress to carry into execution the powers vested in the general government. This is, we think, the unavoidable consequence of that supremacy which the Constitution has declared.

We are unanimously of opinion, that the law passed by the legislature of Maryland, imposing a tax on the Bank of the United States, is unconstitutional and void.

This opinion does not deprive the States of any resources which they originally possessed. It does not extend to a tax paid by the real property of the bank, in common with the other real property within the State, nor to a tax imposed on the interest which the citizens of Maryland may hold in this institution, in common with other property of the same description throughout the State. But this is a tax on the operations of the bank, and is, consequently, a tax on the operation of an instrument employed by the government of the Union to carry its powers into execution. Such a tax must be unconstitutional. . . .

It is therefore adjudged and ordered, that the . . . judgment of the . . . court of appeals of the State of Maryland, in this case, be, and the same hereby is, reversed and annulled . . . and that judgment be entered in the Baltimore county court for . . . James W. McCulloch.

Reversed.

IV. The Brief of the Case

The elements of the case not only constitute a framework of reference for reading a judicial decision, they also provide an analytical outline for reducing the case to its essentials. Such an outline is called a "brief," and it serves as a convenient digest of the case as well as a test of whether or not the material has been mastered. What follows is a sample brief of the *McCulloch* case:

Background: The controversy in 1790 over establishment of a national bank pitted the Hamiltonian Federalists against the Jeffersonian decentralists. The former (representing Eastern mercantile-creditor interests in favor of a strong central government) argued for a broad construction of the Constitution in support of congressional power to create a bank; the latter (representing Southern agrarian-debtor elements fearful of consolidated national authority) based their denial that such a power existed on a strict construction of the fundamental law. The Federalist position prevailed, and the first Bank of the United States was chartered by Congress in 1791. Unchallenged in the courts, it operated until 1811. A second B.U.S. was incorporated in 1816 with less opposition in Congress. But the old controversy was renewed in several Southern and Western states, as the "cheap money" frontier forces joined the agricultural areas in opposition to the conservative Bank. Popular pressure in those states, one of which was Maryland, resulted in restricting the Bank's activities. This case arose out of a challenge to Maryland's anti-Bank law.

Facts: A Maryland act of 1818 imposed a heavy tax on any bank or branch not chartered by the state (i.e. the Bank of the United States, chartered by Congress), or in lieu of the tax a large annual fee, and provided substantial penalties for violation of the law. When the cashier of the Baltimore branch of the United States Bank, McCulloch, refused to comply with this statute, Maryland brought suit to recover the penalties and was successful in the highest state court. The case was then appealed to the Supreme Court of the United States.

    Issues: (a) Has Congress the power to incorporate a bank? (Yes)

          (b) May Maryland tax a bank chartered by Congress? (No)

[*N.B.* The issues in a case should always be stated in the form of questions which can be answered "yes" or "no." They may be stated in varying degrees of specificity or generality to reflect a narrower or a broader view of the Court's holding. Thus issue (a) above might be phrased in increasingly general terms as follows:

(1) Has Congress the power to incorporate *this* bank?

(2) Has Congress the power to incorporate *any* bank?

(3) Has Congress the power to establish *other* instrumentalities in carrying its enumerated powers into execution?

(4) Has Congress the power to use *any* means in effectuating its enumerated powers?]

Decision: The judgment of the Court of Appeals of Maryland was reversed and annulled.

Opinion: (Marshall, C. J.) The Constitution is not a mere compact among sovereign states. It was "ordained and established" by the American people. By the Constitution the people created a national government of limited authority, but within its sphere of action that government's authority is supreme. Congress was expressly granted certain powers, among which are the power to lay and collect taxes, borrow money, regulate commerce, declare war, and raise and support armies. Admittedly the national legislature was not given the express power to incorporate a bank, but not even in the Tenth Amendment does the Constitution limit Congress to its expressly delegated powers, for it was clear to the Framers that the legislature must have incidental authority to select the means for effectuating its enumerated powers if it was to accomplish its purposes. They recognized this need by including such additional authority in the clause empowering Congress "to make all laws which shall be necessary and proper" for carrying its enumerated powers into execution. It follows that the words "necessary and proper," as used in the basic law, do not restrict Congress to the use of those means which are indispensable to making its delegated authority effective, but rather that they allow for resort to all means which are convenient and appropriate. ("Let the end be legitimate, let it be within the scope of the Constitution, and all means which are appropriate, which are plainly adapted to that end, which are not prohibited, but consist with the letter and spirit of the Constitution, are constitutional.") A bank is such a means for carrying into execution the legislature's expressly delegated fiscal powers, and its establishment by Congress is therefore constitutional.

Since Congress acted within its constitutional authority in incorporating a bank, it also has the power to preserve the institution. But a state's use of its reserved powers to tax an instrumentality of the national government might result in the bank's destruction. The resolution of this dilemma lies in the fact that the Constitution, and the laws of the United States made in pursuance thereof, are "the supreme law of the land," and that any state laws repugnant to them are null and void. Whether or not Maryland would use the taxing power to destroy a legitimate instrumentality of the national government is irrelevant; the mere existence of such a power is incompatible with the basic law, and the tax is therefore unconstitutional.

Concurring or dissenting opinions: None. The decision was unanimous.

General principle of constitutional law: This case established the doctrine that the national government possesses "implied powers" related to and flowing from its specifically delegated authority. Chief Justice Marshall's opinion also included a definitive exposition of the idea that the Constitution was established by the American people acting as a single and unified nation, as well as a classic statement of the doctrine of national supremacy. Finally, the case is an important illustration of the Supreme Court's function as umpire of the federal system.

Significance of the case: The doctrine of implied powers ranks in importance with the doctrine of judicial review as an essential factor in the development of the governmental and constitutional systems. For it made possible a continuing expansion of national authority to meet the changing needs of American society. It also raised the serious problem, however, of whether there are any definable limits on the national legislative power—a problem involving the federal principle and ultimately the very concept of constitutional rule.

[*N.B.* A brief may be very concise or quite detailed. This will depend on the difficulty and importance of the case, as well as on individual choice. In general, however, a brief should be *brief.*]

CASES AND SELECTED BIBLIOGRAPHY

(Capitalized case titles refer to the opinions included in this book.)

Introduction

CASES:

Dred Scott v. Sandford, 19 Howard 393 (1857).

EAKIN V. RAUB, 12 Sergeant and Rawle 330 (Pa. Sup.Ct., 1825).

Fletcher v. Peck, 6 Cranch 87 (1810).

MARBURY V. MADISON, 1 Cranch 137 (1803).

MCCULLOCH V. MARYLAND, 4 Wheaton 316 (1819).

BIBLIOGRAPHY:

Beard, Charles, *An Economic Interpretation of the Constitution* (New York: Macmillan, 1913).

Becker, Carl, *The Declaration of Independence* (New York: Vintage, 1959).

Black, Charles, *The People and the Court* (New York: Macmillan, 1960).

Cahill, Fred, *Judicial Legislation* (New York: Ronald, 1952).

Cahn, Edmond, ed., *Supreme Court and Supreme Law* (Bloomington: University of Indiana Press, 1954).

Cardozo, Benjamin, *The Nature of the Judicial Process* (New Haven: Yale University Press, 1932).

Carr, Robert, *The Supreme Court and Judicial Review* (New York: Rinehart, 1942).

Commager, Henry, *Majority Rule and Minority Rights* (New York: Oxford, 1943).

Corwin, Edward, *The "Higher Law" Background of American Constitutional Law* (Ithaca: Cornell University Press, reprint, 1955).

_____, ed., *The Constitution of the United States of America: Analysis and Interpretation* (Washington: Government Printing Office, 1953).

_____, and Jack Peltason, *Understanding the Constitution*, rev. ed. (New York: Holt, 1958).

Crosskey, William, *Politics and the Constitution in the History of the United States,* 2 vols. (Chicago: University of Chicago Press, 1953).

Curtis, Charles, *Lions Under the Throne* (Boston: Houghton Mifflin, 1947).

Frank, Jerome, *Law and the Modern Mind* (New York: Brentano, 1930).

Frank, John, *Marble Palace: The Supreme Court in American Life* (New York: Knopf, 1958).

Freund, Paul, *On Understanding the Supreme Court* (Boston: Little, Brown, 1949).

Haines, Charles, *The American Doctrine of Judicial Supremacy,* 2d ed. (Berkeley: University of California Press, 1932).

_____, *The Role of the Supreme Court in American Government and Politics, 1789-1935* (Berkeley: University of California Press, 1944).

Hamilton, Alexander, James Madison, and John Jay, *The Federalist (Earle edition)* (New York: Random House, 1937).

Hand, Learned, *The Bill of Rights* (Cambridge: Harvard University Press, 1958).

Harris, Robert, *The Judicial Power of the United States* (Baton Rouge: Louisiana State University Press, 1940).

Hart, Henry, and Herbert Wechsler, *The Federal Courts and the Federal System* (Brooklyn: Foundation Press, 1953).

Jackson, Robert, *The Supreme Court in the American System of Government* (Cambridge: Harvard University Press, 1955).

Locke, John, *The Second Treatise of Civil Government* (Sherman edition) (New York: Appleton-Century-Crofts, 1937).

McCloskey, Robert, *The American Supreme Court* (Chicago: University of Chicago Press, 1960).

———, ed., *Essays in Constitutional Law* (New York: Knopf, 1957).

McIlwain, Charles, *The American Revolution: A Constitutional Interpretation* (New York: Macmillan, 1923).

———, *Constitutionalism: Ancient and Modern* (Ithaca: Cornell University Press, 1940).

McLaughlin, Andrew, *A Constitutional History of the United States* (New York: Appleton-Century-Crofts, 1935).

Mason, Alpheus, *The Supreme Court from Taft to Warren* (Baton Rouge: Louisiana State University Press, 1958).

———, and William Beaney, *The Supreme Court in a Free Society* (Englewood Cliffs: Prentice-Hall, 1959).

Mill, John Stuart, *On Liberty* (Castell edition) (New York: Appleton-Century-Crofts, 1947).

Murphy, Walter, and C. Herman Pritchett, *Courts, Judges, and Politics* (New York: Random House, 1961).

Peltason, Jack, *Federal Courts in the Political Process* (New York: Random House, 1955).

Powell, Thomas Reed, *Vagaries and Varieties in Constitutional Interpretation* (New York: Columbia University Press, 1956).

Pritchett, Herman, *The American Constitution* (New York: McGraw-Hill, 1959).

Read, Conyers, ed., *The Constitution Reconsidered* (New York: Columbia University Press, 1938).

Rodell, Fred, *Nine Men: A Political History of the Supreme Court* (New York: Random House, 1955).

Rosenblum, Victor, *Law as a Political Instrument* (New York: Random House, 1955).

Schmidhauser, John, *The Supreme Court: Its Politics, Personalities, and Procedures* (New York: Holt, 1960).

Schubert, Glendon, *Constitutional Politics* (New York: Holt, Rinehart and Winston, 1960).

Schwartz, Bernard, *The Supreme Court* (New York: Ronald, 1957).

Swisher, Carl, *American Constitutional Development,* 2d ed. (Boston: Houghton Mifflin, 1954).

———, *The Supreme Court in Modern Role* (New York: New York University Press, 1958).

Warren, Charles, *The Supreme Court in United States History,* rev. ed. (Boston: Little, Brown, 1928).

Westin, Alan, ed., *The Supreme Court: Views from Inside* (New York: Norton, 1961).

Wormuth, Francis, *The Origins of Modern Constitutionalism* (New York: Harper & Bros., 1949).

Wright, Benjamin, *The Growth of American Constitutional Law* (New York: Holt, 1942).

JUDICIAL BIOGRAPHY:

Beveridge, Albert, *The Life of John Marshall,* 4 vols. (Boston: Houghton Mifflin, 1916).

Christman, H. M., ed., *The Public Papers of Chief Justice Earl Warren* (New York: Simon and Schuster, 1959).

Ewing, Cortez, *The Judges of the Supreme Court, 1789-1937* (Minneapolis: University of Minnesota Press, 1938).

Frank, John, *Mr. Justice Black* (New York: Knopf, 1949).

Frankfurter, Felix, *Mr. Justice Holmes and the Constitution* (Cambridge: Harvard University Press, 1938).

Gerhart, Eugene, *America's Advocate: Robert H. Jackson* (Indianapolis: Bobbs-Merrill, 1958).

Konefsky, Samuel, *The Constitutional World of Mr. Justice Frankfurter* (New York: Macmillan, 1949).

Mason, Alpheus, *Brandeis: A Free Man's Life* (New York: Viking, 1946).

———, *Harlan Fiske Stone: Pillar of the Law* (New York: Viking, 1956).

Pusey, Merlo, *Charles Evans Hughes* (New York: Macmillan, 1951).

Swisher, Carl, *Roger B. Taney* (Washington: Brookings Institution, 1935).

Chapter I   Government and the Economy

CASES:

Ashwander v. Tennessee Valley Authority, 297 U.S. 288 (1936).

Carter v. Carter Coal Company, 298 U.S. 238 (1936).

Cooley v. Board of Wardens, 12 Howard 299 (1852).

Gibbons v. Ogden, 9 Wheaton 1 (1824).

Gold Clause Cases, 294 U.S. 240, 317, 330 (1935).

Hammer v. Dagenhart, 247 U.S. 251 (1918).

Home Building and Loan Association v. Blaisdell, 290 U.S. 398 (1934).

Morehead v. New York ex rel. Tipaldo, 298 U.S. 587 (1936).

Mulford v. Smith, 307 U.S. 38 (1939).

NATIONAL LABOR RELATIONS BOARD V. JONES & LAUGHLIN STEEL COMPANY, 301 U.S. 1 (1937).

Nebbia v. New York, 291 U.S. 502 (1934).

Panama Refining Company v. Ryan, 293 U.S. 388 (1935).

Railroad Retirement Board v. Alton Railroad Company, 295 U.S. 330 (1935).

SCHECHTER POULTRY CORPORATION V. UNITED STATES, 295 U.S. 495 (1935).

Steward Machine Company v. Davis, 301 U.S. 548 (1937).

Swift and Company v. United States, 196 U.S. 375 (1905).

United States v. Darby Lumber Company, 312 U.S. 100 (1941).

United States v. E. C. Knight Company, 156 U.S. 1 (1895).

Virginian Railway Company v. System Federation No. 40, 300 U.S. 515 (1937).

West Coast Hotel Company v. Parrish, 300 U.S. 379 (1937).

WICKARD V. FILBURN, 317 U.S. 111 (1942).

Wright v. Mountain Trust Bank, 300 U.S. 440 (1937).

BIBLIOGRAPHY:

Anderson, William, *The Nation and the States, Rivals or Partners* (Minneapolis: University of Minnesota Press, 1955).

Benson, George, *The New Centralization* (New York: Holt, 1941).

Burns, James, *Roosevelt: The Lion and the Fox* (New York: Harcourt, Brace, 1956).

Corwin, Edward, *Constitutional Revolution, Ltd.* (Claremont: Associated Colleges, 1941).

Dowling, Noel, "Interstate Commerce and State Power," 47 *Columbia Law Review* 547 (May, 1947).

Frankfurter, Felix, *The Commerce Clause Under Marshall, Taney, and Waite* (Chapel Hill: University of North Carolina Press, 1937).

Freidel, Frank, *Franklin D. Roosevelt* (Boston: Little, Brown, 1952).

Jackson, Robert, *The Struggle for Judicial Supremacy* (New York: Knopf, 1941).

Jaffe, Louis, "An Essay on Delegation of Legislative Power," 47 *Columbia Law Review* 359, 561 (April, May, 1947).

Pritchett, Herman, *The Roosevelt Court* (New York: Macmillan, 1948).

Rauch, Basil, *The History of the New Deal* (New York: Creative Age Press, 1944).

Schmidhauser, John, *The Supreme Court as Final Arbiter in Federal-State Relations, 1789–1957* (Chapel Hill: University of North Carolina Press, 1958).

Stern, Robert, "The Commerce Clause and the National Economy, 1933–1946," *59 Harvard Law Review* 645, 883 (May, July, 1946).

Chapter II   Racial Discrimination and Civil Rights

CASES:

Berea College v. Kentucky, 211 U.S. 45 (1908).

Bolling v. Sharpe, 347 U.S. 497 (1954).

BROWN V. BOARD OF EDUCATION, 347 U.S. 483 (1954).

BROWN V. BOARD OF EDUCATION, 349 U.S. 294 (1955).

Civil Rights Cases, 109 U.S. 3 (1883).

Cooper v. Aaron, 358 U.S. 1 (1958).

Cumming v. Richmond County Board of Education, 175 U.S. 528 (1899).

Gong Lum v. Rice, 275 U.S. 78 (1927).

McLaurin v. Oklahoma State Regents, 339 U.S. 637 (1950).

MISSOURI EX REL. GAINES V. CANADA, 305 U.S. 337 (1938).

PLESSY V. FERGUSON, 163 U.S. 537 (1896).

Sipuel v. Board of Regents of the University of Oklahoma, 332 U.S. 631 (1948).

Slaughterhouse Cases, 16 Wallace 36 (1873).

Sweatt v. Painter, 339 U.S. 629 (1950).

BIBLIOGRAPHY:

Ashmore, Harry, *The Negro and the Schools* (Chapel Hill: University of North Carolina Press, 1954).

Bickel, Alexander, "The Original Understanding and the Segregation Decision," 69 *Harvard Law Review* 1 (November, 1955).

Blaustein, Albert, and Clarence Ferguson, *Desegregation and the Law* (New Brunswick: Rutgers University Press, 1957).

Carr, Robert, *Federal Protection of Civil Rights* (Ithaca: Cornell University Press, 1947).

"Civil Rights in America," 275 *The Annals of the American Academy of Political and Social Science* 1 (May, 1951).

Frank, John, and Robert Munro, "The Original Understanding of 'Equal Protection of the Laws,'" 50 *Columbia Law Review* 131 (February, 1950).

Gellhorn, Walter, *American Rights* (New York: Macmillan, 1960).

Greenberg, Jack, *Race Relations and American Law* (New York: Columbia University Press, 1959).

Harris, Robert, *The Quest for Equality* (Baton Rouge: Louisiana State University Press, 1960).

Horn, Robert, *Groups and the Constitution* (Stanford: Stanford University Press, 1956).

Konvitz, Milton, *The Constitution and Civil Rights* (New York: Columbia University Press, 1947).

Murphy, Walter, "Desegregation in Public Education — A Generation of Future Litigation," 15 *Maryland Law Review* 221 (Summer, 1955).

Myrdal, Gunnar, *An American Dilemma* (New York: Harper & Bros., 1944).

President's Committee on Civil Rights, *To Secure These Rights* (Washington: Government Printing Office, 1947).

"Racial Desegregation and Integration," 304 *The Annals of the American Academy of Political and Social Science* 1 (March, 1956).

Ziegler, Benjamin, ed., *Desegregation and the Supreme Court* (Boston: Heath, 1958).

Chapter III   National Security and Civil Liberty

CASES:

Abrams v. United States, 250 U.S. 616 (1919).

Adler v. Board of Education of New York City, 342 U.S. 485 (1952).

American Communications Association v. Douds, 339 U.S. 382 (1950).

Anastaplo, In re, 348 U.S. 946 (1955).

Bailey v. Richardson, 341 U.S. 918 (1951).

Barenblatt v. United States, 360 U.S. 109 (1959).

Barsky v. United States, 167 F.2d 241 (1948).

Beilan v. Board of Public Education of Philadelphia, 357 U.S. 399 (1958).

Braden v. United States, 365 U.S. 431 (1961).

Cole v. Young, 351 U.S. 536 (1956).

Communist Party v. Subversive Activities Control Board, 351 U.S. 115 (1956).

Communist Party v. Subversive Activities Control Board, 367 U.S. 1 (1961).

Debs v. United States, 249 U.S. 211 (1919).

De Jonge v. Oregon, 299 U.S. 353 (1937).

DENNIS V. UNITED STATES, 341 U.S. 494 (1951).

Emspak v. United States, 349 U.S. 190 (1955).

Frohwerk v. United States, 249 U.S. 204 (1919).

Garner v. Board of Public Works, 341 U.S. 716 (1951).

Gitlow v. New York, 268 U.S. 652 (1925).

Herndon v. Lowry, 301 U.S. 242 (1937).

Jencks v. United States, 353 U.S. 657 (1957).

Joint Anti-Fascist Refugee Committee v. McGrath, 341 U.S. 123 (1951).

Konigsberg v. State Bar of California, 353 U.S. 252 (1957).

Lerner v. Casey, 357 U.S. 468 (1958).

Pennsylvania v. Nelson, 350 U.S. 497 (1956).

Peters v. Hobby, 349 U.S. 331 (1955).

Quinn v. United States, 349 U.S. 155 (1955).

Scales v. United States, 367 U.S. 203 (1961).

Schaefer v. United States, 251 U.S. 466 (1920).

SCHENCK V. UNITED STATES, 249 U.S. 47 (1919).

Schware v. Board of Bar Examiners of New Mexico, 353 U.S. 232 (1957).

Service v. Dulles, 354 U.S. 363 (1957).

Slochower v. Board of Higher Education of New York City, 350 U.S. 551 (1956).

Stromberg v. California, 283 U.S. 359 (1931).

Sweezy v. New Hampshire, 354 U.S. 234 (1957).

United States v. Josephson, 165 F.2d 82 (1947).

United States v. Rumely, 345 U.S. 41 (1953).

Uphaus v. Wyman, 360 U.S. 72 (1959).

Watkins v. United States, 354 U.S. 178 (1957).

Whitney v. California, 274 U.S. 357 (1927).

Wieman v. Updegraff, 344 U.S. 183 (1952).

Wilkinson v. United States, 365 U.S. 399 (1961).

YATES V. UNITED STATES, 354 U.S. 298 (1957).

BIBLIOGRAPHY:

Barth, Alan, *Government by Investigation* (New York: Viking, 1955).

Bontecou, Eleanor, *The Federal Loyalty-Security Program* (Ithaca: Cornell University Press, 1953).

Chafee, Zechariah, *Free Speech in the United States* (Cambridge: Harvard University Press, 1942).

Chase, Harold, *Security and Liberty* (New York: Doubleday, 1955).

Conference of Chief Justices, *Report of the Committee on Federal-State Relationships as Affected by Judicial Decisions* (Chicago: The Council of State Governments, 1958).

Cushman, Robert, *Civil Liberties in the United States* (Ithaca: Cornell University Press, 1956).

Emerson, Thomas, and David Haber, *Political and Civil Rights in the United States,* rev. ed. (Buffalo: Dennis, 1960).

Fellman, David, *The Defendant's Rights* (New York: Rinehart, 1958).

Fraenkel, Osmond, *Our Civil Liberties* (New York: Viking, 1944).

Gellhorn, Walter, ed., *The States and Subversion* (Ithaca: Cornell University Press, 1952).

Griswold, Erwin, *The Fifth Amendment Today* (Cambridge: Harvard University Press, 1955).

Hook, Sidney, *Heresy, Yes — Conspiracy, No* (New York: John Day, 1953).

Konvitz, Milton, *Fundamental Liberties of a Free People* (Ithaca: Cornell University Press, 1957).

Lasswell, Harold, *National Security and Individual Freedom* (New York: McGraw-Hill, 1950).

Meiklejohn, Alexander, *Free Speech in Its Relation to Self-Government* (New York: Harper, 1948).

Mendelson, Wallace, "Clear and Present Danger — From Schenck to Dennis," 52 *Columbia Law Review* 313 (1952).

Pound, Roscoe, *The Development of Constitutional Guarantees of Liberty* (New Haven: Yale University Press, 1957).

Pritchett, Herman, *Civil Liberties and the Vinson Court* (Chicago: University of Chicago Press, 1954).

_____, *Congress versus the Supreme Court, 1957–60* (Minneapolis: University of Minnesota Press, 1961).

_____, *The Political Offender and the Warren Court* (Boston: Boston University Press, 1958).

Spicer, George, *The Supreme Court and Fundamental Freedoms* (New York: Appleton-Century-Crofts, 1959).

Stouffer, Samuel, *Communism, Conformity, and Civil Liberties* (New York: Doubleday, 1955).

Taylor, Telford, *Grand Inquest: The Story of Congressional Investigations* (New York: Simon and Schuster, 1955).

United States Senate, Committee on the Judiciary, *Hearings before the Subcommittee to Investigate the Administration of the Internal Security Act and Other Internal Security Laws.* 85th Congress, 2nd Sess. Hearings on S. 2646. (Washington: Government Printing Office, 1958).

United States Senate, Committee on the Judiciary, Hearings on S. 2646, *Limitation of the Appellate Jurisdiction of the United States Supreme Court.* 85th Congress, 1st Sess., part 1, 1957; 2nd Sess., part 2, 1958.

Chapter IV Government in Time of War

CASES:

Bowles v. Willingham, 321 U.S. 503 (1944).

Duncan v. Kahanamoku, 327 U.S. 304 (1946).

Employers Group of Motor Freight Carriers v. National War Labor Board, 79 U.S. App. D.C. 105 (1944).

Endo, Ex parte, 323 U.S. 283 (1944).

Hirabayashi v. United States, 320 U.S. 81 (1943).

KOREMATSU V. UNITED STATES, 323 U.S. 214 (1944).

Lichter v. United States, 334 U.S. 742 (1948).

Merryman, Ex parte, 17 Fed. Cases 9487 (1861).

Milligan, Ex parte, 4 Wallace 2 (1866).

Oetjen v. Central Leather Company, 246 U.S. 297 (1918).

PRIZE CASES, 2 Black 635 (1863).

Steuart and Brothers v. Bowles, 322 U.S. 398 (1944).

United States v. Bethlehem Steel Corporation, 315 U.S. 289 (1942).

United States v. Macintosh, 283 U.S. 605 (1931).

United States v. Peewee Coal Corporation, 341 U.S. 114 (1951).

Vallandigham, Ex parte, 1 Wallace 243 (1864).

Yakus v. United States, 321 U.S. 414 (1944).

YOUNGSTOWN SHEET AND TUBE CO. V. SAWYER, 343 U.S. 579 (1952).

BIBLIOGRAPHY:

Anthony, Garner, "Martial Law, Military Government, and the Writ of Habeas Corpus in Hawaii," 30, 31 *California Law Review* 371, 477 (1942, 1943).

Berdahl, Clarence, *The War Powers of the Executive in the United States* (Urbana: University of Illinois Press, 1921).

Bureau of the Budget, Committee on Records of the War Administration, *The United States at War* (Washington: Bureau of the Budget, 1946).

Corwin, Edward, *The President: Office and Powers*, 4th rev. ed. (New York: New York University, 1957).

————, "The Steel Seizure Case: A Judicial Brick Without Straw," 53 *Columbia Law Review* 53 (1953).

_____, *Total War and the Constitution* (New York: Knopf, 1947).

Dunning, William, *Essays on the Civil War and Reconstruction* (New York: Macmillan, 1910).

Grodzins, Morton, *Americans Betrayed: Politics and the Japanese Evacuation* (Chicago: University of Chicago Press, 1949).

Hirschfield, Robert, "The Problem of Crisis Government in the United States," 6 *Public Policy* 66 (1955).

_____, "The Power of the Contemporary Presidency," 14 *Parliamentary Affairs* 353 (Summer, 1961).

Koenig, Louis, *The Truman Administration* (New York: New York University Press, 1956).

McWilliams, Carey, *Prejudice: The Japanese-Americans* (Boston: Little, Brown, 1944).

Randall, James, *Constitutional Problems Under Lincoln,* rev. ed. (Urbana: University of Illinois Press, 1951).

Rankin, Robert, *When Civil Law Fails: Martial Law and Its Legal Basis in the United States* (Durham: Duke University Press, 1939).

Roche, John, "Executive Power ·and Domestic Emergency: The Quest for Prerogative," 5 *Western Political Quarterly* 592 (1952).

Rossiter, Clinton, *The American Presidency,* rev. ed. (New York: Harvest, 1960).

_____, *Constitutional Dictatorship* (Princeton: Princeton University Press, 1948).

_____, *The Supreme Court and the Commander in Chief* (Ithaca: Cornell University Press, 1951).

Rostow, Eugene, "The Japanese-American Cases – A Disaster," 54 *Yale Law Journal* 489 (1945).

Schubert, Glendon, *The Presidency in the Courts* (Minneapolis: University of Minnesota Press, 1957).

Smith, Malcolm J., and Cornelius Cotter, *Powers of the President During Crises* (Washington: Public Affairs Press, 1960).

Sutherland, Arthur, ed., *Government under Law* (Cambridge: Harvard University Press, 1956).

Tanenhaus, Joseph, "The Supreme Court and Presidential Power," 307 *The Annals of the American Academy of Political and Social Science* 106 (1956).

Ten Broek, Jacobus, Edward Barnhart, and Floyd Matson, *Prejudice, War, and the Constitution* (Berkeley: University of California Press, 1954).

Truman, Harry, *Memoirs,* 2 vols. (Garden City: Doubleday, 1955–1956).

United States, Library of Congress, Legislative Reference Service, "Acts of Congress Applicable in Time of Emergency," *Public Affairs Bulletin,* no. 35 (Washington: Government Printing Office, 1945).

United States, White House Press Release, "Digest of Laws Which Would Become Operative Upon Proclamation of a National Emergency by the President," *New York Times* (December 17, 1950).

Westin, Alan, *The Anatomy of a Constitutional Law Case* (New York: Macmillan, 1958).

Wilson, Woodrow, *Constitutional Government in the United States* (New York: Columbia University Press, 1917).

INDEX